Fearing
CHINA

Asking the question: Should we fear China?

Terry D. Wittenmyer

Zebra CAT Publishing

Published by Zebra CAT Publishing
Boca Raton, Florida U.S.A.

Fearing China
Asking the Question: Should We Fear China

Copyright Terry D. Wittenmyer 2015
ISBN 978-0-9963435-1-0

Editors:
Mary Gentry
Jerri Trammel
Osa Marie Wittenmyer

TABLE of CONTENTS

Fearing China

Introduction

It was my first trip to China. I tucked my laptop under the seat in front of me as the flight attendants walked down the aisle checking that everything was in order for the long flight. The first thing that struck me was the operation of this Chinese airline; it was the cleanest I had ever been on, and the crew functioned like clockwork, courteous and efficient. Not what I had expected.

For years I had kept an eye on newspapers and other media, listening to the politicians and commentators reporting on this far away country. From the news reports it was clear that China was a dirty, dangerous, and threatening place. The source of toys laced with lead. A place that had no regard for the environment. A place where human rights were ignored. I was told that China was a threat to its neighbors and even a threat to the U.S. I had read of the buildup of the Chinese military, of questions as to how many nuclear weapons they had developed, and of significant concerns about their military intent. I was told that the Chinese economy could one day be bigger than the U.S. economy, and that China was accomplishing this through things like currency manipulation, unfair trade practices, and subsidies to industry. I read that China was taking jobs from U.S. manufacturers and forcing under age children to work in factories under terrible conditions at unreasonably low pay. I read how the Chinese government was using computer hackers to plan technological warfare. I intently followed the stories of how China stole U.S. intellectual property, like software and movies, as well as technological secrets from U.S. corporations and our military. I heard about how the Chinese Communist government controlled all Chinese people and Chinese businesses.

The commentators and politicians, who were all clearly experts on the topic, informed me that China was a threat to my country in every way, and that China and its people were not to be trusted—that we had to take action to stop this growing monster that threatened our way of life. Even as I sat on the airplane on my way to this place, the day's newspapers headlines warned: "Chinese Military Buildup Continues with Purchase of Aircraft Carrier," "Chinese Toys Recalled after Investigation," "U.S. Trade Commission Pressures China on Solar Subsidies," "Currency Manipulation by China Threatens U.S. Economy," "U.S. Hit Hard by Chinese Labor," "Internet Search Company Refuses Chinese Government Censorships," and "Chinese Human Rights Activist Takes Refuge in U.S. Embassy."

As I sat comfortably in the plane that would take me across the Pacific Ocean, I focused on what I saw around me. I observed a Chinese family, the mother and father working to keep their two young children entertained during the long trip. In another row, a Chinese businesswoman worked on her laptop. In another, a young Chinese man, possibly college aged, listened to music on his headphones. Next to him sat an elderly Chinese couple preparing for the long flight. In the aisle, a Chinese flight attendant, smartly dressed, smiled politely as she served the passengers. As I read each article in the newspaper, I glanced up to see the faces of China around me. The articles told me one thing, but these faces told a different story. Between what I was told and what I could see there appeared to be a conflict. Was I seeing only the privileged elite? Were the news stories true? What would I find in the real China?

As the soft tone alerted me to the light above, "Fasten Your Seatbelt," I asked myself: *Should I fear China*? *Should we fear China*? With the click of a seatbelt, my journey began. It would be a journey through time, exploring the history of China, a journey of places, and a journey of relationships, getting to know a people and their culture. Finally, it would be a journey of facts as I explored the truth behind the headlines. My experience in the real China and my personal look at the real data started to paint a picture inconsistent with what I had been told. As I learned more, I began to keep a closer eye on news stories and started to do my own fact checking. With each expert opinion I looked closer at the evidence I'd uncovered, and with each premise I questioned the assumptions. The journey that started on my flight to China caused me to ask the question. My journey since has given me the answer to that question: *Should we fear China*?

1

Fearing China's Growing Economy

Is China an Economic Threat? (Fox News)
China Seeks to Upend Economic Power of US (The Standard)
How the U.S. Should Counter China's Economic Power Play (Fortune)
U.S. Eclipsed as Allies Line Up to Join China's Asia Bank (Newsweek)
China Gaining on U.S., Now World's Second Largest Economy (CBS)
At Global Economic Gathering, U.S. Primacy Is Seen as Ebbing (New York Times)

[1]

1959

*

The year was 1959 and there was no choice. She lit a small fire under the pot where she would boil enough soup to fill two small bowls. Her three children sat quietly on the dirt floor, two on the verge of death by starvation and the third only slightly better off. She struggled to decide how to allocate the insufficient portions. Her husband refused any for himself, knowing he would be dead within days. The mother stirred the pot slowly, questioning whether or not her decision would even matter in the end. She looked into the eyes of each child as she reflected upon the growing knowledge that she had failed her ultimate duty as a mother, but there was no choice, there was no food.

"What else can we do?" she said to her husband, as she placed into the pot the small remnants of nutrition he had scavenged from the cold.

"I don't know," he said, as he stepped out the door for one last hope of finding something that was not to be found. His feet were bleeding, as his shoes had long been gone and not replaced.

It was not news when two of the children died just a few days later and the father shortly after. It was only news many years later when historians began debating the estimated statistics, whether 25 million or 45 million people had died of starvation during what became known as "The Difficult Three Year Period." It was the darkest of days in China.

In that same year, 1959, and in another place, a woman called her children to the table for dinner.

The small boy pulled up his chair and took a look at the chicken casserole, green beans, and a whopping bowl of creamy mashed potatoes placed prominently in the center of the table.

"I don't like that," he announced. "I won't eat it." He squirmed in his seat, eyeing the butter as it melted into the green beans.

"Give it a try," the father instructed. "I think you'll like it. And either way, that's what we're having tonight. You should be grateful."

The boy grabbed his fork and began poking at his food, thinking about the ice cream sundae that would follow if he could just force himself through the main meal.

The father handed the mother a wrapped box tied with a bow. "Happy Birthday," he said.

She opened the box to find a beautiful new pair of shoes in her favorite color. "Do you have room in your closet for another pair?" he joked. "I'll make room," she said smiling. "You can never have too many pairs of shoes." She leaned forward to give him a kiss on the cheek.

Economists later would refer to this period as the Golden Age of the United States.

*

In 1959 the world saw the highest of highs and the lowest of lows. In one part of the world, a place of abundance, closets were filled to the brim with every fashion whim, and the selection of food was so broad that a young boy could complain about having too many choices. Here, families lived in the most modern of homes equipped with electrical appliances that eased daily chores, and garages were filled with shiny new cars that boasted all the latest features. The United States was experiencing a grand economic boom.

In China, life was quite different. Still working to recover from the devastations of WWII and a civil war, economic and political missteps by the Chinese government caused mass starvation as tens of millions died from lack of basic necessities. While China tried to make their own path, it was not working; the country floundered, stepping from one disaster to the next, hitting a low point in 1959, the same year the U.S. was at the top of the world, ranking number one in almost every economic and social indicator.

The U.S. Path

The United States has been the world's largest economy since 1871. The birth of U.S., almost one hundred years earlier, coincided with the beginning of the Industrial Revolution, as machinery and improved manufacturing processes rapidly increased the productivity of labor. While the old worlds of Europe and Asia, entrenched in centuries of established rule, struggled to adapt to the new political and economic realities, the U.S. leveraged its advantage of building from the ground up. The old worlds were burdened with the task of changing from old to new; the U.S. simply started fresh, with the added benefit of being geographically isolated from conflicts in European and Asian.

Like a child born into the right family, the benefits of a good beginning allowed the U.S. to build and maintain its position as the largest economy in the world for well over a century. At one point, the U.S., which represents only five percent of the world's population, was producing roughly sixty percent of the world's goods and services. Even today the U.S. produces about twenty-two percent of the world's goods and services.

The China Path

China, however, was not so fortunate. In the early 1900s, while industrializing nations were implementing new technologies, China was caught up in the task of ridding itself of 4,000 years of dynastic rule. For over fifty years Chinese society had been disrupted by rebellions against the dynasty as they sought to rid themselves of ineffective rulers. By 1912, the dynasties had been removed; however, civil war broke out as competing groups sought to establish the new order. The civil war was interrupted by the foreign invasions of WWII, but then quickly resumed at the end of the world war.

Once the dust of war had settled, political and economic

missteps further prevented China from participating in the advantages of the Industrial Revolution, and thus the modern world. By 1959, China had experienced a century of wars, instability, and questionable leadership. If the century leading up to 1959 was fertile ground for success in the U.S., it was a full one hundred years of disruption and instability for China. Relief was not to come for almost another twenty years as the leaders of China desperately sought to find the key to economic success.

Finally in 1978, with new leadership, China began to turn the corner. China began to make substantial changes away from the political and economic structures of the early years of the republic. Despite the early mistakes of the Chinese government and the setbacks caused from wars waged by foreign nations, by 1980 China was breaking out of its troubled past. At long last, China was making its entrance into the modern world, a process that Western nations had entered into more than a two centuries prior. As these changes took hold, the Chinese economy began to quickly improve. In 1980 the Gross Domestic Product (GDP) of China, which is the dollar value of all goods and services produced, was $189 billion per year. By 2000 it was $1.2 trillion and by 2014 China's GDP had exceeded $10 trillion.[2]

Economic and political changes have created a rapid shift in China's performance. And today we find ourselves watching as China grows exponentially, progressing quickly in economic growth and standard of living. In 2009, China surpassed Japan as the world's second largest economy. Looking at economic growth trends, it's clear that China is on the path to surpass the U.S. as the world's largest economy in the very near future.

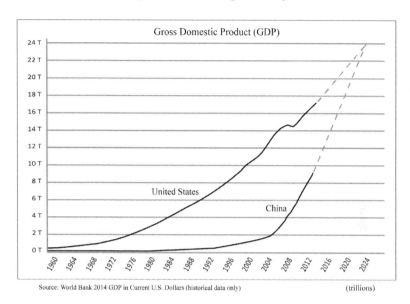

Source: World Bank 2014 GDP in Current U.S. Dollars (historical data only) (trillions)

U.S. Economic Influence

For over a century the U.S. has been the dominant force in world economic leadership. At the end of WWII, nations met to establish a new and more stable world financial system. The U.S. and Great Britain were the two major players at the conference and therefore controlled the agenda and its outcome. At the conference the World Bank and the International Monetary Fund (IMF) were established, it was decided that all currencies would be pegged to the U.S. dollar, and the decision was made that the U.S. dollar would be backed by gold. The World Bank and IMF headquarters were located in the U.S. and have remained there for over fifty years. The U.S. has more voting units in the World Bank and IMF than any other country. Since its founding in 1945, the president of the World Bank has always been from the U.S.[3]

In addition to controlling the World Bank and the IMF, the U.S. is the largest economy in the world, the largest capital market, the largest consumer market, and the U.S. dollar is used as the currency of international trade. The combination of these things gives the U.S. massive influence in world finance and economics. This financial power has given the U.S. the ability to influence and form world economic structures and relations for decades, often to its own advantage. With the U.S. dollar being the reserve currency of the world, the U.S. is able to influence and often control world exchange rates. As other nations buy up the all-powerful dollar, the U.S. is able to deficit spend without causing inflation. U.S. economic power is used to negotiate trade agreements as well as to define international banking and finance policies.

In 1971 President Richard Nixon took the dollar off the gold standard, which caused the dollar to quickly devalue. Using U.S. economic power, he negotiated with Saudi Arabia to ensure oil sales were denominated in U.S. dollars, thus saving the dollar from rapid devaluation. This is just one example of how U.S. economic power is used to sway the international rules to its advantage. However, the era of U.S. economic dominance is slowing.

China's Growing Influence

In 2012, China became the world's largest trading nation. In 2013, the European Union (EU) received $351 billion in imports from China, while only importing $262 billion from the U.S. While the U.S. is still the EU's largest export market (exporting $387 billion to the U.S and $148 billion to China), its exports to China are rapidly growing.[4] As China's consumer class expands, eventually the EU will export more to China than to the U.S., which will in some ways make their relationship with China more important than their relationship with the U.S. The sheer volume of trade between China and its trading partners has a huge impact on every economy in the world. As China becomes more connected to the world economy, world consumers become more dependent on Chinese imports, and world businesses become more dependent on sales to China. While the U.S. dollar may continue to be the world's dominant currency of exchange, the Chinese *yuan* will grow in strength as countries bypass the U.S. dollar and begin to do more direct exchange with China, which will cause the dollar to lose influence. China's export economy has caused it to be the fastest growing economy in the world.

Falling Out of the Number One Spot

Today numerous books, TV commentators, and newspaper

headlines warn of our impending doom as the U.S. "falls into decline" and cedes to China our position as the world's largest and most powerful economy. Estimates vary, but most economists agree that by 2024 China will have the world's largest economy, taking from us the number one position. What a difference thirty years has made.

Certainly there can be nothing good about falling to the number two spot: right? We've been told that this is the beginning of the end and a sign of our ultimate demise—the end of the American era. But what does this threat truly mean to the U.S., our position in the world, our security, and ultimately our standard of living?

The threat of falling out of the number one position, which we have held for almost 150 years, must be taken seriously. We are not accustomed to second place, as generations of Americans have only known a life at the top as part of the world's largest and most powerful economy. How could we allow China, this very recently "backwards" nation, to suddenly take our position? Was it neglect or overconfidence that caused us to slip? Have we become lax and inefficient, allowing China to become more productive than the U.S.? Should we sit passively as China takes our position, or should we fight to maintain what we have held for so long? Will China abuse its new position of power? Will China's rise cause instability in the U.S. and in the world? Will the international structures created by the U.S. begin to crumble? Let's take a closer look at the assumptions and arguments and consider the implications of China surpassing the U.S. to become the world's largest economy.

GDP Per Capita

Gross Domestic Product (GDP) is a measure of productivity and thus also a measure of a country's ability to consume and accumulate wealth. But a more important measurement is GDP per capita, which is a country's GDP divided by total population. The country of Norway has a GDP of about $500 billion, which by world standards is quite small. However, Norway has a small population, so the GDP per capita (per person) is one of the highest in the world, exceeding $100 thousand per person. On the other end of the spectrum, Brazil has one of the largest economies with a GDP of $2.2 trillion. However, because the population is very large, the GDP per capita is only $11 thousand per person.[5] In evaluating a society's standard of living, GDP per capita is a much more critical measurement than GDP.

While incomes may vary within a society, GDP per capita gives a reasonable measure of a nation's standard of living. The chart below compares the GDP per capita of eleven countries. Note that because the population of China is four times that of the U.S, even when China reaches a GDP equal to the U.S., the GDP per capita will be one quarter of that in the U.S. due to China's larger population. As China's Vice-Premier Wang Yang said, anything multiplied by 1.3 billion people is huge, while anything divided by 1.3 billion is tiny.[6]

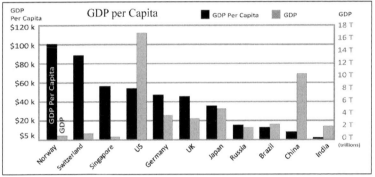

Source: International Monitary Fund 2014 GDP in Current U.S. Dollars

For those who hope the U.S. will maintain the number one position and always have a larger economy than China, a higher GDP than China, then what they're seeking is that the U.S. always have a GDP per capita of more than four times that of China, and that the Chinese standard of living be a quarter of what we've accomplished in the U.S. Is that truly what we wish for?

Generous Americans

The American people are generous in their contributions to help others throughout the world. In the U.S., over $200 billion is given to charity every year, and the government of the U.S. spends billions on poverty relief around the globe. The Millennium Development program has as its goal the elimination of extreme poverty by the year 2015; the U.S. contributes anywhere from one to three billion to this organization each year.[7] Americans do have concerns for their fellow humans around the world, and this fact is illustrated by our generous private and government programs. From these programs and contributions it's clear that we hope for an improved standard of living for others.

But what is our hope for the people of China? Do we hope for their economic success and an improved standard of living? Or do we hope that the children of China will never be able to afford higher education that could give them the opportunity to be as productive as those in London, Paris, or Boston? Do we hope that the people of China will never be able to afford the medical technologies that save lives in the U.S., Germany, England, and Canada? Do we hope that those in the rural western areas of China will never have access to running water or electricity, a cell phone or a washing machine? Do we hope that a Chinese family in central China will never be able to afford to buy a car or travel to a foreign land?

Nations can lack economic success for a variety of reasons, ranging from the interruptions of war to poor political and economic structures, and such was the case for China; causing them to miss the opportunities of the early Industrial Revolution. However, China is now adopting the methods and machines of the modern world, which is rapidly propelling them forward, increasing their GDP per capita and thus their standard of living. In 1985 the average income in China was equivalent to $300 per year, by 2000 it was $1,000 per year, and by 2013 $6,800 per year.[8] Being free from the disruptions of foreign invasions and breaking out of the failed economic and political structures of the past, over the last thirty years, China has truly improved the standard of living of the average Chinese family. As each person's productivity increases, GDP per capita increases, and as GDP per capita increases, so does the total GDP.

Again, given the fact that China's population is over four times that of the U.S., if we hope that their standard of living and productivity reaches that of first world nations, then we would be hoping that the GDP of China is at least four times that of the U.S. So we must decide if we want to remain in the number one position as the world's largest economy, or if we would like the standard of living for those in China to advance to what we have accomplished. We cannot have both.

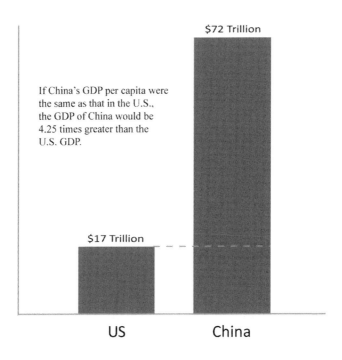

$72 Trillion

If China's GDP per capita were the same as that in the U.S., the GDP of China would be 4.25 times greater than the U.S. GDP.

$17 Trillion

US   China

Given our history of working to help others and our pursuits of eliminating poverty around the world, we should be anxious for China to be the world's largest economy. We should be hoping for an increased standard of living for all in China, and we should be enthusiastic about the idea of hundreds of millions of people moving out of poverty and progressing rapidly towards the standard of living that we've achieved.

Power to Make the Rules

In the 2015 State of the Union Address, President Obama said:

"As we speak, China wants to write the rules for the world's fastest-growing region. That would put our workers and businesses at a disadvantage. Why would we let that happen? We should write those rules."[9]

Obama made it very clear that there's an advantage to being the one who writes the rules, and that we should maintain that advantage. Even though China is the driver and the heart of that "fastest-growing region," Obama said the U.S., not China, should write the rules. He did not propose working with China to develop rules that would be mutually beneficial to the U.S., China, and the world. He proposed that the U.S. write the rules for Asia, to ensure our advantage.

As China grows in economic size and power, U.S. economic power will be relatively diminished, ultimately giving China more power and voice in the world. The era of "We should write those rules" is quickly coming to an end. China will use its new economic size and power to ensure that rules are not simply written by the U.S. and imposed on others, but that China is a part of writing those rules, ensuring that the rules are to the benefit of all, giving no "advantage" to one side or the other. In contrast to Obama's statement, consider the statements of China's president Xi Jinping when he said in a speech to Mongolian leaders: "We will never do things that could result in 'one wins and the other loses' or 'one wins more and the other gets less.'"[10]

In our relations with other countries, too often we look to find the winner and loser as if economic competition is a zero sum game, but not only is it not a zero sum game, it's a network of synergistic relationships. A healthy economy in Germany helps the economy of the U.S. A healthy U.S. economy is good for Mexico. A solid Taiwan economy is a benefit to Singapore. A strong Chinese economy is good for the world. In sports there is a winner and a loser; in the real world of economics, it benefits all when all economies succeed. If we're keeping score, then let's keep score against poverty as emerging economies rise to productivity. Let's keep score against disease as more around the world gain access to medical technologies. Let's keep score against ignorance as the poor gain access to education that will give them the opportunity to gain security and the other advantages of our modern world. All countries should be on the same team going up against the opponents of poverty, disease, ignorance, and war.

Those that hold onto the hope of maintaining our position as the world's largest economy should question the actual benefits of being the world's largest economy. Is it that negotiations can be leveraged in our favor? When sitting down at the world table is the U.S. able to construct unfair treaties simply due to our size? If our hope is to continually be the largest economy in the world, we should question what we find to be the benefit of that position and truly understand the implications of retaining our position as the largest.

While pundits will continue to predict doom for the U.S. as our rank as the world's largest and most powerful economy sinks, the question becomes how will China use its new economic power? As we explore China's history and character in this book, their intent will become clear. It will be evident that China will continue the trend of using its economic power to improve the lives of the Chinese people as well as to level the playing field. China will continue to insist that negotiations take place between equals and not allow those negotiations to be skewed by one dominant player. As China grows in economic power and influence, they will increasingly reject the proposition of a U.S. President when he says: "We [the U.S.] should write those rules."

Africa and Other Hopes

While China's economic growth has already brought over 300 million people out of poverty, their continued growth will improve the lives of millions inside and outside of China. Even today China has significant influence in the continent of Africa as it invests in African economic development. The West's approach to Africa has been aid driven, providing grants or loans that, although sometimes helpful, often simply enrich political leaders. China, although providing some aid, has taken a more active approach of building infrastructure in exchange for raw materials. China has shown itself to be very capable of rapid infrastructure development, from high-speed rail to new bridges, as well as commercial and residential construction. Bringing their expertise in infrastructure development to third world countries such as those in Africa may have a dramatic influence on reducing world poverty. As third world and emerging nations seek to break out of the poverty trap, they will begin to look to China as an example of how to implement rapid development for true economic improvement, resulting in a higher standard of living for the people.

As we can see, the economic influence of China will be two fold. First, as developed nations become economically connected to China, they will become dependent on sales to and imports from China. This mutual dependency will give China growing bargaining power in negotiations with individual nations, but also in international organizations like the World Trade Organization (WTO) and the United Nations. Second, China's influence will be by example as struggling economies will look to the ideas of China as an alternate path to the rapid elimination of poverty.

It is this alternate path that causes great concern from the West, in particular the U.S. But it's critical to understand that while China's path may be different from ours, their hopeful destination is the same as ours: security, tranquility, prosperity, and liberty. Before we assume this to be the goals of all nations, or the goals of all leaders, consider those who have come to power in some of the Arab nations. Their goal is often to force a religious creed, or simply to obtain and maintain power with little or no care for the standard of living of the people. Too often their goals are incompatible with our own, sometimes even to the extent that they strive to destroy our nation or our way of life. China does not share this destructive mentality. Their goal, like ours, is continued improvement for all.

The advances that China has made over the last thirty years cannot have come by chance; these advances are a product of intent—bringing 300 million people out of poverty in three decades does not come by luck, but by purpose. We'll explore this alternate path in subsequent chapters, because it's this difference that causes much of our conflict with China. But know that our common goals are a great advantage in our relationship with China, and that our concerns are more about method and choice of path than about destination.

As we consider China becoming the world's largest economy, it appears we have a catch-22 on our hands. We can hope for the improved standard of living for all in China as they move towards a GDP per capita equal to that of the U.S., but due to the size of China, a parity in GDP per capita ultimately means that China will have a much larger economy than the U.S. Thus, the U.S. will lose some influence and power, while China gains influence and power. However, in the end, fearing that the U.S. will lose its place as the world's largest economy is a position of ill will towards those who would attain a standard of living similar to our own. Not only should we abandon our fear of a growing Chinese economy, but we should celebrate as millions are freed from the shackles of poverty.

The Real Effect of China's Economic Growth

China's economic growth is a young man moving from the demanding physical labor of farming in his hometown to a more profitable and less demanding job at a factory. While we may think of Chinese factories as a hard way of life, young people are moving to the cities to take these jobs in droves. Factory work is a big step up from the opportunities available in their rural hometowns. The growing economy of China is a young woman moving from the factory floor to the factory accounting department, learning to use computers and modern tools which make her more productive and valuable to the factory, while also improving her pay and thus her standard of living. The Chinese growing economy is a student graduating from Huazhong University of Science and Technology in Wuhan, going on to take a job with Huawei developing communications technology, and then making ten times what his father could ever have dreamed. It's a family acquiring their first phone, which allows them to stay in touch with friends and relatives. It's a family moving into a house with electricity and running water. It's a family buying their first car, which gives them the freedom to travel locally and saves them time because they can now drive where they once biked or even walked. The growing Chinese economy is a couple taking their first trip abroad, traveling to faraway places, and gaining life experiences that were unavailable to prior generations of Chinese.

Leading by Size or Leading by Greatness

To fear China's growing economy is to hope for less than the best for China, and it is to believe that our standard of living is contingent on the U.S. being the biggest economy in the world. While there may be some advantages to leading through size, our advantage cannot and should not remain our mere size. Our strength must come from leading through innovation and great ideas that benefit us as well as others.

Leading by the brute force of size may have been easy, but leading by great ideas will be more advantageous. China's economic success does not have to mean U.S. economic failure. In many ways China's economic success is U.S. success, because an improved standard of living for all is our true hope.

The late Steve Jobs, founder of Apple Computer, was possibly the most focused business leader of our time. However, it was rare to hear him talk of being number one, or having the largest market share. What Steve Jobs spoke of was "insanely great" products and groundbreaking innovation.[11] This ultimately resulted in Apple being a true leader. There is something to be learned from his focus. If our goal is to be number one (meaning the biggest economy), then it's quite possible that our efforts are misplaced.

Taking inspiration from Steve Jobs, we should focus not on being the largest economy, but on creating "insanely great" education systems. On developing "insanely great" technologies that improve everyone's standard of living, or on improving government functionality that would make the best use of our resources. We should focus on developing great medical technologies that can improve lives around the world. We should focus not on power and control, but on bringing great ideas to the world that will improve our lives as well as the lives of others. If instead we focus on maintaining our power through size, and if we continue to fear China's growth, we will miss out on truly historic opportunities to partner with China to address problems that are common to all.

But What About...

But economic success is not all that matters. What about the dangerous products from China? What about the environmental damage? What about intellectual property rights? What about the threat of Chinese technological advances? What about human rights issues like democracy and the one-child policy? What about communism? What about threats to our jobs? What about China's growing military threat?

Yes, these issues must be addressed, but let us address them from a foundation of hoping the best for the people of China. This means a continually improving standard of living, even as we realize this will ultimately result in China having the world's largest economy—a growing economy that makes the China of 1959 a distant memory, a growing economy that we must celebrate and not fear.

*

The year was 2009. He watched as the men unloaded the new washing machine from the truck and wheeled it into his mother's home.

"*Nǐ chīfàn le ma,*" he said, greeting his mother.

The mother watched in amazement as her son twisted a simple knob that caused fresh water to rush into a device that would save her hours of daily labor. He didn't know much about her past. She didn't like to talk about it, but he did know that she had lost a brother, a sister, and her father to starvation in 1959. But he and his mother preferred to think about the future rather than the past.

Before he left to go back to the city he handed his mother a box with a shiny blue bow. She smiled at him knowing what was in the box.

"Another pair of shoes?"

"You can't have too many," he replied as he walked out the door and got into his car.

In China, a typical greeting among the older generation is, "*nǐ chīfàn le ma.*" It means: have you eaten? If you understand 1959, then you can understand "*nǐ chīfàn le ma.*" And if you understand "*nǐ chīfàn le ma,*" you understand why we must celebrate, not fear, China's growing economy.

*

2

A Very Brief History of China

History can tell us a lot about the character of a person or a nation, so an understanding of the history of China is important as we explore the question of whether or not we should fear China. If we do not have at least a basic understanding of Chinese history, we can be easily misled, as some may attempt to characterize China as something it's not. We'll focus more on recent history, as it's more relevant to our question. If you are one who finds reading history a chore, hopefully this summary of Chinese history will do you no harm, and it should be easier than reading a 500 page book on the Ming Dynasty. In a way, students in America who study U.S. history have it quite easy; there are only several hundred years of U.S. history to keep track of. A student in China has a much more formidable task; the history of China spans almost four thousand years. Because of this, a brief history of China is not really possible, but this summary should suffice for our purposes.

2070 BC

The history of China can be traced back about four thousand years, with the first dynasty beginning in 2070 BC. The Xia [pronounced Shyah] dynasty was a very small part of what we know as China today. For the next two thousand years, China oscillated between relatively unified dynasties to periods characterized by divided kingdoms run by warlords. Some of the dynasties lasted only 15 years, while others held power for over 500 years. See, not bad so far. We just covered two thousand years.

The first imperial dynasty, which is often referred to as the "First Dynasty," was the Qin Dynasty pronounced [Chin] established in 220 BC by Qin Shi Huang. Qin forced a standardization of language and measures that helped to unify a larger area of China. A series of dynasties followed for almost another 2,000 years, with each dynasty expanding or contracting in size depending on its power.

Many wars were fought as one dynasty was forced out by the next, or as subjects not happy with their leaders rebelled. It's impossible to get an accurate count, but there have been easily hundreds of civil wars within China, and over 100 million lives lost as one dynasty or warlord attempted to take over another. The Mongol conquests in 1206 AD cost 50 million lives, while the Qing dynasty's conquest over the Ming Dynasty in 1616 racked up a death toll exceeding 20 million people. China had to contest with internal difficulties for many years, but in the 16th century external forces also began to exert themselves. Europe had begun expanding trade and commerce to the Far East. Portuguese traders first settled in Macau, a city in South East China, in 1513.

1592 Japan Attacks

Learning from the European empires, in 1592 Japan invaded Korea, a country on the northeast border of China. Korea requested help from China to stop the Japanese invasion, and it was in the interest of China to help fight back the Japanese invaders, as China was their ultimate target. Japan's hopes of taking over China were crushed when China joined forces with Korea to stop the invasion.

1711 The British Come to China

In 1711 the emperor of China, Enkh Amgalan Khaan, gave permission for the British East India Company to come to Canton to trade silver for Chinese silk, porcelain, spices, and tea. The trade soon caused a problem. China had little interest in European goods, so Europe continued to trade silver for the Chinese products it desired. This resulted in a trade imbalance as China gained silver while Europe, in particular Britain, lost silver. The British traders had a solution to this trade imbalance. They found that they could develop a market in China for a different product. That product was the drug opium, and it quickly replaced silver as payment for goods exported out of China.

1787 France Invades Vietnam

In 1787, around the same time The United States was finally finishing up with the Revolutionary War, France invaded Vietnam, a country on the south border of China. The French were working to grow their empire. The government of Vietnam requested the assistance of China to help them repel the foreign invaders. Most of Vietnam was lost to France by the time China stepped in and stopped further northern advances. China was recognizing that, similar to the prior war with Japan, foreign powers were invading their close neighbors to get to *them*. These foreigners obviously had no limit to their imperial ambitions—the invaders had their sights on China and the emperors knew it.

1839 The Opium Wars

Meanwhile, by 1810 the British were sending huge quantities of opium into China. The drug was illegal according to Chinese law, but the foreign traders had no consideration for the rules set by the Qing Dynasty. China worked to enforce the law, but because so many of their population had become addicted to the drug that the British were smuggling into China, the Chinese government felt that they had lost control. By 1820 British traders were sending 900 tons of opium into China each year. Seeing the great damage the drug caused for society, in 1839 the Qing Dynasty began to confiscate the illegal cargo. They issued a decree which in part read: "Opium has a harm. Opium is a poison, undermining our good customs and morality." The actions of the Qing Dynasty to stop the drug trade caused Britain to send naval ships to Hong Kong and the surrounding area. The British military attacked the coast of China to protect the drug trade. This was the first Opium War.

China, recognizing the overwhelming power of the British navy, retreated from their attempt to stop the illegal trade. But the drug continued to damage the Chinese society, so again, about thirty-five years later in 1856, the Qing Dynasty made an attempt to stop the trade. Sadly, they failed once more. The British navy forced China to accept the drug as payment for goods exported back to Europe. This was the second Opium War.

1851 Taiping Rebellion

In 1851, around the time of the U.S. Civil War, rebels in the south of China, discontent with Qing Dynasty leadership, and facing growing threats from foreign powers, began to organize. The Qing

Dynasty had originated from Manchuria in northeast China, and those in the south considered them foreigners. So as the Qing Dynasty flailed, those from the south of China readied to throw them out. The Taiping Rebellion grew into a huge civil war as inhabitants of south and central China fought to overthrow the Qing Dynasty. To give some perspective, the American Civil War cost about six hundred thousand lives, while the Taiping Rebellion cost between twenty and thirty million lives. After fourteen long years, the Qing Dynasty won and put down the rebellion. But the Chinese people were still dissatisfied with the Qing leadership, which was continuously bullied by foreign imperialists. They had lost the Opium Wars and were unable to suppress foreign missionaries who were increasing in number; these missionaries forced their ways onto the Chinese, often supplanting Chinese laws with their own legal systems.

1894 Japan Attacks

Because China had its hands full with the French in Vietnam and the British along the Southeast coast in the Opium wars, Japan again set its sights on Korea. In 1894 Korea was on the verge of a civil war due to political unrest. Japan seized upon this opportunity to once again try to annex Korea. And once again, China got involved. This effectively meant that two outside countries, China and Japan, fought a war against each other on Korean soil. But this time Japan had superior military and naval forces, as they had been buying ships from Britain and France. Japan, as China had feared, was not just interested in Korea; after taking Korea they marched into China. Although Japan had won, they quickly realized the impossibility of actually taking all of China's land mass. Due to this, Japan negotiated a settlement wherein they would control many Chinese ports, and take control of the island of Formosa (Taiwan).

The Qing dynasty became unpopular with the people of China because they were not showing strength in the face of imperialist aggression from Europe and Japan. They were constantly forced into unequal treaties because the foreign powers had more technically advanced armies and could extract unreasonable concessions. Simply threatening with superior militaries was also an effective way for foreign invaders to continue plundering China. China was stuck gazing down the barrel of a gun as they futilely attempted to negotiate from a position of military weakness. They lost territory and sovereignty. It seemed only a matter of time before China would be taken over by a foreign power, whether by Japan, Britain, France, or possibly even the U.S.

1898 The Boxer Rebellion

In 1898 a group of martial arts fighters, referred to as "Boxers" by westerners, were fed up and started attacking and killing foreigners living in China. The movement grew and many joined the Boxers as resentment against foreigners grew exponentially. At first the Qing Dynasty was split on which side to take. Empress Dowager Cixi originally instructed her forces to protect the foreigners as she cautiously watched foreign military troops enter China, in an effort to protect their missionaries. There were eight nations that sent troops into China to put down the Boxers: Japan, Russia, Great Britain, France, the United States, Germany, Austria-Hungary, and Italy. These foreign powers ultimately ordered Empress Cixi to hand over her military and financial powers to them. The empress of China knew then that she must side with the Boxers; it was clear that the foreigners were using the situation to take control of China. The combined forces of the foreign militaries, totaling over 49 thousand troops, not only put down the Boxer Rebellion, but they also marched through China, looting cities and raping women.

The Westerners took control of Beijing, Tianjin, and other cities. They occupied these cities for a year, ransacking the Summer Palace, which had been previously attacked by British and French troops forty years earlier during the Second Opium War. In 1901 the Western Allies offered the Empress a deal. They would allow her to stay in power if she agreed to pay reparation and meet other demands of the eight countries. She had little choice—she could continue a war against eight of the largest militaries in the world, or she could allow them to assume even more power in China.

China's sovereignty was degrading at a rapid pace as European and American powers exerted increasing authority over the fragile nation. Russia took territory in northeast China, and France was expanding in south China, having already taken control of Indochina and Vietnam.

China's perception of Western powers was being solidified. For almost two hundred years Western nations had not been knocking at China's door; rather, they had been breaking the door down. They saw Great Britain force opium on the people of China. They saw the Japanese invasion of 1894 enabled by military technology from the West. They witnessed forty-nine thousand Western troops enter Shanghai and Beijing to put down the Boxer Rebellion. They saw their palaces ransacked by Western nations. While some Chinese profited from the foreign trade, overall the people of China saw no good come from the West as these nations flouted Chinese laws, ransacked their nation, and took increasing power from their Empress. They also watched as foreigners invaded neighboring countries like Vietnam, Indochina, and Korea. The people of China saw those from the West not as some great hope, but as *the* biggest threat to their peace and prosperity. While time can heal, as we explore our relationship with China, it's important to remember that China's first introduction to the West was brutal and violent.

1912 End of the Dynasties

The political power of the Qing Dynasty was weakened from external attacks, but it was also crumbling internally as divisions emerged within the ruling dynasty. A sequence of power struggles, complete with death by poisoning and a childless emperor, left the 264 year-old Qing Dynasty in the hands of Puyi, a two year old child. Cabinet members of the government attempted to keep the dynasty together, but it was too weak to survive. In October of 1911 forces within China established a new government with Sun Yat-sen as its leader. Sun Yat-sen negotiated with the imperial government and in February of 1912 they issued an edict abdicating the child emperor Puyi from the throne. Two thousand years of imperial rule in China had come to an end.

Following the end of the last dynasty in China, a void in leadership was created. The fall of the Qing Dynasty had left each region of China under the control of warlords; China was no longer unified. Sun Yat-sen, who was instrumental in the revolution and was the first post-dynastic president of China, worked to unify the country. But it was a daunting task. Educated by western missionaries in Hong Kong and Shanghai, he was fluent in English, an advantage the dynasties never had, and he had learned the ways of western cultures and economies. Seventy-Five years before the true opening of China to the world, he articulated the importance of foreign capital to create the factories that would give productive ability to the large population of China. He knew that the hard working Chinese people, in combination with the capital and technologies of the West, would make China an economic success.

While Sun Yat-sen tried to focus on economic development and trade, the reality of the circumstances required his attention to be focused on the unification of China. The remaining thirteen years of his life were spent in political battles as numerous groups attempted to take control of China. Warlords were carving out their domains and numerous political parties were fighting for control. Although not a supporter of communism, Sun Yat-sen partnered with the Communist Party of China to work towards a stable and unified government.

Upon Sun Yat-sen's death in 1925, Chiang Kai-shek took over as head of the Nationalist party, the KMT. Chiang Kai-shek did not like the influence of the Communist Party within the KMT, so he began to rid the party of Communists. Chang Kai-shek was supported in this endeavor by the Western powers such as the U.S. and Great Britain. This, along with other factors, caused many to oppose him. The Chinese people felt that Chang Kai-shek had the same problem as the dynasties in that he was unable to stand up to foreigners. After having been forced out of the government, the Communist Party began to build power and quickly gained the support of the people, especially in the central and western provinces of China. While the Nationalist party controlled the eastern cities, the Communist Party marched west, gaining the support of the common people.

1927 Civil War

Because so many of the Chinese people sided with the Communists, in 1927 civil war broke out between Chiang Kai-shek's Nationalist Party and the Communist Party of China, ultimately led by Mao Zedong. Seeing the trouble that China was having, Japan once again attempted to take over China.

1937 Japan Attacks

In 1937 Japan attacked China with a full military invasion, ultimately sending 3.9 million troops into China. The invasion was a horrifically brutal attack on a civilian population. The Japanese soldiers routinely raped Chinese women and it's estimated that over 20 million Chinese died in the war. The battle of Nanking is well documented and is referred to as the "Rape of Nanking" because of the sheer amount of rape Chinese women suffered at the hands of the Japanese. 300 thousand Chinese died in the Nanking battle alone.

Due to the Japanese invasion, the Nationalist Party formed an alliance with the Communist party to fight Japan. This put a temporary halt to the civil war in China. The Japanese made it all the way to Hong Kong and down into Vietnam in the south of China, controlling all the major cities along the coast, including Shanghai, Nanking, and Beijing.

In 1945 the United States dropped two atomic bombs on Japan; simultaneously, the Soviet Union sent troops to fight the Japanese in northern China. These two events caused Japan to unconditionally surrender. Upon surrender, Japan was forced to relinquish the island of Taiwan, which it had controlled since 1895. With the assistance of the U.S., Taiwan was handed over to Chiang Kai-shek and the KMT Nationalist party.

With the Japanese problem solved, China resumed their civil war. By 1949 the Communist Party of China controlled most of mainland China. Chiang Kai-shek's Nationalist Party was forced to move its government to Taiwan, but still claimed to be the official government of China, even though the mainland was under the control of the Communists.

1949 Mao Declares the People's Republic of China

In October of 1949 Mao Zedong declared the People's Republic of China (PRC) and began working with the Soviet Union to make China a truly communist society. As Mao sought to establish a communist political and economic structure, China underwent many changes. At first he pursued the structure of the Soviet Union, but by 1958 Mao began to see problems with the Soviet style system. Because of this, he created a new system unique to China. Mao was persistent and often brutal in eliminating landowners and anyone else who opposed the Communist Party or its way of thinking.

1959 The Great Leap Forward & 1966 The Cultural Revolution

In 1959 Mao instituted a plan called The Great Leap Forward, which focused on industrialization and agricultural collectivization—private farming was prohibited. The social and economic policies were a disaster and resulted in the deaths of 18 to 30 million people, most due to starvation. Characterized by coercion and violence, it was a very dark period in modern Chinese history. As central government economic policies failed, China was starving but refused help from the West. They had no interest in begging from those who had caused them so much harm in the past.

Because of the program's failure, Mao was beginning to be marginalized and others such as Deng Xiaoping were gaining power in the Communist Party. To counteract this effect, in 1966 Mao initiated a plan called the Cultural Revolution. He claimed that some in the government were turning against Communist principles and pursuing a more capitalist structure, and he was correct, they were. The Cultural Revolution was intended to remove all elements of capitalism as well as traditional Chinese culture from the society. This included historical landmarks and artifacts, religious sites, and traditional religious teachings such as Confucianism. The ultimate aim was to bring the population in line with Maoist philosophy and the principles of Communism.

The youth of the country accepted Mao's claim and formed the Red Guard which went on to persecute political leaders and any citizens thought to be lacking in commitment to the beliefs and practices of Communism. This resulted in class struggle and social unrest. Historical, cultural, and religious documents were destroyed and buildings were ransacked. Mao instructed the police to not interfere with the activities of the Red Guard, and the youth became increasingly violent. Deng Xiaoping and many other political leaders were sent away for "re-education." The social instability brought on by the Cultural Revolution caused the economy to suffer. Mao recognized that the movement was getting out of hand and so began to phase out the Red Guard. He eventually brought Deng Xiaoping back into the party, and because of his leadership ability, Deng, along with other reformers, was able to make improvements to the economy. However, hard line Communists again became concerned that Deng and others were turning against Communist principles. The Communist Party worked to turn public opinion against Deng, but the people were supportive of the reforms he was making. The people began to turn against the hardliners.

1978 Deng Xiaoping

Mao died in 1976 and in a surprise move the military arrested the top leaders in the Communist Party for their abuses during the Cultural Revolution. The successor to Mao was not fully up to the task of leadership and slowly relinquished power to Deng and his associates. By 1978 Deng Xiaoping was the new leader of China and began a movement to open China to the world. He began implementing pragmatic political and economic reforms.

Deng once said, "It doesn't matter whether the cat is black or white, as long as it catches mice." This statement indicated that he was more concerned about the results of the political and economic structure than he was in advancing a particular political philosophy. The changes Deng made, which became known as a socialist market economy, had a huge impact on China—this was the beginning of China's swift economic advancement. In 1980 Deng began opening the doors of China to U.S. trade. In 2000 President Clinton granted China "Permanent Normal Trade Status," and in 2001 China joined the World Trade Organization (WTO). These changes caused some of the most rapid economic development ever seen worldwide. In a span of thirty years, the GDP of China increased by nearly 50 times, bringing the people out of starvation and setting them on a path to quickly become a developed nation.

For the history phobic: congratulations, you just covered 4,000 years of Chinese history. Well, at least a summary. But hang in there, we have just a few more events to cover, then we can get back to the question of whether or not we should fear China. In studying the history of what China has done, it is also important to study the history of what China has not done. For this reason it's important to understand the Philippine war, the Korean War, and the Vietnam War, because these events define much of China's perception of the U.S. We'll finish up with the Tibet issue.

1898 Philippine War

The Philippine Islands were taken as a colony by Spain in 1565. The Spanish developed and unified the islands into a single political entity, bringing trade and education to the islands while fighting off other European imperialists. The Philippine revolution began in 1896 as a secret organization that sought to gain independence from Spain. In 1898 the Spanish-American war was fought as the U.S. helped Cuba to gain independence from Spain. The short war ended with the U.S. as victor, causing Spain to give independence to Cuba and to hand over colonial control of Puerto Rico, Guam, and the Philippine Islands to the United States. The U.S., despite having just fought to gain independence for Cuba, made the rather strange decision to step in where Spain had left off and take over the Philippines as a colony. Those in the Philippines who had been fighting for independence from Spain then began fighting the United States for independence. The war lasted three years and caused over 6,000 U.S. deaths and over 200,000 Philippine deaths. When the war ended in 1902 the U.S. gave the Philippines some control and limited voting rights, but the U.S. continued to administer the Philippines while levels of autonomy were gradually extended. The Philippines did not gain full independence from the U.S. until 1946—forty-eight years after the U.S. took the Philippines from Spain.

1950 Korean War

After the WWII surrender of Japan in 1945, Korea, which had been controlled by Japan since 1895, once again became independent; however, because the United States and the Soviet Union had contributed to winning the war against Japan, it was agreed that North Korea would be under the control of the Soviets and South Korea would be under control of the United States. The Korean leaders were not allowed to negotiate on their own behalf. Although the ultimate goal was that the two re-unite, under the Soviet influence North Korea became communist, and with the U.S. influence South Korea became capitalist. Tensions simmered on the border between North and South Korea until North Korea invaded South Korea in 1950 in an attempt to force the two countries to reunite. North Korea nearly won this war; however, the United States feared the conflict would grant the communist countries of Soviet Union and China control of Korea. In order to avoid this, the United States sent 300,000 troops to South Korea to help push back the North Koreans. China did not want to get involved, but citizens and the government became increasingly concerned about their own security.

China made it clear to the United States that it would not get involved as long as U.S. troops did not go further than the original border between North and South Korea. In the meantime, United States President Truman told General MacArthur to go ahead and take North Korea as long as China and the Soviet Union were not there. The U.S. military thus not only pushed the North Korean army back to the original border, but pushed them all the way back to the border with China, effectively giving South Korea and the United States full control of Korea. Once the U.S. went north of the original border between North and South Korea, China sent 200 thousand troops to North Korea. With Soviet air support, the Chinese pushed the American troops all the way back to Seoul, the capital of South Korea. The war was then at a stalemate for two years as neither side gained territory, at which point the two sides agreed on an armistice that resulted in the approximate original border being restored between the North and South. The death toll reached well over two million people.

1963 Vietnam War

Since 1887 Vietnam had been a colony of imperialist France, under full control of the French government. The people of Vietnam, dissatisfied with foreign rule, had for many years tried to regain their independence. During WWII Germany took control of France and thus Vietnam; however, Germany chose to hand over control to their ally Japan who was attempting to take over all of Asia. A group called the Viet Mihn was first organized to gain freedom from France, but once Japan invaded Vietnam, the group's mission was expanded to removing the French *and* the Japanese.

In 1945 Russia, the U.S., and Great Britain defeated Japan in WWII. Ho Chi Mihn, who had led the Viet Minh against the Japanese and the French, proclaimed independence for Vietnam and was beginning to gain full control of Vietnam and to recover from years of foreign occupation. However, foreign superpowers U.S.,

Russia, and Great Britain agreed that control of the country should be given back to France. British and non-Communist Chinese military were sent to help regain control of Vietnam for France. By 1946 the British troops left Vietnam after regaining power in the south and handing over their fragile control to the returning French troops.

By 1949 Mao's power in China was solidified, and he decided to help Vietnam gain independence from France and the Western Powers. The Soviet Union was simultaneously realizing that Great Britain and the U.S. were working to gain influence in the region. Due to this fact, the Soviet Union switched from supporting the French to supporting the communist leader Ho Chi Minh. From 1950 both the Soviet Union and Communist China provided support, but not troops, to the North Vietnamese, while at the same time the South was supported by the Western powers. The Soviet Union and Communist China recognized Ho Chi Minh's government as the leader of Vietnam, and the U.S. and Great Britain recognized Bao Dai in the south as the leader of Vietnam.

By 1954 the Viet Minh had beaten the French and the French military left Vietnam. South Vietnam was still under the control of a government established by the French and supported by western powers. But the Viet Minh were making their way south to take full control of Vietnam and re-unite the country.

At the Geneva Conference of 1954, the Soviet Union, U.S., Great Britain, and Taiwan agreed to divide Vietnam into two states. The nation would be split until an election could take place, then the people would decide who would lead, and finally the country would be re-united. Sound familiar? Yes, this exact tactic was implemented in Korea just a few years earlier. For Vietnam, Ho Chi Minh was given authority over the North and Ngo Dinh Diem was given control of the South.

Vietnam Split Between North and South

Both North and South Vietnam had difficulties as they attempted to weed out opposition within their ranks. However, it was believed that if an election was held, Ho Chi Minh and the Communist North would win, so the U.S. did not want an election. In the North, the Viet Minh had made tactical errors, so they were being replaced by other political leaders. At the same time, a group from the South called the Viet Cong were gaining strength in their rebellion against foreign influence and power, working to rid the South of a government backed by the U.S. The U.S. had about 900 advisors in Vietnam at that time. By 1963 the U.S. had 16,000 military personnel in the country.

The Viet Cong gained support and power from within the South, as North Vietnam prepared to invade. The U.S., seeing the impending invasion from the North, began bombing North Vietnam, and by 1965 they had placed 200 thousand troops in Vietnam to fight both the Viet Cong and the approaching armies from the North. At the peak of the war, the U.S. had over 500 thousand troops in Vietnam. By 1971 the U.S. began withdrawing troops and abandoning their pursuit of supporting the South. By 1975 the last of the American troops and military personnel left Vietnam—the North took the capital of Saigon and proclaimed it Ho Chi Minh City.

In all, the U.S. spent over $100 billion on the Vietnam War, equivalent to about one trillion in today's dollars. Over 58 thousand Americans were killed in the war, but more importantly, it's estimated that the total death toll of the war was over two million people. China's involvement in the war was limited as they supplied some arms and advisors to the Communist leaders. In all, they spent several hundred million (as opposed to the $100 billion spent by the U.S.). Likewise, the Soviet Union supported the North Vietnamese with arms and advisors with totals also in the hundreds of millions; however, neither China nor the Soviet Union sent ground troops to Vietnam.

Tibet

Tibet is a region in the southern part of China and is currently considered part of China. Since the Yuen Dynasty (1271-1368), Chinese dynasties have had various levels of control over Tibet. There is much debate about the status of Tibet through the dynasties, but in general, the Yuen Dynasty had a reasonable amount of control and a friendly relationship with Tibet. Then the Ming Dynasty (1368-1644) lost influence and Tibet was largely independent. The last dynasty, which was the Qing (1644-1912), saw renewed influence and control over Tibet. However, towards the end of the dynasty, rulers were forced to send troops to assert their control. When the Qing Dynasty fell in 1911, Tibet expelled all Chinese troops and refused to submit to the new Chinese government. Meanwhile, Great Britain, in its drive to build its empire, invaded Tibet in 1903 due to the fact that it borders India, which Britain had already taken as a colony.

In 1914 China, Great Britain, and Tibet worked to establish a treaty and to set borders. Although they almost came to an agreement, only Tibet and Great Britain signed the final treaty. From 1916 to 1949 Tibet was independent; this was very much due to that fact that China was preoccupied with its own internal strife and civil war. Once China's civil war ended, and the Mao led Communists had taken control of most of China, Mao sent troops back into Tibet to reestablish China's control. China regained control, but many groups in Tibet began to rebel against Chinese rule, and in 1959 the conflict came to a boiling point. Mao had begun implementing the same land reforms and socialist programs in Tibet that were proliferating in China. As China continued to force changes, they decided to remove the Tibetan leader, the Dalai Lama. When the Chinese military came within range of the palace, the Dalai Lama escaped before he was taken. In the following few years, China destroyed many of the monasteries and worked to eliminate religion from Tibet, imprisoning and killing many monks and religious leaders. Over the past 20 years, China has relocated many of the Han Chinese into the Tibet area to dilute the population and to help integrate Tibet into China. In 1998 imprisoned monks held uprisings. As recently as 2008 major protests have occurred with the people demanding independence for Tibet and the release of imprisoned monks.

This brief review of China's history is important. If we are to evaluate China's place in the world, and the "threat" they pose, we must understand at least the last few hundred years of China's history. And special attention must be devoted to China's rocky relationship with the West, which began with the Opium Wars and continued through the Boxer Rebellion to the Korean and Vietnam wars. With this history in mind, let's now get back to our question: Should we fear China?

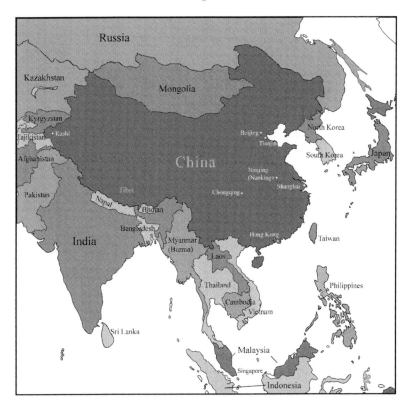

A timeline of China's History may be found in appendix A

3

Fearing China's Military Power

How Threatening are China's Missiles? (The Diplomat)
U.S. Plans Naval Shift Towards Asia (Wall Street Journal)
How Many Nukes Does China Have? (Wall Street Journal)
China Navy Makes Waves in South China Sea (USA Today)
For Xi, a 'China Dream' of Military Power (Wall Street Journal)
How to Neutralize China's Military Threat (The Washington Times)
China, U.S. Head Toward Faceoff in South China Sea (USA Today)
U.S. Official Warns About China's Military Buildup (New York Times)[12]

The newspaper headlines paint a narrative that the Chinese military should be feared and kept under close watch. Recently, President Obama announced that the U.S. navy would "pivot" to the Pacific and position sixty percent of naval resources in Asia; this is instead of the fifty percent that has been the norm since WWII. His most recent political opponent, presidential candidate Mitt Romney, said that this was not enough and he would do even more to counter China's growing military.

There's no question that the politicians and media would like Americans to believe that China is a military threat. Are they right? Should we fear China's growing military and its increasing power and influence? An exploration of China's past, its current activities, and its claimed objectives will be a good guide to determine whether or not China's military power is truly a threat to be feared. To evaluate the threat of the Chinese military, we must first examine what rights countries should have to build and maintain their militaries. When we talk about "rights" we must presuppose that other countries or groups of countries can work to impose limitations on the military of sovereign nations. Thus, organization like the U.N. or NATO might confirm a "right" to have a certain size military or may work to restrict a nation's military.

Militaries throughout the ages have been used to defend the homeland, defend allies, expand territory, and influence negotiations. If our goal is a more peaceful and free world, the international community should allow and encourage all nations to defend themselves. We should work together to discourage and prevent aggressive action and expansions of territory. An international community focused on the well-being of all should watch closely to ensure militaries are not used to intimidate or extort unfair concessions or treaties upon weaker nations.

Defending the Home Land and Allies

The right to defend a homeland is one of the most basic rights of a nation. The size and strength of the military required to accomplish security and defense depends upon what is to be defended and what threats exist. Measuring what is to be defended is more quantitative in that it's easy to measure such things as population size, length of border, and amount of coastline. Determining threats may be more elusive, but could be derived from an analysis of the current political climate as well as a review of the country's history to see if a country has been attacked or invaded, and if so, when and by whom.

Let's begin with what is to be defended. China has a landmass of approximately 9.6 million square kilometers (km), which is roughly the same size as the United States—only Russia and Canada are larger. However, because Russia and Canada are further north, much of their land is not reasonably inhabitable. The coastline of China is about 14.5 thousand km long, while the total coastline of the United States is about 20 thousand km. Starting with these basic elements, it's instructive to compare the top military spenders in the world.[13]

The U.S. spends about $620 billion per year on national defense. China currently spends about $216 billion. If we look at landmass, and dollars per km spent, China spends approximately $22 thousand per square km, compared to $64 thousand per square km in the U.S. On this measurement, China only spends more than Russia. But if we factor in that Russia has a large amount of uninhabitable land, then effectively China is the smallest spender of the big six when it comes to military dollars spent per square km. Regarding how much is spent per km of coastline, China spends about $15 million per km of coast line, ranking second in the category, while the United States spends over two times as much, at $31 million per km of coastline. Dollars spent per km of land borders indicate the same discrepancy. China spends about $10 thousand per km of land border compared to the U.S. at about $51 thousand.

But perhaps defense dollars spent per square km, length of coastline, or land borders are not really what we should look at. Maybe population is more important. How many people must be protected? The population of China in 2013 was just over 1.3 billion (1,357 million). The United States had a population of 316 million, so China's population is over 4 times the size of the U.S. population, while the total land size is about the same.

China spends approximately $160 per person, per year on national defense, ranking only behind Japan on the list. The United States, in contrast, spends about $2,000 per person, per year on national defense; this is an astounding thirteen times more per person spent on defense.

Let's move on to GDP and compare what countries spend on defense as a percent of their entire Gross Domestic Product. China spends less than two percent of GDP on national defense, ranking again almost last on the list (just ahead of Japan which spends only one percent of their GDP on national defense). The United States spends 3.4 percent of GDP on national defense, the highest on the list of top spenders.[14] At the peak of the Iraq and Afghanistan war, the U.S. was spending an additional one hundred billion per year on military, equating to approximately 4.7 percent of GDP.

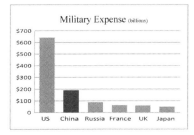

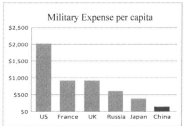

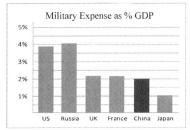

Source: SIPRI Military Expenditure Database 2013. http://milexdata.sipri.org

When looking at these most basic measurements, we can see that China is not a big spender on military. When it comes to the amount of land, coastlines, and borders they need to protect, they spend very little compared to other nations. When it comes to population, they're almost the lowest spender on our list, and as a percent of GDP they likewise rank very low. However, when it comes to national defense, the size of territory, population, or size of the economy are less important than the actual threat faced by that nation.

If a country wants to know how much of its resources should be spent on defending itself, perhaps it should look at the true threat of attack or invasion. One critical factor to consider would be how many countries border the homeland and how friendly these neighbors are. China shares borders with sixteen countries. Are these stable and friendly countries? You can formulate your own analysis, but to name a few that may not be easy neighbors to contend with, consider: North Korea, Russia, Afghanistan, Burma, and Pakistan. Let's contrast these neighbors with the neighbors of the United States, which are Canada and Mexico. Who would you rather share a border with: Canada or North Korea? Or maybe select between Mexico verses Afghanistan. Great Britain borders only one other country and that is the Republic of Ireland. Across the water are France and Germany, and to the north, Norway. France has neighbors such as Spain and Germany. Looking at these neighborhoods, there's no doubt that China has more difficult neighbors than the United States, Great Britain, and many other first world nations.

Objectively determining the defense requirements of a country using the measurable criteria of landmass, length of coast line, length of land border, size of population, GDP, and the character of the neighbors, reveals that China arguably should have a national defense on par with the U.S. and Great Britain.

But the most important factor in analyzing a nation's defense requirements is history. If a country hasn't been attacked or invaded by an outside power for many years, then their defense needs may be smaller, while a country with a history of being invaded, attacked, and abused by foreigners would be well advised to maintain a stronger military defense. So let's refer back to some highlights from of our Brief History of China to see how China has been treated by foreign nations around the world.

In 1592 Japan invaded Korea with the intent of taking China. In 1787 France invaded and took control of Vietnam, a neighbor of China. In 1839 Britain attacked China in the first Opium War in an attempt to control China's trade. In 1856 Britain again attacked China in the Second Opium war. In 1894 Japan invaded Korea for a second time and also took the island of Taiwan from China with the ultimate goal of taking all of China. In 1898 eleven countries, including the U.S. and Great Britain, joined together and invaded China to put down the Boxer Rebellion. In 1931 Japan once more invaded China in one of the most brutal attacks on a country in modern history with over 22 million civilians killed in the war. In 1950 the U.S. invaded China's neighbor Korea, and at one point considered going into China. And finally, in 1955 the U.S. invaded Vietnam, a neighbor of China. In looking at China's history and the number of times China has been invaded and attacked by foreign powers, we can clearly see that the country has a need and a right to a strong military defense.

For comparison, let's look at the history of the United States. Since winning its war for independence from Britain in 1776, the

U.S. has never been invaded by a foreign power. WWII saw the attack on Pearl Harbor by the Japanese, although the Japanese did not land troops on the islands. Likewise, on September 11, 2001 Arab radicals used commercial airplanes to attack New York City and Washington DC, but did not invade with troops. The geographic position of the U.S., far from Europe and Asia, gives it a distinct advantage for protecting the homeland. In addition, because our only bordering countries are Canada and Mexico, which are friendly to the U.S., there is no true threat to the U.S. homeland other than terrorist attack, which is a common threat to all countries. Throughout its short history, the United States has shown to be quite immune from invasion and direct attack.

When put side by side, these contrasting histories paint a very clear picture. China has been brutally attacked and invaded by foreigners for over two centuries. The U.S. has suffered several small attacks and has never been invaded in its entire history. Considering these facts it would be hard to conclude that China should have a smaller military defense than the U.S. And in fact, one could argue that history indicates China should have a larger military than the U.S.

Expanding Territory

But does the world community and the U.S. have reason to be concerned about China's growing military strength and size? The history of the world is one of fluctuating borders, as kingdoms, empires, and dynasties fought to expand territory and grow their influence. Think of the Roman Empire, the Hungarian Empire, and the colonial pursuits of European nations in the 17th through 20th centuries, wherein Great Britain, Spain, and France controlled countries such as India, the Philippines, Vietnam, and Hong Kong.

Due largely to the devastation of WWI and WWII, our modern world has worked to stop aggressive military actions by expansionist states. Great Britain and France thought empire building was a good idea until they were the ones being bombed. Through alliances such as the UN and the NATO, the world community attempts to limit the military capacity of countries that are thought to be aggressive and to have expansionist ambitions. At the end of World War I, the international community put limits on the size of the military that

Germany could maintain, capping their armed forces at 100,000 troops. At the end of World War II, restrictions were put on Japan's military. In a similar fashion, Germany, which was responsible for the deaths of an estimated 50 to 70 million people in WWII, was banned from maintaining a standing military for about 10 years. Other examples include the aggressions of North Korea in 1950 and the attack on Kuwait by Iraq in 1990. These examples all illustrate how acts of aggression necessitated that the international community monitor and restrict a fellow country's military.

In addition to responding to actual aggressive military action, the world community also often attempts to put military restrictions on nations that are seen as unstable or unfriendly to their neighbors. The former leader of Iran periodically made remarks indicating he would prefer Israel not exist. Due to his unfriendly tone, the world community believed him a threat to Israel, and so the UN worked to prevent Iran from obtaining nuclear weapons. When the world community tries to determine if there should be limits on a country's military, we look at that country's history of aggressive behavior and at the statements made by their political leaders. So what is the history of China as an aggressive neighbor? How many countries have they invaded and what threats have they made to other countries? Although China has had many civil wars over history, in the last 200 years China has only sent troops into one country for military action. That country was Korea, which China has worked to protect from Japanese invasion on several occasions. China also sent troops into Korea to prevent the U.S. from taking North Korea and to prevent the U.S. from entering China. Additionally, China assisted North Vietnam in gaining independence from France and in slowing the U.S. troop movement to the north. However, most of this assistance was in equipment and advisors.

Tibet

Tibet is often mentioned as an example of the aggressive nature of China. This conflict has been addressed in our "Brief History of China," but in this context, a review is important. China was aggressive in retaking Tibet in 1950; however, it's important to realize that Tibet had been a part of China on-and-off for many centuries. Tibet was only independent from China for about 37 years.

This is not to argue for a position on one side or the other, but simply to give context for the conflict. It's not comparable to Germany marching into Poland, or Iraq attacking Kuwait, or even the U.S. fighting in Vietnam. At the time China re-asserted its authority over Tibet, even Great Britain agreed that Tibet was part of China.

Taiwan

Taiwan is also used as an argument that China is aggressive with its military. But the island of Taiwan only became separate from China in 1949 when, after the Chinese Civil War, the losing party retreated to the island and retained control of this strategically located resource. This was only made possible with the help of the United States. China would like to reincorporate the island back into the nation in the same way Hong Kong was reincorporated back into China, but so far China has been very peaceful and has not asserted military force in the matter. Think of it this way; in the American Civil War, the pro-slavery Confederates lost, but what if they had retained the state of Florida, effectively defending the peninsula and turning it into a separate political and economic system, while all the time claiming to be the legitimate head of the United States? This is the situation between Taiwan and China, with the additional insult that an independent Taiwan was only made possible with the support of the U.S.

History Based Analysis

History tells us that for hundreds of years China has not been a military aggressor and has been very cautious in its use of military force. On the few occasions it has sent troops outside its borders, it has been to close neighbors that have requested help in repelling a foreign aggressor. China's military and international affairs position has been one of non-intervention, and they've held to that quite well. The chart at the end of this chapter shows a timeline of countries that have invaded China, along with a timeline of countries that China has invaded. Although the U.S. media and politicians attempt to characterize the Chinese military as aggressive and overreaching, history does not show any evidence to support this claim, and quite to the contrary, the actual evidence shows that China adheres to its stated policy of non-intervention.

If it's fair to ask if the U.S. and the world have reason to be concerned about China's military, then we also need to address whether or not China and the rest of world have reason to be concerned about the U.S. military. Since its founding in 1776, the U.S. has sent troops into military combat in over twenty countries. To list and address all the military actions that the U.S. has taken, or to get into the reasons for each action, is well beyond the scope of this book. But consider the following major conflicts.

In the war of 1812 the U.S. attacked Canada. 1846 saw the U.S. attack Mexico as the U.S. expanded territory. In 1898 the U.S. sent over 3,000 troops to China in the Boxer Rebellion. Also in 1898 the U.S. military spread throughout Latin America, in what came to be known as the Banana Wars, in which the U.S. sought to exert economic and legal control over numerous neighbors to the south. 1898 was also the year the U.S. fought the Spanish American War, ultimately taking the Philippines from Spain, and then one year later the U.S. fought the Philippines for control of their country. In 1914 the U.S. sent troops to Europe to fight Germany in WWI. In 1918 the U.S. sent 13,000 troops to Russia during the Russian Civil War. The U.S. had troops in Europe and Asia for WWII from 1931 to 1945. In 1950 the U.S. became involved in the Korean War. In 1955 the U.S. deployed troops to Vietnam to help train Vietnamese soldiers, thus beginning our participation in the Vietnam War. In 1983, Grenada; in 1986, Libya; in 1989, Panama. In 1990 the U.S. fought to prevent Iraq from taking Kuwait. In 1993 the U.S. entered conflict in Somalia. In 1999 the U.S. dropped bombs on Serbia. In 2001, after the 9/11 attacks on the U.S., the war in Afghanistan began. In 2003 the U.S. once again invaded Iraq.

The purpose here is not to critique U.S. military actions or foreign policy, but simply to contrast the fundamentally passive nature of China's military history with the very aggressive U.S. military. The U.S. has had its reasons for each war that it's fought. Looking back, some of these wars were of benefit to the world, like the U.S. involvement in WWII wherein Hitler and his bloody regime was ended and Japan was expelled from China. Even the Chinese would agree that U.S. intervention in the Pacific WWII was to the advantage of China and the world. But U.S. military interventions in places like the Philippines, Vietnam, Korean, Iraq, and Afghanistan have had much less definitive results—it's also clear that the original motive for each of these wars was questionable at best.

China's Growing Military Power and Influence

China now has the second largest military in the world in terms of dollars spent, and due to the size of its population, it could potentially have the largest number of troops. China's national defense budget, while still less than half of that of the U.S., has allowed China to become a regional power.

Over the last thirty years we can see that China's focus has been internal, giving priority to improving the standard of living of the Chinese people. When given the choice to allocate resources to military involvement in foreign lands or to invest domestically, China chooses domestic over and over again. In other words, given the choice between spending a trillion dollars on high-speed rail or spending a trillion dollars on a foreign war, they will consistently choose improvements at home.

Some may think that this is only a temporary condition, and that as China's wealth and military ability increase they may turn their power outwards. However, there are two reasons to find this to be improbable. First, the history of China does not support this position; we've seen that China's history reveals sustained policies of non-interference in the internal affairs of other nations. Second, a nation's wealth and prosperity does not make them more militant or aggressive. Both Germany (prior to WWII) and the Soviet Union (following WWII) had poor economies and plummeting standards of living. Despite this, both committed a very large percent of their GDP for outward expansion. It's the characteristic of leaders, not nations or wealth, that determines how military power is used. As China observes the difficult and expensive situations the U.S. has created in foreign wars, its leaders have ample evidence that military entanglement on foreign soil should be avoided whenever possible. Our examples confirm their already held belief that sending troops into foreign wars is rarely beneficial.

Given China's history, the statements of its political leaders, and its character, it's clear that China will likely be using military power for defense. China will work to ensure that the atrocities like the Japanese invasion in WWII and the British attacks in the two

Opium Wars never happen again. China will also use its increased military power to re-assert itself in international relations and negotiations, preventing others from bullying them into unequal treaties.

The Diaoyu Islands and The Expanding Japanese ADIZ

The media has reported on the increased aggressiveness of the Chinese navy in the South China Sea as China moves towards being a new "superpower." However, those recent events deserve a closer look to see what is meant by increased aggressiveness. One such issue, which is indicative of many of the tensions, is the dispute over the Diaoyu Islands. While both Japan and China claim historical rights to the islands, the U.S. controlled the islands following WWII.

Neither the Republic Of China (ROC - Taiwan), nor the People's Republic of China (PRC - mainland China), were invited to negotiations or the signing of the Treaty of San Francisco that dealt with the islands. The treaty was unclear on whether the island belonged to Japan or China. Distracted by domestic concerns, the PRC and ROC did not make issue of the islands until the U.S. handed over administrative control of the islands to Japan in 1971. Until that time, China had assumed the islands were a part of China.

In September 2012 the nation of Japan bought the islands from a private owner in an attempt to formally annex the islands to Japan. This action caused China to step up its claim in the form of political protest and naval presence. While the U.S. government said little of Japan's action to annex the islands, they heavily critiqued China's actions in claiming the islands and increasing naval patrols. A review of the geographic location of the Diaoyu Islands shows suspicious intent by the U.S. and Japan. The islands are 170 km from Chinese Taiwan, and 410 km from the closest Japanese island. By allowing Japan to take the islands, the U.S. has assisted Japan in creating a political barrier blocking China from the Pacific Ocean. While the U.S. politicians and media portray this as aggressive action by China, it is the unilateral actions of Japan and the U.S. that were the instigators, as they sought to incorporate the islands officially into Japanese territory. China's political and military response was simply to say: *No. These actions are unacceptable.*

Following WWII, the U.S. set up an Air Defense Identification

Zone (ADIZ) around Japan. An ADIZ is a mapped area for which a nation attempts to monitor air traffic; in ADIZs, foreign airplanes are required to report and request permission for use from the host country. The U.S. administered the Japanese ADIZ until 1969 then turned administration over to Japan, which enlarged the zone in 1972 and again in 2010. By claiming islands far from the homeland, a country can stake out a larger ADIZ, in effect claiming rights to control air space across a potentially much larger area. The dispute over the Diaoyu Islands is partly about the actual islands, but it's more about who controls the area.

A look at the Japanese ADIZ, which was established by the U.S and then expanded by Japan, reveals a dubious claim; the area reaches far from Japan and arrogantly within arm's length of China, at points less than 100 miles from mainland China and Taiwan. From China's point of view, the ADIZ is not about defending Japan, but about containing China within a wall of military and political surveillance. It's easy to see why they believe this to be the case.

Following the 2012 purchase of the Diaoyu Islands, in November of 2013 China established their own ADIZ which, while much smaller than the Japanese area, overlapped the Japanese ADIZ. While the media made little mention of Japan's purchase of the Diaoyu Islands and their expansion of ADIZ space, the U.S. politicians and media sounded all the alarms when China established their own ADIZ. Headlines blared that this was an overreaching, provocative, and aggressive military move by China. However, when we consider that it was Japan that attacked and invaded China in WWII (and on several other occasions prior), and not the reverse, the ADIZ map is not only suspect, it's manifestly offensive. The ADIZ maps tell us a lot about why China claims the West is biased towards Japan. The maps also support China's claim that the U.S. is attempting to contain China.

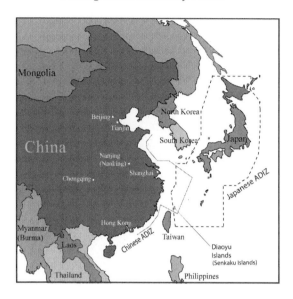

U.S. Military in Asia

U.S. military presence in Asia has been overwhelming since WWII. The U.S. maintains about 80 thousand troops in East Asia including: Korea, Japan, throughout the coastal waters of China, and Australia. This presence has caused tension between the U.S. and China— it's a game of cat and mouse as each side works to display their military power and authority.

In 2001 a U.S. EP-3 spy plane collided with a Chinese fighter jet 70 miles off the coast of the Chinese island of Hainan. In 2007, after being refused port in Hong Kong, a U.S. naval fleet transited through the Taiwan Straits. This placed armed U.S. naval vessels within 100 miles of the coast of China. In 2013 the U.S. navy complained that a Chinese naval ship had cut across the bow of a U.S. naval vessel, nearly causing a collision. The U.S. naval vessel was the USS Cowpens. The Cowpens is a ship with a provocative history, as it was the first ship to fire weapons at Iraq during the first Iraq war. The near collision with the missile armed Cowpens was off the coast of China. In 2014 the U.S. complained of Chinese fighter planes harassing U.S. spy planes as they flew off the coast of China.

If we're keeping an eye on the map, the trend is quite evident;

the events reported as growing aggressiveness on the part of the Chinese military almost always take place off the coast of China. These events are precipitated by U.S. military in the East and South China Seas, not Chinese military near the U.S. or other parts of the world. A fully armed U.S. aircraft carrier cruising through the Taiwan Strait would be at about the same proximity as a Chinese fully armed aircraft carrier cruising between the U.S. and Cuba. The spy planes flying near Hainan China would be like Chinese spy planes flying around the Gulf of Mexico or the New York coast.

From China's point of view, the guns of the USS Cowpens are reminiscent of the British ships off the coast of Hong Kong during the Opium Wars. Then as now, China may find it difficult to believe we are interested in friendship and negotiating in good faith when we have guns pointed at them. China's pushback against U.S. military in the region is their way of saying: "We no longer negotiate under intimidation. We do not sign because you have a gun pointed at us, we sign because the agreement is truly beneficial."

No Longer Bullied

Since WWII, and in many ways for a hundred years prior, the U.S. and Great Britain have effectively been the world's mapmakers, exerting force in setting borders and writing treaties. As the Chinese military grows, it will be used to push back against U.S. domination and assumed authority in the region. As China's military power grows, disputes over territories will become matters of true negotiation and discussion rather than unilateral decisions and intimidation made by foreign powers. Though the narrative has been that a Chinese military buildup will be a destabilizing force, consider that it actually may be a stabilizing and equalizing force. If our idea of stability is having complete control over all international issues through military superiority, we may need to re-think our position.

China does not build military strength to force treaties on others; rather, they build military strength so that none will dare abuse them in negotiations as was done in the Opium Wars, the Boxer Rebellion, and many other conflicts since. They do not build military to expand and acquire territory, they build so that none will dare attack and invade their land, and yes, to push back against recent abuses wherein Western powers dictated borders and international agreements as we have seen with the Diaoyu Islands and the ADIZ issue. They do not build military so that they can control foreign seas, but so they can push back against others who try to control the seas off China's coast.

Remember the little kid in elementary school who was always bullied by the bigger kids? As he got older he grew in size to the point that no one dared bully him anymore; he didn't suddenly become the bully, yet he could no longer be bullied. China is the neighbor who works out to build size and muscle not because of an interest in fighting, but as a deterrent to any who would threaten harm. China is the gentle giant, not seeking conflict, but ready and able to defend itself. China has shown itself to be very cautious in the use of military power and all signs point to the fact that they will continue to be so; however, as their military strength grows, they will not be as timid in defending their interests.

China's Military Intent

U.S. media and politicians question why China continues to grow its military power, but history proves their questions tone deaf and the answers quite easy to see. The Japanese invasion of China and the brutalities that took place during WWII are ample reasons for anyone to agree that China should have one of the largest militaries in the world. But if one thinks 1931 is not enough, then simply look deeper into the history books with special attention to 1592, 1787, 1839, 1856, 1894, 1898, 1931, 1950, 1955. In every single one of these years, China or a bordering ally of China was invaded by a foreign power.

While it may not be productive to pursue unfounded conspiracy theories, it does seem that the continued Cold War mentality of justifying massive U.S. military expenses should give us pause. We might question whether or not there is some absurd ulterior motive causing the U.S., a country which has never been invaded by a foreign power, to expend such vast amounts on defense, especially when looking at the fact that the U.S. has had as many foreign policy failures as successes.

Should we fear the influence of a growing Chinese military power? There's no doubt that in time the U.S. will lose its unilateral authority over East Asia and the Chinese coast as China rebuffs

Western domination off their shores. When China brings its first aircraft carrier to Cuba and starts flying spy planes off the coast of New York, it will not be for preparation of attack on the U.S., it will be to demonstrate to the American people what it feels like to have a major military power flexing its muscle off your shores.

The fear mongers will tell us about the threat of China's growing military power and influence. The president will talk of a pivot to Asia as we shift military resources towards China to counter their growing military power. The media will cite conflicts off the coast of China as cause for great alarm. However, as we've seen, while China is a military power to be respected, it's not a military power to be feared. A military superpower to be feared is one that is trigger-happy and too quick to send troops abroad, one that too often sends soldiers and guns around the world, a nation that uses military power to bully foreign lands into acquiescing to unfair ultimatums. This isn't the character of China. In time, the rising power of China's military influence will be a stabilizing force in the world. While many think this is a time to increase U.S. military presence in Asia, to posture, and to show force, this is actually the time to make friends. If we seize the opportunity, the influence of the Chinese military in combination with the U.S. military can be the most stabilizing force the world has ever seen. If we treat them as enemies and work to counter their strength, we'll waste resources and miss a historic opportunity. If we can look past the headlines, we will see the benefits of China's growing military influence and the opportunities presented to our generation for a more stable and peaceful world.

The U.S. media and politicians will continue working hard to make U.S. citizens fear China's growing military power. Does this mean we should? For many years China has said that it is a peaceful nation and that it believes in a policy of non-interference with the internal affairs of other nations—for many years they have been true to this position. History has shown that China is not an aggressive nation or an aggressive people. This country, which has been battered and abused by foreign nations, has remained steadfast in focusing on internal issues and advancements. Attacked and raped by foreign powers such as Japan, forced into unequal treaties by Great Britain and the U.S., they have nevertheless steadfastly refrained from lashing out against others. On the contrary, they maintain focus on their own peace, tranquility, and prosperity.

China's recent economic success and manufacturing power has put them in a position to act against those who have treated them so poorly, but instead of building planes and tanks and ships to retaliate, they're building bridges and high speed trains, a much more productive use of resources.

Looking at Chinese history and current events, it's reasonable to conclude that China's growing military power should not be feared. Furthermore, it's quite likely that China's military expansion should be welcomed as a stabilizing force—China's growing military may not just be a benefit to China, but to the whole world.

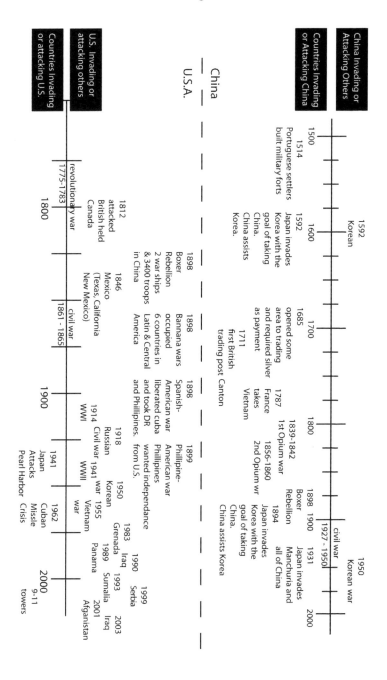

China Invading or Attacking Others

Countries Invading or Attacking China

China

U.S.A.

U.S. Invading or attacking others

Countries Invading or attacking U.S.

1500

1514
Portuguese settlers
built military forts

1592
Korean

1592
Japan invades
Korea with the
goal of taking
China.
China assists
Korea.

1600

1685
opened some
area to trading
and required silver
as payment

1711
first British
trading post Canton

1700

revolutionary war
1775-1783

1800

1812
attacked
British held
Canada

1846
Mexico
(Texas, California
New Mexico)

civil war
1861 - 1865

1787
France
takes
Vietnam

1839-1842
1st Opium war

1856-1860
2nd Opium wr

1800

1898
Boxer
Rebellion
2 war ships
& 3400 troops
in China

1898
Bannana wars
occupied
6 countries in
Latin & Central
America

1898
Spanish-
American war
liberated cuba
and took DR
and Phillipines.

1898
Boxer
Rebellion

1894
Japan invades
Korea with the
goal of taking
China.
China assists Korea

1899
Phillipine-
American war
Phillipines
wanted independence
from U.S.

WWI
1914

1918
Russian

1900
Boxer
Rebellion
Manchuria and
all of China

1931
Japan invades

civil war
1927 - 1950

1900

WWII
1941

1950
Korean
war

1941
Japan
Attacks
Pearl Harbor

1962
Cuban
Missle
Crisis

1950
Korean war

1955
Vietnam
war

1983
Grenada

1989
Panama

1990
Serbia

1993
Sumalia

2001
Afganistan

2003
Iraq

1999
Iraq

2000

2000
9-11
towers

4

Fearing China In Cyberspace

Chinese Hackers: No Site is Safe (CNN)
How Does China Censor the Internet (The Economist)
China Military Involved in U.S. Hacking (USA Today)
Is Your Gmail Being Hacked from China? (The Guardian)
China Hacking is Deep and Diverse, Experts Say (Wall Street Journal)
U.S. Says China's Government, Military Used Cyber espionage (Wall Street Journal)

[15]

The U.S. Department of Defense recently stated that the biggest security threat we face may be a cyber attack.[16] This is great news considering school children in the 1950s had to practice taking cover under their desks should the Soviet Union drop a nuclear bomb. Now we simply need to drill our children on how to survive a day without access to their Facebook or Twitter accounts. Certainly a cyber attack is capable of more damaging consequences, such as threatening a banking system or power grid, but if cyber attacks are truly the biggest threat to our security, then we have made great progress over the last 50 years.

Since the early days of the Internet, the U.S. has been accusing China of hacking into government and private computers, but in February of 2013 they had proof. Years of baseless allegations were finally legitimized when Mandiant, a Washington D.C. company that specializes in cyber security, released a report "confirming" that China was hacking into computer systems. The report confirmed that China was hacking to spy on the U.S. government and acquire plans for top military systems. The report also confirmed that China was hacking to steal valuable information from U.S. corporations. China responded to the allegations by countering that it was actually the U.S. who was guilty of spying. However, that response fell on deaf ears, because in early 2013, who would have believed that the U.S. was hacking into Chinese computers?[17]

On May 6th of 2013, the U.S. government explicitly accused

China of hacking into government computers and government subcontractors. On May 29th U.S. Defense Secretary Chuck Hagel accused China of waging cyber espionage against the United States. In today's world, espionage, which is the illegal gathering of information, means hacking into computer and phone systems.

On June 8th of 2013 President Obama was to meet with the president of China, Xi Jinping. High on Obama's list of things to discuss was China's cyber spying and attacks. For many months prior U.S. politicians, supported by the media, had been complaining about the problem. Along with accusing China of hacking into U.S. government and corporate computers, they accused China of spying on its own people and of censoring the Internet. On June 5th, just three days before the President of the U.S. was set to lecture the President of China on the evils of hacking, former U.S. government contractor Edward Snowden disclosed the extensive spying activities of the U.S. government—the U.S. had been spying on its own people as well as hacking into Chinese telephone and computer systems. Snowden reported that the U.S. had access to Chinese computers, text messaging, emails, and telephone data. Although Obama did meet with President Xi of China, the agenda was abruptly changed by Snowden's disclosures. The game had changed due to this unforeseen event. The moral high ground had been lost.

What is clear about cyber spying is that many, if not all, governments do it. And what is more recently clear is that the U.S. government is the most active organization, spying both internally and externally.

The United States Cyber Command, which is part of the U.S. Department of Defense, has made it clear that they're not only a defensive organization, but also an offensive group planning and training to attack enemy cyber structures.

The Source of Cyber Attacks

In the third quarter of 2012, Akamai Technologies, which monitors cyber attacks, reported that the number one source for cyber attacks was China, with 33 percent of all attacks originating there. But guess who the number two source was. Russia? Iran? India? No. The number two source for initiating cyber attacks according to their study was the U.S., which accounted for 13 percent of all attacks. This is not to argue that China is blameless, but the number two violator can't lecture the number one violator with much credibility. Add to the mix that it is difficult to identify the true source of attacks and you have a questionable claim. While the U.S. media talks of cyber attacks from China, China's Cyber Emergency Response agency reports that most cyber attacks on China are from the U.S., Japan, and South Korea; they also noted that at least 20 percent of the Chinese computers commandeered for cyber attacks can be traced back to the U.S.[18]

If the Akamai Technologies analysis is correct, then 18 percent of the world's population (China) accounts for 33 percent of the cyber attacks, while 4 percent of the world's population (the U.S.) accounts for 13 percent of the attacks. On a per capita basis that means there were more cyber attacks coming out of the U.S. than China. While the U.S. is unable to control the large number of attacks coming from within its borders, it nevertheless seeks to put pressure on China to control the hacking coming from within China. The U.S. is home to the most sophisticated technology companies in the world, and inventor of most cyber technologies. To expect China to control its hackers while we cannot control ours might be an unrealistic expectation.

More recent reports from Akamia show that Indonesia has moved up to the number one source for cyber attacks. While only a year or so earlier they accounted for only one percent of all cyber attacks, suddenly in the fourth quarter of 2013 they had surpassed China and were the number one source of cyber attacks, accounting for 38 percent of all attacks. While some in the media did report the findings, it was not reported with the same vigor that the media had reported when China was the primary culprit. Likewise, the U.S. government's reaction to the news was devoid of any condemnation of Indonesia or calls for immediate action—as they had done with China.[19]

It's suspicious that such a shift in the source of cyber attacks could occur so quickly. Did tens of thousands of hackers suddenly move from China to Indonesia? Or does this indicate how easy it is to remotely commandeer computers in a foreign place to make it look like the attacks are coming from a place other than where the true hackers are located?

If one wanted to generate a fear of cyber attacks from China and get the U.S. media to initiate and perpetuate that fear, what would be the best way to accomplish that aim? The quickest and best way may be to perform a cyber attack on major U.S. news organizations like the *New York Times*, the *Wall Street Journal*, and the *Washington Post*, hop through an anonymous proxy server in China, and fake the return address as a Chinese Internet Protocol (IP) address. Interestingly enough, these three news organizations have reported recently that they had been hacked by China. It's nearly impossible to determine the true source of the attacks, but if we consider motive, we may find some clues. In this elusive game of who-done-it, there's great danger in inconclusive allegations. And most accusations regarding cyber attacks *are* inconclusive.[20]

In March of 2013, 30,000 computers in South Korea were hit by a cyber attack. The attack successfully breached security at three major banks, causing them to close for two days. After a brief investigation, South Korea announced that the cyber attack had come from China. Shortly after, they apologized for the accusation, admitting that they had made an error, and that the attack had not originated in China. With the Western media constantly proclaiming that China is a hacking threat around the world, all are quick to assume China is the guilty party when a major attack occurs, an instinctual reaction developed by media and political influence.

Life Is Better When We're Connected

A bank advertisement recently proclaimed, "Life's Better When We're Connected." When we contrast our Internet connected world with that of our pre-connected world, it's easy to see that we're certainly better off in many ways. Travel flight times and prices can be compared from the convenience of home or office. That car you've been wanting can easily be found on the Internet. A note can be sent to a friend without having to find a stamp or envelope, and that note will be received on the other side of the world within seconds. A video of the grandkids can be sent to grandma in the blink of an eye. And of course even true love can be found using online dating sites.

But in other ways we are not better off. Before online banking we had to keep a tally of our bank account balance in the back of a checkbook. Now we simply login to see our balance and activity. While that seems much more convenient, it must be contrasted with the threat of an anonymous person half way around the world hacking into our account and stealing our money, and the time and aggravation it would take to get the money back if it even could be retrieved. Suddenly, keeping a hand written balance on a piece of paper doesn't seem quite so bad. Likewise, back in the 1980s the power grid appeared to work quite well; the biggest threat of a power outage was a major storm or simply an overload of the grid. Today the threat to the power grid is that some 17 year old kid in a far away country could hack into the system and bring New York City to its knees.

Even as late as the 1970s, if a competitor of Boeing wanted to steal technical drawings for an aircraft, they would have to physically get into a Boeing building and steal that long tube of paper with the drawings. Now only 40 years later a competitor need only hack into the corporate system to retrieve those plans. A large team of hundreds could be stationed in a far away country working 24-7 to steal the plans, or if they preferred the conventional method, they could get someone on the inside and sneak out millions of documents all on a very small, easily hidden flash drive—a flash drive that could be purchased at any local convenience store for less than ten dollars. "Life's better when we're connected?" Not always.

It's important to understand the nature of cyber attacks and what makes them possible. The Internet is inherently an insecure system and is structured to guarantee anonymity. With four billion Internet addresses and over one billion computers in the world, tracing the source of a cyber attack is very difficult, and often impossible. When something is sent over the Internet, it has an address like a return address on an envelope, which is called an IP (Internet Protocol) address. But that return address can easily be spoofed or faked, making it nearly impossible to trace back to its origins. Hackers can use anonymous proxy servers to have other computers submit requests without revealing the original requester's IP address. Another thing that makes cyber attacks difficult to trace is that they can use unsuspecting computers to do the attacking. In this method, a criminal or spy agency installs a virus on a server, effectively turning that computer into a robot that can do damage or steal information from other computers. Meanwhile, the computer used to create the virus has been destroyed, the criminal has collected his fee, and he's sitting on a beach drinking something with a small umbrella perched at the edge of the glass. All this while your unsuspecting computer does the damage. Not only is it difficult to find the originator of a cyber attack, but it's also quite simple to make the attack look like it came from another place. Like a magician, attention is misdirected and once the trick is over it's often too late to figure out how it actually happened.

In 2003 the U.S. was unequivocally convinced that Iraq had weapons of mass destruction. At the time, the budget for the CIA and other intelligence gathering was over $25 billion per year. Such weapons are physical things that can be seen, touched, and verified when found. With the largest and most expensive intelligence agencies, combined with the largest and most expensive military in the world, the U.S. got it wrong. In the end there were no weapons of mass destruction. Consider how much more difficult it is to find something that could be hidden on one of a billion computers in the world, replicated on thousands of unsuspecting computers—then consider that the originating computer has a fake return address going through an anonymous proxy server. What are the odds that U.S. intelligence will get it right when trying to identify the original source of a cyber attack?

With the fundamental security flaws we've discussed, one has to question why the power grid, banking, or any other such system would be connected to the Internet in the first place. If a bank with no alarm system leaves its doors open at night and then is robbed, although the thief is chiefly to blame, the bank also shares the blame because they've failed to protect the money. In the drive to provide customers with convenience, many consumer, commercial, and government services (such as online banking) have been implemented before they've been made truly secure. This is the fault of the institution, but in the end it's your problem. If a power plant, mass transit, air traffic control, or other important system is exposed to security threats through the use of our public Internet, then there has quite possibly been an error in judgment—maybe that system should not have been tied to an anonymous, insecure network in the first place. This is not to say that all security breaches are through the Internet, but the Internet is the most vulnerable part of our newly connected world.

The use of this "connected" world is a voluntary choice made by governments, businesses, and individuals. If the threat of cyber attack is bigger than the threat of conventional war or even a nuclear attack, then we could revert back to our pre-connected world and have effectively no real threat to our security. Although it's important to work to prevent cyber crime and attacks at the source and to go after the perpetrators, the real answer to cyber security is to develop secure systems and networks.

Prior to the 20th century, cities were plagued with great fires. The great London fire of 1666 resulted in the loss of homes for 85 percent of the population. In 1872 the Great Boston Fire claimed over 700 buildings. The Great Chicago Fire of 1871 burned three square miles to the ground. While major cities of the day worked to create more effective fire departments and makeshift firewalls, the core of the problem was that the underlying infrastructure was not built to withstand fire. The buildings were made of wood and lighting was provided by candle or Kerosene lamp, which made for a most dangerous (and combustible) combination. Why would they build such a fragile infrastructure? With the threat of fire, why would anyone build a wooden house and light it by candlelight? The reason: because it was the cheapest and fastest way to build. This is the same reason your bank encourages you to use the Internet and a common browser to access your bank account. It's cheap and fast to create. Like the wooden houses of the past, it's not very safe, but it's definitely cheap and fast. Why would a U.S. defense contractor keep top-secret plans for a stealth bomber on a computer server with a connection to the Internet—a connection easily hacked by an interested party? That would be crazy, right? Except that it's very convenient, cheap, and fast to create. You're using a network which already exists, servers and workstations that are cheap, and off the shelf software from your local store. And as may have been predicted, in June of 2013, the U.S. military admitted that top secret plans for our F-35 stealth fighter had been stolen by hackers. Oops. Over time and after a many great tragedies, cities began to be built with steal, stone, and cement. And fire was no longer used for lighting. The core infrastructure was altered to make life safer for citizens.

There are and will be cyber criminals and cyber spying. It doesn't matter where they're from; they do the same damage regardless of host country. No country has a monopoly on malicious hackers or foreign spy agencies attempting to gain information. The only true way to protect against these attacks is defensive, which means truly secure systems. It is said that the Chicago fire of 1871 was started when a cow kicked over a lamp in Mrs. O'Leary's barn. Trying to find and stop every cyber criminal or government spying organization would be like telling 1871 Chicago to eliminate all their cows. Not a practical solution when the real problem is wooden houses lit by fire, or in our cyber world, critical functions placed on insecure systems and networks.

Why We Spy

As Snowden continues to reveal additional activities of U.S. government spying, our relations with foreign countries continues to deteriorate. It has been disclosed that the National Security Agency (NSA) has tapped the phones of leaders of Germany, France, Spain, Brazil and Mexico, as well as the World Bank and the United Nations. Does the United States consider the World Bank a security threat? What about the U.N.? Do U.S. officials believe that Brazil is planning to invade the U.S.? Should we be preparing for an attack by France or Spain? What about Mexico? As it becomes clear who the U.S. is spying on, it becomes more evident *why* the U.S. is spying.

In November of 2013, Indonesia discovered that Australia was tapping the phone of their president. The Indonesian government demanded an apology and discontinuation of spying. The president of Australia responded: "We make no apology for spying for security and our national best interest." His statement is critical to understand. If spying is not just for security but also for "national best interest," then a country spying on a foreign corporation and passing information to a domestic corporation to give it a better chance of winning a lucrative contract would be in the national best interest. Right? Under the guise of national security, the mission creeps into the broader realm of "national best interest," which can encompass industrial espionage and cheating in negotiations.

In January of 2014, Snowden told a German TV network, ARD, that the U.S. does not limit its espionage to issues of national

security, but pursues any intelligence that's beneficial, citing
Siemens as an example of companies that the U.S. spied on. "If
there's information at Siemens that's beneficial to U.S. national
interests – even if it doesn't have anything to do with national
security – then they'll take that information nevertheless," Snowden
said. His claims appear to be consistent with other disclosures and
information that clearly indicate that U.S. spying goes beyond
security. In March of 2015 the BBC reported that the German spy
agency BND had worked with the United States NSA to spy on
companies such as Airbus. It was also reported that the NSA had
even requested help from the BND to spy on the German company
Siemens. Germany of course refused.[21][22]

Often the parties the U.S. spies on are not security threats, but
instead are people or groups with whom we negotiate trade
agreements and other economic arrangements. Spying on Hitler is
for security. Spying on the U.N., Airbus, Siemens, the president of
Brazil, the president of Mexico, the president of Spain, the president
of Germany, or the president of France is for cheating—to obtain
inside information and to learn the other side's strategies. Snowden's
revelations don't just tell us who we spy on, they tell us why we spy.

The hyperactive spying machine in the U.S. is driven by the
media and by politically generated paranoia; ultimately, spying does
far more harm than good to our international relations. As each
relationship is damaged, the general reputation of the U.S. is
likewise damaged. The motives and objectives of the military and
spying machine of the U.S. must be questioned, not by the military
or the NSA, but by the American people and their representatives.

New World Standards Set by the NSA

The NSA has set a new world standard that would allow the
tapping of foreign leaders' phones as well as full collection of all
citizen's emails and phone logs. Is that the standard we choose? And
if so, would we propose a different standard for Brazil, Mexico,
France, Germany, China, and others? By spying on the U.N. and
World Bank we have set a standard that spying is not just for
security, but for whatever purpose we choose. The U.S. spies on all
correspondence and collects information on private companies. To
what use is this information intended? Is this economic espionage

acceptable?[23]

In 2010 the U.S. and Israel infected computers in Iran's nuclear centrifuges with the Stuxnet virus, causing the mechanical devises to spin at such high speeds that they destroyed themselves. Neither the U.S. nor Iran had declared war, but the CIA took covert action, which by most standards would be considered an act of war. The U.S. military has said that cyberspace is the new battleground. If this is true, then the U.S. has fired the first shots on the battlefield—not just against Iran, but against any country that we may disagree with. While destroying with bombs is considered an act of war, does it make sense that destroying with technology and hacking is not?[24]

The U2 and The End of Hope

On September 15th 1959, the leader of the Soviet Union, Nikita Khrushchev, visited the United States for 13 days. During his visit U.S. President Dwight Eisenhower, who had been a general in the U.S. military, hosted the Russian leader, and the two were quite friendly. There was hope both in the U.S and in Russia that the relationship between the two contentious countries would improve. The trip culminated with Khrushchev inviting Eisenhower to visit the Soviet Union. Eisenhower accepted the invitation and began making plans for his visit. As the Soviet people prepared for the visit of the U.S president, they were also excited and hopeful that this would be the end of the Cold War.

The U2 spy plane was a highly advanced plane used in the 1950s by the U.S. military to fly at high altitudes while taking spy photos over foreign countries. Each flight had to be approved by the president. Military leaders, fearing a Soviet military buildup, pressed the president for another fly over the Soviet Union.

The president planned to meet the Soviet leader in May, at a conference in Paris, and then travel on to visit the Soviet Union. On May 1st 1960, with the president's permission, the U2 spy plane flew over Soviet air space once again for the purpose of accumulating additional spy images. The plane was shot down by the Soviet Union and the pilot captured. The incident caused the immediate cancelation of Eisenhower's trip to the Soviet Union. The event flung the U.S. and USSR back into the depths of the Cold War, a conflict that would continue unabated for another thirty-one years at a cost of billions of dollars.

The cost of spying is very high, not only in the actual expenditures, but even more so in the cost of damaged relationships and reduced prospects for peace. It is one thing to spy on true evils, such as Hitler's Germany, but we must more cautiously define who our enemies are and weigh the costs of these activities against the benefits. We must evaluate the costs not just in the massive amounts of dollars spent, but also in the cost of moving further away from our goal of a better world.

In Eisenhower's last few days in office he gave a speech; in it he warned of the influence of the military-industrial complex saying: "In the councils of government, we must guard against the acquisition of unwarranted influence, whether sought or unsought, by the military-industrial complex." Perhaps the warning was not so much about how military action often is not as beneficial as claimed; rather, perhaps he warned that military action can be a true detriment to peace and security. Eisenhower watched first hand as the "unwarranted influence" of the military-industrial complex influenced him to approve the last U2 mission that destroyed his best hope of a solid and lasting peace with the Soviet Union.

A report by the U.S. congressional committee called the 'U.S.-China Economic and Security Review' issued on May 8th 2012 stated: "China almost certainly would mount a cyber attack on the U.S. in the event of a conflict, and the U.S. has no clear policy to determine how to respond appropriately." The report was written for the congressional commission by Northrop Grumman, which is the fourth-largest defense contractor in the world and provides Information Technologies (IT) services to the U.S. government, including cyber security.[25]

As long as U.S. politicians form their opinions based on reports from companies, groups, and individuals who have a huge financial incentive to create fear, they will continue to overspend and over-react on all "security" and military issues. Taking their cues from companies like Northrop Grumman and Mandiant, politicians will always be led to believe there is an imminent danger, and that the worst-case scenario is highly probable. Eisenhower's warnings of the influence of the military industrial complex could not be more clearly on display. When a company sells airplanes and high-technology to the U.S. Department of Defense, they will surely increase their profits if they can convince the U.S. government that China is a cyber threat. And what better way to influence Congress than to write the actual report that the congressional committee will deliver? Eisenhower's warning is ignored as these influences cause our political leaders to engage in cyber spying that ultimately does more damage to our prospects for peace than good.

Stopping the Real Threat

Framing the question is often the first step to misleading the public. In the same way that asking a child if they stole a piece of candy suggests the child's guilt, the question presumes an answer. Politicians and the media are experts at framing the question for the purpose of assuming or implying an answer. The question that has been consistently posed from Western media is: should we fear China in cyberspace? However, the more objective and beneficial questions would be: what should we fear about our newly connected world, and is China an exceptional threat?

It's inexcusable that it's even possible to infect your computer with a virus through the simple act of opening an email, or that by landing on a web site a virus can install itself on your computer. It's our country and our companies that design and build these programs and systems. U.S. technology companies decide what an email can and can't do. Yes, we can continue to fear the thief, but it would be much more beneficial to fear the unlocked safe, the wide open bank vault door—we should fear that we're using insecure technologies on a mass scale for functions that must be secure.

China's Defense

Military defeats in China over the last several hundred years have been due to China's inferior military technology. British naval superiority and armament left China vulnerable to the demands of unequal treaties. Japan learned from the West and also gained technologies that were more advanced than China, thus allowing Japan to attack and invade China on several occasions. Leaders of China know this history, and as they grow in economic power, they are watching to ensure that foreign powers will not have a technical advantage in a military conflict. When the U.S. tells the world that cyberspace is the new battleground, certainly China will take notice and work to ensure that they are not left behind on the technologies of cyber warfare.

While the U.S. builds up its cyber weapons in preparation for this new battlefield, it requests that China stay idle and not engage in like development of cyber war capability. To ask China not to hack while the U.S. government shows itself to be the world's most active hacker is a fool's request—it's also the largest of all hypocrisies. The relative quietness of China on this issue is possibly their response. The implied response is: "We no longer accept unequal treaties. We will not sit idly by while you develop cyber warfare capabilities and show yourself to be the world's largest cyber spying organization."

China observes the actions of the U.S., whether it be tapping foreign leader's phones or spying on an entire country's emails and text messages, and has cause to question the position and motives of the U.S.; China may very well look at Google, Facebook, Twitter, and the iPhone as technical means of spying on China's leaders as well as its population. Given the revelations about U.S. spying activity, it may be amazing that China still allows companies like Apple and Cisco to operate within their borders.

The danger of this tit for tat exchange, with accusations flying, is the unfriendly relationship it creates. The U.S. consistently calls it cyber warfare. Just the definition of this is inflammatory and creates a Cold War tension, and as this new cyber war unfolds, the hope of good relations is diminished. With the prospect of this new tension, a reasonable fear would be that a new Cold War is beginning with China. China will refuse to be at a technological disadvantage, so if we want a cyber Cold War, we will have it. China will work to ensure they're not at a disadvantage.

The United States often defines world standards through our negotiations and actions. When the U.S. spies on foreign leaders and hacks into emails and phone systems, it sets a standard for the world; we should expect nothing less from others. We should fear that we're setting a dangerous standard that other nations will follow.

Is China a Particular Cyber Threat?

Cyber attacks come from everywhere. From the history of China we know that China is not an aggressive, expansionist nation.

In the same way China is not a military threat, they are not an exceptional cyber threat. But we also know that China will no longer accept unequal treaties, the game where each player is subject to different rules. In the same way that they move toward parity with the U.S. military to eventually ensure that their military is not at a disadvantage, they will monitor U.S. actions to determine their position on cyber activity. The U.S. military has stated that they're preparing for a cyber offensive. This can only be seen as a security threat to China, and China will seek to keep up in this newly defined military arena—to not do so would be irresponsible.

When China observes that we're listening in on the phone calls of the World Bank, the U.N., and most foreign leaders, they can be clear that we are not spying for security, but spying for purposes beyond security. With this observation, China must decide their course of action. Do they adopt the new standard set by the NSA that hacking and cyber spying by governments is OK, and even potentially a necessity, in our modern world? Do they contest our action? Do they attempt to change or clarify the rules? These conflicts, like many others, are instigated by the position and actions of the U.S. China has suffered the consequences of inferior technology in the past, and as the cyber world becomes the new battleground, they have no choice but to be prepared. Thus any cyber threat from the Chinese government is simply a reaction to our cyber threats against China. In the area of national spying, the NSA has shown that China is more of a victim than a threat. In the non-governmental world of cyber criminals and malicious hackers simply attempting to do damage, both the U.S. and China are at risk.

The sequence of events beginning with massive allegations of Chinese hacking and culminating in revelations of the NSA's activities should very possibly be our biggest fear. This is due not so much to the hypocrisy of the accusations made against China, but to the tactic of attempting to divert the attention from our own misdeeds to the misdeeds of others.

When it comes to the question of fearing China in cyberspace, it's easy to see that our fears are misplaced. We should fear that we are using insecure technologies that make us vulnerable in so many ways. We should fear that we're starting a new, wasteful, and damaging cyber Cold War driven by our paranoia and the military industrial complex. We should fear that as a leader in the world, we're setting poor international standards in the area of spying and espionage.

It's convenient to look outward to find threats, but when it comes to cyberspace, we need to look inward instead. Consider that if all the Chinese hackers and cyber threats from China were eliminated, it would do little to solve our cyber security problem. It's the U.S.'s decisions and actions that should be our biggest concern and our biggest fear. All the legitimate fears about cyberspace can be resolved from within. China is not an exceptional threat to U.S. cyber security—to fear China in cyberspace diverts our attention and resources from finding true solutions to cyber security.

5

Fearing China's Intellectual Property Rights

US Report Warns on China IP Theft (BBC)
How China Steals Our Secrets (New York Times)
Cheap 'Apple Watch' Copies On Sale Via Alibaba Site (BBC)
Microsoft's Ballmer: Piracy Killing Our China Revenue (ZDNet)
China's Theft of Business Secrets is Beyond Espionage (USA Today)
Chinese Hackers Steal U.S. Weapons Systems Designs, Report Says (NBC)[26]

The typical Hollywood movie costs about $50 million to produce, while blockbusters can cost over $200 million. If it were legal for anyone to copy a movie onto a DVD and sell the copy, then movies would never be made—not only would there be no profit motive, but every dollar invested in a movie would be lost.

Intellectual property (IP) is a legal concept wherein the inventor or creator of a product is given exclusive rights of ownership to that creation for a period of time. This covers original works like music, art, movies, and books as well as inventions, discoveries, and trademarks. While copyrights and trademarks are used to protect original works, patents are used to protect inventions and discoveries. The purpose of intellectual property rights is to encourage these activities by giving to the creator the benefits of ownership. If a person or company goes to the effort and expense to make a movie, they are given ownership to that movie so that they can profit from it. Therefore, intellectual property rights are critical to encourage creations such as movies, music, and books.

Likewise, IP law is used to encourage innovation by granting the inventor a temporary monopoly on the invention so they can recoup the investment and potentially make a profit. If there were no patent laws, then an individual or company could work years and spend millions to develop a new technology, but once complete, another company could simply copy and profit from the idea.

Patent and copyright protection gives the creator incentive to create because it provides the opportunity to benefit from their labor and investment. The challenge of a society is to use patent and copyright law to encourage original works and innovation, and to advance technologies.

Hidden Danger in Patent Law: The Selden Affect

The automobile we know today is a culmination of many inventions, the initial work of which began as early as 1769 with French inventors. By 1877, the internal combustion engine, which is the fundamental design we use today, was invented by Nikolaus Otto. And by 1885, Karl Benz had created an automobile with a gasoline engine. By the 1890s, cars were being produced in the U.S., and in 1896 Henry Ford built his first. As Ford developed his automobiles, he also sought to mass produce them. Prior to Ford, cars were a rich person's luxury, and each was custom built by hand. Ford wanted to drive the price down by changing the way automobiles were made, making them affordable to the common person, but here he ran into a problem.

Shortly after forming the Ford Motor Company in 1903, he was sued by a group of car manufacturers who claimed to hold the patent on the automobile. The ALAM group, which held the Selden patent, sued Ford to force him to stop making cars. Regardless of the fact that the first gas powered cars were being produced in Europe as early as 1889, a lawyer by the name of Selden filed and was granted a U.S. patent in 1895 for the gas powered automobile.

Ford fought the patent in court, but the court ruled against him. The history of the Selden patent is a good case study to understand the dangers of bad patent law. The Selden patent was filed by a lawyer, not because he was a great inventor or actually invented anything; it was filed simply to create a monopoly on an industry that was inevitable given the direction of the current day's technology. In addition, the ALAM group, which bought the patent, also simply used it in an attempt to prevent competition. Their actions were not born of an impulse to protect some groundbreaking invention they'd created, but was instead a simple strategy to create a monopoly. To Ford's benefit, he won on appeal and the patent was declared unenforceable. But for a period of time, the Selden patent actually slowed innovation in the automobile industry as would-be inventors were forced to discontinue their pursuits. To coin a term, this "Selden Affect" shows that poor patent law can actually slow or stop innovation, the exact opposite of the purpose of patent law.

Race to Monopoly

When the race for innovation becomes a race for monopoly, the purpose is destroyed. If a patent is granted for an idea that is obvious or is a natural progression of a basic technological idea, then a monopoly has been formed that will slow innovation as others are forced to abandon use of the idea. If it's too easy to obtain a patent, then ideas become locked up, which prevents further innovation. Patents should only be issued for inventions and innovations that are truly groundbreaking and outside the natural progression of a technology.

As an example, imagine that fifteen companies are working on a similar idea for an improved antenna for cell phones. Each company has many scientists working on the idea, and due to other recent technological breakthroughs, they're all headed toward a very similar innovation; a solution to the puzzle that will take cell phone reception to the next level. If one company reaches the finish line first and successfully files a patent, then the other fourteen companies will have to stop pursuing their ideas. It's a winner-take-all system.

The LED is an electronic light that's very small and requires little energy to operate; thus, it's uniquely suited to a variety of applications. It's obvious that it could be incorporated into any object that would be convenient to have a light attached such as a knife, a watch, a dog collar, a bookmark, a pen, and thousands of other products. The uses are simple and obvious and do not require any groundbreaking innovation, but due to poor patent law, a company was issued a patent on "the light pen." This was not some groundbreaking innovation, and in fact this was not even the first company to incorporate an LED into a pen, but the company filed for a patent for the purpose of creating a monopoly on this obvious product. This patent application prevented others from selling pens with a built-in LED light.

In 2012 a U.S. court ruled that a French shoemaker could have a trademark for shoes with red soles, preventing other shoemakers from making shoes with red soles, even though shoes with red soles have been made for centuries.

The world of genetics is a fast growing technology that offers great promise to progress in medical advancement. Companies spend a great amount of resources to identify genes that can be used in testing for specific diseases, and companies are attempting to patent those genes. If a company is allowed to have a patent on a gene, then other scientists will be prohibited from doing research on that gene. Imagine the consequences of this lack of collaboration; the costs and benefits of our patent law truly need to be reevaluated.

Shorter Patent Life

The world population in 1800 was about one billion people, with a large percentage of the population working in agriculture. Today the world population is over seven billion; and every year fewer and fewer work in agriculture and more and more are work in technologies and innovation. As our world gets larger and more resources are applied to research and development, it becomes even more important to watch for the Selden Affect.

With a world population of over seven billion, it's likely that someone else has also thought of that brilliant idea you had, but credit goes to the one who either registered the idea with a patent office, or created the product. In the 17th century, technological innovation moved at a very slow pace as few were working on technology, and the world population was 20 percent of what it is today. But today there are thousands of technology companies with millions working on new ideas and new products. As new technologies stimulate even newer technologies, and millions work on these ideas, it's critical that patent laws be monitored and adjusted to prevent the Selden Affect. Also, because in today's economies companies have access to the entire world for their markets, it's quicker to recover costs or make a profit on new inventions. For these reasons, governments should be very cautious in granting patents.

Graphene, which is a single layer of carbon, is a newly discovered substance that holds great promise for a variety of applications. Graphene is also a prime example of how patent laws have created a race to monopoly, instead of promoting true innovation. Like the LED light where companies simply filed patents for obvious uses of a technology, companies and research universities are scrambling to file patents on any use of grapheme that they can find. They're hoping to create a monopoly on a use or method that will lock out the competition and/or require the competition to pay royalties. One scientist called it a "land grab," a very appropriate description—a land grab is a situation where nothing is truly being created; rather, it's simply a race to get there first and put your name on it.

The China Blitz

So what does all this have to do with China? As China becomes more incorporated into the world economy, they often must accept the rules that have already been established, but in the area of patent law, it may be reasonable for China to contest the establishment. Certainly China will gain from better enforcement of intellectual property rights at home, but moving to the system used by the U.S. will most likely slow growth and innovation in China. Furthermore, in the end the U.S. patent system will ultimately hurt the U.S. more than it'll hurt China.

Consider that China has over four times the population of the U.S. If our system finds it acceptable to file patents on simple and obvious ideas, then China would do well to develop a patent system that creates millions of patents. With 1.3 billion people, they could effectively lock up millions of simple ideas. For example, maybe this week could be Cell Phone Case Design Week, during which the government encourages millions to submit design ideas. The Chinese government could then file these patents. As a result, the next time Apple or another cell phone company comes out with a new phone, China could simply go to their database of a million cell phone case designs and say: *Oh, sorry, you can't use that, we already thought of it. See design #A4476289921. A kid at a grade school in Hubei province thought of it last year.*

By the way, Apple did in fact file and receive a patent for rounded corners on the cell phone and electronic pad.[27] The patent was granted as though rounded corners had never been thought of. That old laptop in your closet that you bought ten years before the iPhone came out probably has a screen with rounded corners, so clearly this isn't a new idea, and a long way from groundbreaking. Apple has attempted to create a monopoly on a simple and obvious progression, and now competitors like Samsung must have teams of lawyers trying to find a legal way to sell a phone with rounded corners. However, Apple and others are already feeling the challenge of this flawed structure—they were forced to pay a Chinese company $60 million to buy the rights to the name iPad because a company in Shenzen had already registered the term. Likewise, a company in Southern China is suing Apple for patent infringement over Siri, Apple's voice command program, claiming it's an idea they'd already invented and patented. So over time, companies will learn that this is a two edged sword, and a particular challenge when 1.3 billion people are competing against 300 million. In 2013 over 501,000 patents were granted by the U.S. Patent and Trademark Office. In China, over 734,000 patents were issued in that same year.

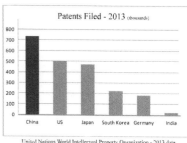

United Nations World Intellectual Property Organization - 2013 data

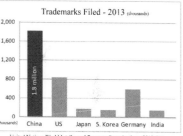

United Nations World Intellectual Property Organization - 2013 data

Race to Monopoly

Patent and trademark law can't simply be a race to gain a monopoly; this is destructive to the advancement of innovation. We must create incentives for companies and individuals to pursue truly groundbreaking inventions. Changes in our patent laws would not only be an advantage to the U.S., but also to China and the rest of the world, because they would actually promote innovation worldwide. China is actively working to improve their patent law and its enforcement and has made great progress in the last fifteen years, but as they work on their system, we need to also be working on ours.

To improve our intellectual property system, focus must be placed on protecting four things: original works, complete products, corporate identity, and groundbreaking ideas. Original works such as a song, a movie, a book, and even software must be protected from being reproduced without the owner's permission. As mentioned, if a production company spends $50 million to produce a movie and others can simply copy the DVD and sell it, then there is no incentive to create.

The same goes for a completed product. If a company can simply pull apart an iPhone and reverse engineer and reproduce it exactly, then the incentive to create new products is lost.

A company's identity must also be protected through trademarks. As companies work to create a reputation for design and quality, they need to be able to protect their brand. If someone wants to buy an Apple iPhone, they need the legal assurance that they are buying an Apple iPhone. Companies should be protected from the theft of their identity as criminals pretend to be someone they are not. In China a company was making tennis shoes with a logo very similar to the New Balance logo. The intent was clearly to trick customers into believing they were buying the New Balance brand. New Balance fought to protect their identity and won in the Chinese courts.

And as previously discussed, groundbreaking technology needs to be given patent protection, but great caution must be taken, because if patents are too liberally granted, invention and innovation will be stifled, creating the Selden Affect.

The Art of Imitation

In China, to copy something is not looked down on, and is, in fact, a form of flattery. Across China there are replicas of European landmarks like the Eifel tower and a full town replicating a German village—to learn from and imitate others is held as a value. Even in the U.S., we learn from each other and, yes, we copy each other. These variations on a theme can be seen when Microsoft Windows imitated the look and feel of Apple's operating system, or when Ford imitates the look of a Chevy. Take a look at the cars on the street. It's difficult to tell them apart because they often look the same. But there is a delicate balance between learning from each other and outright stealing others products and designs.

The China IP Dilemma

There is no doubt that some Chinese companies steal intellectual property from the U.S. and other countries. AMSC, a Massachusetts company that provides wind-turbine control systems, discovered that one of their main customers in China had copied all their software and was using the illegal software to run their wind-turbines. Sinovel, the Chinese wind-turbine company, eventually stopped buying the control systems from AMSC once they were able to simply copy the software. Steve Ballmer, the CEO of Microsoft, estimates that up to 90 percent of the Microsoft software used in China was not paid for. It's estimated that 20 percent of software in the U.S. is pirated.[28]

China recognizes the benefits and necessity of patent law to stimulate innovation. But they also see the dangers of monopoly, which can inhibit competition and multiple players. For the last fifty years there have effectively been only three or four automakers in the U.S. In China there are about 170 automakers. Did U.S. patent law promote innovation in the auto industry or hinder that innovation?

For China to more strongly support intellectual property protection, we must create better IP laws here in the U.S. and in international institutions, keeping that which promotes innovation while eliminating that which suppresses it. Patent terms must be shortened from their current 20-year length to a more reasonable amount of time, and the issuing of patents must be limited to groundbreaking invention and innovation.

Manufacturing is a basic first step for industrialization, and it proves to be a valuable way to quickly grow an economy. But there is a limit to what manufacturing can provide. To make the transition from an emerging market to a first world country, a nation must become an innovator in science and technology as well as a creator of original works like movies and software, and they must become a builder of world-class corporations. As China transitions from a manufacturing economy to a technology driven economy based on research and development, intellectual property rights become critical to their advancement.

It's not our lecturing and complaining about China's lack of IP law that is driving them to improve their laws, it's the reality that solid intellectual property laws and law enforcement is the only way to continue their economic advancement. China doesn't act in reaction to our pressure on IP, they act out of their own necessity as they transition from an emerging market to a first world country.

Should we fear China's intellectual property (IP) theft? China is making fast progress in improving their laws and law enforcement in this area as they move towards being an even more innovative society. Twenty years ago they copied with no regard, but as they advance they are seeing the advantages of protecting intellectual property. As they learn from us, we should be learning from them. The dysfunction of our current IP law should be feared possibly more than China's lack of IP enforcement. However, China recognizes that to become a first world nation they must become technology innovators. And to become technology innovators, their intellectual property law and enforcement must continue to improve. In the end, we both have a lot of work to do in improving our IP laws.

6

Fearing Chinese Technology

NASA Banned From Working With China (Discovery)
US Panel: China Tech Giants Pose Security Threat (Yahoo News)
US Admiral: China Counter-Space Threat Is 'Real' (The Diplomat)
A123 Sale to China: Threat to US Security? (Christian Science Monitor)
China's Huawei and ZTE Pose National Security Threat, Says US (The Guardian)
*Lawmakers Press Huawei, ZTE Amid Probe About Possible Threats to U.S.
Security* (Wall Street Journal)[29]

We Refuse to Buy

It was a phone call from then Secretary of Commerce Gary
Lock to the CEO of Sprint Nextel in 2010 that strongly encouraged
Sprint not to buy network equipment from the Chinese company
Huawei, the second largest network equipment provider in the world
at the time. Secretary Lock explained the grave security threat that
could arise if Chinese equipment were used in U.S. cell phone
networks. The CEO of Sprint took the warning and didn't buy
equipment from Huawei.[30]

Three years later, in 2013, Sprint Nextel, the third largest cell
phone network provider in the U.S. with over 54 million subscribers,
was to be purchased by Softbank Corp., a non U.S. company.
However, government officials were again concerned about security.
They expressed the fear that if the company were no longer U.S.
owned, there could be a security risk, as the new owners could
purchase networking equipment from Chinese companies like
Huawei or ZTE, exposing the cell phone networks to security threats.

If Sprint Nextel was no longer owned by U.S. interests, a call
from the Commerce Secretary probably wouldn't have the same
impact. Because of this security concern, before approving the
Softbank Corp. purchase, the U.S. government received guarantees
that they'd have oversight over equipment purchases. This would

ensure that the new owner couldn't buy equipment from China.

It's not the U.S. government's concern about Chinese network equipment that's the most interesting aspect of the Sprint Nextel story. It's who the buyer of Sprint Nextel was. Sprint was not being purchased by a Canadian company, a British company, or some other company with a history of friendly relations with the U.S. The purchase was by the Japanese company Softbank Corp. Yes, Japan, the only country that has ever initiated a full-scale military attack on the U.S., and the Japan that invaded China on three major occasions. There were virtually no concerns raised that a Japanese company was buying a cell phone network that hosted 54 million U.S. cell phone users. The concern was that the Japanese company might use Chinese-made equipment.

In March of 2013, a law was passed in the U.S. that prohibited the U.S. government from buying information technology from companies owned directly by or subsidized by the People's Republic of China. This law was specifically directed towards Huawei, which by that time had become the largest network equipment supplier in the world, passing their Swedish competitor Ericsson.[31]

It's clear that the U.S. government wants businesses and consumers to fear the importing of Chinese technology, as they overtly work to stop companies like Huawei, ZTE, and others from selling their products in the U.S. Let's consider three possible reasons that the U.S. is working to prevent Huawei and others from entering the U.S. market.

1) The concern that the Chinese government may use the equipment to spy on the U.S. 2) The U.S. needs control over the networks to be able to spy within the U.S. 3) Huawei and other Chinese tech companies are a competitive threat to U.S. technology companies.

The first possible reason is the one claimed by the U.S. government. The U.S. government claims that if Chinese-made network equipment was used in the U.S. it would give the Chinese government the ability to spy on us. While there is little, if any, evidence that this has occurred or would occur, what's clear from Edward Snowden's disclosures is that network equipment can be the key to spying. If the U.S. government believes that network equipment is used for spying, and as the U.S. has been identified as the most active spying organization in the world, then following the logic of the U.S. legislators, no country or organization should ever buy U.S. made networking equipment. Even U.S. corporations probably shouldn't buy network equipment from U.S. suppliers. If simply the fear of being spied on through network equipment is reason enough to prevent purchases from a country, then at this point no country should buy network equipment from the country known to be the biggest spying organization in the world.

It's quite questionable whether or not government officials from the U.S. actually believe the Chinese government would use network equipment made in China to spy on U.S. interests and government—perhaps their fear is exaggerated because they're so familiar with the ability of this equipment to be used for spying. However, it must be asked; why this particular concern about China? Why not a concern about equipment from Japan, Europe, or other places? The instinct of suspicion shown by U.S. legislators towards China is the result of a Cold War mentality developed through 50 years of media and politically self-perpetuated fear, but with little foundation in facts or history.

The second possibility is that when the U.S. says Huawei equipment could be a security threat, it's from the odd view that if Chinese equipment is used, it would be difficult for the U.S. to spy on the world. Perhaps spying requires the cooperation of the equipment vendors, and to ask Huawei and others might be just a little awkward.

The third possibility is the most likely reason the U.S. has prevented the sale of Chinese networking equipment to the U.S., and that is trade protectionism. Huawei, in a short period of time, has become the world's largest network equipment company. By allowing them access to U.S. markets, they would certainly grow larger and would be a competitive threat to U.S. companies like Cisco.

While European countries and others buy from Chinese tech companies like Huawei, our misguided paranoia causes us to miss opportunities for the mutual benefit of trade and technology exchange with China. As members of Congress and other decision makers are manipulated by higher level government officials and lobbyists from major corporations, they're sent to the front lines to make the arguments as to why Chinese equipment is a security threat. But keep in mind that studies and reports provided to political decision makers are written by U.S. consultants and corporations—they're written with a keen interest in making us fear Chinese tech equipment.

We Refuse to Sell

In the pursuit of transitioning to the electric car, many companies are investing great deals of capital to develop the technologies that'll be the foundation of this new electric auto world. A123 Battery, established in 2001, had worked on those technologies for eleven years. Despite subsidies of $129 million from the U.S. government, the company eventually filed for bankruptcy as they weren't able to generate a profit. Contributing to their demise was the fact that their most important customer, Fisker, an electric car manufacturer, was on the verge of bankruptcy itself. Another customer was Chrysler, which announced agreements with A123 in April of 2009, the same month Chrysler filed for bankruptcy. The liquidation of A123 resulted in an auction of its assets that included the patents and technologies it had developed. There was little interest at the auction except for two bids. One was a joint bid by U.S. based Johnson Control and Japan's NEC. The other bidder and winner of the auction was a Chinese company Wanxiang.

Foreign purchases of technology and other companies require review by the U.S. government to ensure there are no national security technologies or secrets being disclosed. Although the company was a simple battery company, when a Chinese company won the bid, hypersensitivity kicked in. In an interview with *The Daily Ticker* about the Chinese company buying A123, Congresswoman Marsha Blackburn, who led the opposition to the sale, said: "Do you really want people that do not wish you well having access to your technology?" Fox News reported on the issue that: "The concern among U.S. lawmakers was that if the sale goes through the Chinese would have access to years of high-tech advancements."[32]

These two quotes exemplify the unfortunate beliefs of U.S. leaders regarding China and why they fear China becoming technologically advanced.

The first belief, as expressed by Congresswoman Blackburn, is that China does not wish us well. Despite the U.S. and other Western nations' poor treatment of China over the last several hundred years, China has maintained an even temperament and continues to focus on improving their own condition. With no hint of ill will towards us, and a very restrained opinion of Japan, their most brutal neighbor, they continue to focus inward. There are many places in the world where leaders and people of nations actually do wish us harm, and they display this through inflammatory statements, flying planes into buildings, and anti-American protests complete with the burning of American flags. China is not one of those places. From our history of China and a review of our current dealings with China, we can see that there is no evidence or indication that China "does not wish us well." Despite our best efforts to turn them into an enemy, so far they have refused to accept that role. The actions of China continue to show a nation interested in friendship, peace, and prosperity.

While the reporter failed to question the grounds for Blackburn's statement, the American people should not. Ignoring the spin from the media and politicians, it's critical that we look at the actions and history of China, which clearly indicate that the congresswoman's statements are without merit. While it's a manipulative trick of politicians and the media to repeat unfounded accusations in the hope that the people will come to believe them to be true, it's incumbent upon us to challenge such unfounded positions.

Fox News' reporting on the issue was just as distorted. Their quote that: "the Chinese would have access to years of high-tech advancements" reveals the implication that there's a hope China won't advance in technologies, and that in some way they should be held back from modern technologies that provide great benefits to our world. Do we really believe that China shouldn't have access to years of scientific advancement? Fortunately, despite great opposition from many politicians and the media, the sale of A123 Battery did go through.[33]

We Refuse to Talk

In 2013, NASA held its second Kepler Science Conference, an event organized by NASA to bring international scientists together for the exchange of ideas on space exploration. When several Chinese scientists applied to register for the conference, NASA rejected their applications—China wasn't welcome. Congress members like John Culberson had been perpetuating the fear of Chinese involvement in space projects when he told the president in 2010 that: "I have grave concerns about the nature and goals of China's space program and strongly oppose any cooperation between NASA and CNSA's human space flight programs without Congressional authorization."[34]

To their credit, upon hearing of the rejection of the Chinese scientists from the conference, many U.S. scientists called for a boycott of the event; unfortunately, the damage had already been done. Once again China was treated as an enemy, a nation to be feared, a nation to be excluded from the advances of science.

Whom to Trust

The U.S. media and politicians sound all the alarms and show unwarranted concern for every technological advancement of China, scrutinizing every sale or sharing of information, fighting to prevent China from participating in the advances of science and technology. At the same time the U.S. denies China the most basic access to scientific information, we sell or transfer technologies to questionable nations throughout the world. In addition to these technologies, the U.S. sells military weapons to nations with questionable motives, character, and history.

In December of 2011, the *Navy Times* announced that Japan would be buying four F-35 stealth fighters from the U.S. However, the sale was delayed, not due to security concerns, but because Japan decided they might build the U.S. designed F-35 fighters themselves. The *Navy Times* went on to say: "Lockheed is offering a production line final assembly and checkout facility in Japan, as well as component and subcomponent assembly work." While we restrict even the most basic non-threatening technology transfer to China, we sell not only weapons, but the ability to manufacture F-35 stealth fighters to Japan, the nation that attacked the U.S. islands of Hawaii and caused the death of over 30 million people in WWII just seventy-five years ago.

To Iraq, an unstable nation, we sold $5.6 billion in arms. And

ISIS, the Muslim terrorist group, now has about one billion dollars worth of U.S. arms in its possession taken from Iraq. To Egypt, a nation that was run by a repressive totalitarian dictator up until 2012, the U.S. sold $7.8 billion in arms. To Pakistan, the country where Osama bin Laden was found by U.S. special forces, while the leadership of Pakistan claimed no knowledge of his location, we sold $4.1 billion in arms.

Saudi Arabia, the largest arms customer of the U.S., was home to fifteen of the nineteen 9/11 hijackers. All this is to say that, if you want to think of a people who wish us harm, there are many nations which are much more qualified than China for that description. While we refuse to allow the sale of a car battery company to China or refuse to buy network equipment from China, the list of nations that we have no issue selling our most sophisticated military weapons is worth noting.

Turkey $3.8 billion	Egypt $7.8 billion
Pakistan $4.1 billion	Saudi Arabia $10.8 billion
Iraq $5.6 billion	

When it comes to technology, our Cold War paranoia prevails. While we engage in technology and weapons commerce with questionable nations throughout the world, when it comes to China, we refuse to buy as we did with Huawei, we refuse to sell as we did with A123, and we refuse to discuss as we did with the NASA convention. These are not exceptions to how we treat China; rather, these are examples of our standard treatment of them—we take every opportunity to prevent China from becoming a technologically advanced nation.

Is it possible that the common thread of limiting technology to China is more about protecting domestic industries than it is about security? While the true motive may be difficult to ascertain, our concern and focus should be on dispelling unsubstantiated claims, because for each agreement that's rejected, we miss opportunities for mutual benefit and advancement.

In 2014, the EU-China Joint Steering Committee meeting on Science and Technology held its 11th annual meeting. Representatives from China and the European Union met to discuss science, technology, and how China and Europe can cooperate for advancements. As the rest of the world works with China to advance technologies in joint ventures and the sharing of information, we're too often frozen by fear. The U.S. and China continue to negotiate on these issues and occasionally find common ground to move forward, so there has been some progress, but that progress has been (and continues to be) greatly inhibited by our groundless fear of China's advancement in science and technology.[35]

Tech Threat or Tech Opportunity?

In May of 2014 at a speech at the U.S. Air Force Academy, U.S. Vice President Joe Biden challenged the audience: "China—and it's true—is graduating six to eight times as many scientists and engineers as we have. But I challenge you, name me one innovative project, one innovative change, one innovative product that has come out of China."[36]

While Mr. Biden certainly lacks enthusiasm for what China can contribute to the world, China's trend is evident and even typical. Emerging economies start with imitation and low-end manufacturing, then move on to more complicated manufacturing, and then finally to true invention and innovation. Manufacturing has allowed China to rapidly grow its economy; invention and innovation will increasingly be a part of China's future. Taiwan, Singapore, Japan, and South Korea have gone through that process, and China is following the same path.

China already boasts the fastest high-speed trains, 14 of the top 20 longest bridges, and the fastest supercomputer in the world. In Shanghai, a 277,000 square meter building houses 10,000 Huawei engineers working on telecom hardware and software development, as Huawei spends over five billion a year on research and development. In addition, and what may be the most important factor for China's technological future, hundreds of thousands of Chinese young people are interested in the STEM (Science, Technology, Engineering and Mathematics) fields and are pursuing degrees in these areas. Over time, China will excel in scientific and technological advancements because they understand its value to their economy and the broader standard of living.

The sheer pace of infrastructure development as well as economic development itself requires innovation in procedures, process, and management. These may be the most influential innovations over the next decade as others seek to learn from China's success in rapid economic development. Like the other areas of influence and power, China's coming leadership in invention and innovation can either be thought of as a threat or an opportunity. If we think that the benefits of new inventions only goes to the inventor, then we should fear China's strategy of pursuing invention and innovation. However, if we believe that invention and innovation are of benefit to the entire world, then we should embrace China's advancement and leadership in these areas.

What if the engineers at Huawei can create communications hardware and software that's impervious to hackers? What if software engineers at Lenova can create an operating system that's completely immune to viruses? What if the Chinese can create a credit card system that makes credit card and identity theft a thing of the past? What if scientists in China can develop medical technology that reduces or eliminates autism or cancer? Is it truly our desire to suppress China's advancements in technology? Is it our hope to stifle their ability to innovate and invent when the benefits of their achievements could have a great impact on solving world problems and improving the lives of millions?

While U.S. inventions and innovations will continue to influence the world, China will soon join the nations that contribute not only technological advancement but social, economic, and political innovation as well. While the U.S. has benefitted greatly from being the world's main source of invention and innovation for over 100 years, we must recognize that it's to the advantage of all if more are contributing to solving the problems of our world and bringing new ideas to the market. Is there room for two Thomas Edisons or two Steve Jobs in the world? Not only is there more than enough room, but more innovators could greatly improve our world. As the most basic illustration, when we attempted to stop China from gaining the A123 battery technology, we attempted to slow the advancement of the electric car, a technology that may very well be the key to addressing our energy and pollution concerns. Imagine a nation of 1.3 billion people anxious to join us in solving real problems. Is fear our best response? No, fearing China's technology is the worst thing we can do.

7

Fearing China's Trade

Are Chinese Exporters Cheating? (NPR)
US Questions China Aviation Subsidies (Leeham News)
Chinese Steel Subsidies Out Of Control (Industry Week)
Obama Gets Tough On China's Auto Subsidies (NPR)
U.S. to Impose Tariff on Tires From China (Washington Post)
Trade with China has Cost 3.2 Million American Jobs (Washington Post)
Chinese 'Currency Manipulation' and What it Means for U.S. Trade (PBS)
U.S. Solar Panel Makers Say China Violated Trade Rules (New York Times)[37]

From Closed to Open

The history of Chinese trade is one of challenge and conflict. Although there was some trade as early as 200 BC on the Silk Road which connected China to Europe and the Middle East, Chinese trade accelerated when European ships were finally able to reach China in the early 16th century, but because much of the trade was forced by the military powers of Europe, China often tried to stop or limit trade with the outside world. As discussed in chapter two, the Opium Wars were caused by Great Britain forcing China to accept opium as payment for traded goods. Because of the consistently poor experiences with the outside world, following WWII China's international trade was small as the country worked to isolate itself from the influence of the U.S. and Europe. During the 1950s, '60s, and '70s, trade with China was mainly for essentials like agricultural products when China experienced food shortages; other than this, China worked to be self sufficient. This arrangement caused China to fall behind on technology, but also caused them to miss out on the economic benefits of trade.

During and shortly following World War II, European and Asian economies and productive capacity were decimated. The U.S., due in large part to its geographic isolation, was one of the few manufacturing centers left in the world, and the world not only needed the regular flow of goods, but also additional goods to rebuild from the devastation of war. By the late 1940s, the U.S. was manufacturing 60 percent of the world's goods. If this was a competition, no one else showed up, and thus the U.S. was the easy victor in economic strength, manufacturing, and exports. Over the next thirty years the war-devastated countries eventually rebuilt and reentered the world economy. There was a general balance between nations by the early 1970s as Germany, Great Britain, Japan, Taiwan, and others regained their productivity and began trading on an equal footing with the U.S.

We like to think very highly of our manufacturing strength in the 50s, 60s, and 70s—we look back at the "good old days," attributing our strength to strong unions, hard work, and innovation. However, much of our economic success on the world stage was actually due to a lack of competition. Spoiled by the misfortune of others, we gave little thought to the fact that the U.S., which represented five percent of the world's population, was producing sixty percent of the world's manufactured goods. In many ways, we were the only store in town. As other countries came online, tensions arose as competition from around the world put pressure on U.S. manufacturers to cut cost, which often meant cutting labor cost.

By the late 1970s we were somewhat content with the status of manufacturing and trade as we settled into a more reasonable balance than we had seen following WWII. However, the 1980s brought a huge shock as Japanese automobiles hit the roads of American cities. Almost comfortable with the new reality that Japan and the Asian Tigers (South Korea, Taiwan, Singapore and Hong Kong) would be in the game the biggest shock was yet to come.

The new leadership of China, which came to power in 1976, observed the economic success of its neighbors like Japan, Hong Kong, and Taiwan, and realized that an economy based on trade would be key to China's advancement. However, given the problems of past trade, they approached the transition with caution to ensure that the abuses and manipulations of the past would not be repeated. Deng Xiaoping promoted a new openness and began making trade agreements with various countries and trade organizations. Under this new openness, China slowly began to grow its economy, which had struggled for over thirty years. In 2001, twenty-five years after Deng Xiaoping became the leader of China, China applied for and was admitted to the World Trade Organization (WTO). This moved China from moderate growth to explosive growth driven by trade. According to the WTO, goods and services exported from China in 2001 were $266 billion and by 2011 the number had grown to $1.9 trillion; over seven times more exports in ten years.

This explosive growth, primarily in manufacturing, had a large effect on the world's import-export economy. While the world economy did grow during those ten years, it did not grow by a multiple of seven, so manufacturers around the world definitely felt the competition. A toy now made in China damaged sales of a toy that may have previously been made in Japan, the U.S., or Germany. A tire previously made in Lima, Peru may now be made in Shanghai—a tennis shoe made in Mexico may now be made in Beijing.[38]

Led by companies like Walmart, retail prices began to drop, causing other retailers to seek out lower wholesale prices to be able to compete, and lower wholesale prices meant buying from China. A company can't stay in business if they're spending four dollars on a shoe for which their competition pays one dollar, and once the ball is rolling, it can't be stopped. The dramatic change in sourcing caused the U.S. and other Western manufacturers to push back any way they could, and that often meant politically. While politicians spoke of "Fair Trade," Western manufacturers fought to maintain their position by any means necessary. They worked to find a way, find a method, find a reason to get the law to slow the competition; thus, the trade wars.

Subsidies

The Western headlines tell us that the Chinese government is subsidizing its domestic manufacturers, creating an unfair trade advantage. In 2011, a group of seven solar companies in the U.S. brought suit against Chinese solar manufacturers. They claimed that China was subsidizing their solar industry and thereby giving them an unfair advantage over the U.S. companies. Some of the U.S. manufacturer's complaints against the Chinese companies were that

Chinese companies were: "dumping their product at artificially low prices" and that these companies also received: "unfair subsidies from their government." The largest company in the suit was the German company SolarWorld, which has locations in the U.S. and around the world. While filing suit against Chinese manufacturers for taking government subsidies, SolarWorld's entire business model was based on receiving its own government subsidies. In its Hillsboro, Oregon plant in the U.S., management signed two "enterprise zone" agreements with the state that exempted it from paying property taxes on buildings and equipment. Ultimately, six manufacturing tax credits were given by the state allowing SolarWorld to be subsidized $22 million in taxes. Later SolarWorld took $2.4 million in Federal government Department of Energy subsidies.

Another U.S. company that filed suit against Chinese solar manufacturers for dumping and taking government subsidies was Solyndra. But while the legal department at Solyndra was busy filing suits against China for taking government subsidies, their lobbying department was hard at work lining up their own Federal subsidies. They were so successful that they received $528 million from the U.S. Department of Energy to help finance development and production of their solar work, filing for bankruptcy shortly after receiving the massive government handout.

The persistent suits by the U.S. solar industry against China have been for its alleged subsidizing and dumping. However, it's clear that U.S. solar companies are sustained by generous government subsidies of their own. When testifying before Congress about Solyndra, the head of the U.S. Department of Energy, Steven Chu, said: "The government should play a role in this because it's a competitive world out there. Other countries are helping their companies. In order to even just level the playing field, the U.S. government should play a role." The statement by Chu reveals that we are confused. Do we think subsidies are OK, or not? The message is clear. Subsidies by the U.S. government to U.S. companies are OK, but subsidies from the Chinese government to Chinese companies are not. Things certainly get complicated with such a double standard—U.S. companies file complaints against the Chinese for subsidizing their solar industry, and then use that same pen to request subsidies of their own.[39]

U.S. government agencies, from the Department of Commerce to the U.S. International Trade Commission, typically rule in favor of U.S. corporations due in no small part to the efforts of lobbyists who put a great deal of pressure on these political organizations; nevertheless, more often than not these biased rulings are overturned by the WTO, which typically takes a far more objective approach. In the case of the solar suits, U.S. government agencies ruled in favor of the U.S. solar companies, and in doing so instituted huge tariffs on solar panels imported from China. However, in 2014 the WTO ruled that the tariffs were illegal, and that the U.S. was simply attempting to protect their own industry—they found no proof that China was breaking WTO trade rules.

SolarWorld's persistent suits against Chinese solar manufacturers even became an annoyance for other U.S. solar companies working to lower prices and install more solar panels. The Coalition for Affordable Solar Energy (CASE) was formed by other U.S. solar industry companies to push back against SolarWorld and others chasing tariffs against China.

GM and Chrysler Subsidies

On Sept 17[th,] 2012, the U.S. filed a complaint with the WTO accusing China of unfairly subsidizing its auto industry with over one billion dollars from 2009 to 2011. This is a fascinating claim when the history of the U.S. auto industry is reviewed. In 1979, with Chrysler on the verge of bankruptcy, the U.S. government loaned Chrysler $1.5 billion. In addition to the loan, the U.S. military then bought thousands of Chrysler vehicles, generating badly needed revenue for the failing auto company. Fast forward 30 years, and once again the U.S. government was subsidizing the U.S. auto industry with billions of dollars. Chrysler and General Motors were on the edge of bankruptcy, and in 2009 the U.S. government actually agreed to back the warranty of Chrysler cars, so that if Chrysler went out of business, the U.S. government would cover the cost of warranty repairs on the cars. When the dust had settled and Chrysler had undergone bankruptcy restructuring, the government had spent $1.3 billion that would not be recovered. Chrysler had been saved once again by government subsidies, but the Chrysler subsidies were small compared to that of General Motors—in 2009 General Motors was taken over by the U.S. government and was subsequently granted $33 billion in financing from the government.

Cash for Clunkers

Along with the financial support provided directly to the U.S. automakers, the U.S. spent three billion on its cash-for-clunkers program. In this program, the government gave U.S. citizens money to assist them in buying cars in an attempt to stimulate car sales. U.S. government subsidies to the auto industry are the largest in the world and have been going on for decades. For the U.S. to file suit against China for providing one billion in subsidies to their auto industry is indefensible given that U.S. government subsidies to automakers over the last thirty years easily exceeds $40 billion. China should hire the tennis player John McEnroe as their spokesperson; he's famous for throwing his tennis racquet to the ground and screaming: "You cannot be serious!"

Import Export Bank

The Boeing Company sells airplanes around the world, and to do so, they must often make loans to buyers. Because it's often difficult to get banks to make such loans, and because the banks would charge very high interest rates for such risk, the U.S. established the Import Export Bank of the U.S. The Import Export Bank subsidizes the loans, which Boeing uses to sell airplanes around the world. In addition, there's an even bigger subsidizer involved, and it's the U.S. Military, which buys billions of dollars in military aircraft from Boeing each year. So far, Boeing has not sued China for aviation subsidies, but it should be expected once China is able to compete with Boeing's production of large aircraft. The question is: should China file a complaint against Boeing for the large subsidies provided to them by the U.S. government?

It's clear that all governments subsidize industry—the fact that the U.S. is the world's largest economy naturally makes it the largest subsidizer as well. The main difference between subsidizing in the U.S. and China should be our biggest concern. That difference is that in China, most subsidies are part of a cohesive, well thought out economic plan, while in the U.S., subsidies are determined by special interest groups like: the farm lobby, the real estate lobby, the oil industry, and the auto industry all fighting for their hand out. While there is debate over whether subsidies are ultimately good or bad for an economy, certainly the method we use to determine who gets the subsidies deserves our attention. However, there can be no doubt that the U.S. is the leader in government subsidies to business.

Dumping – Labor Rates

Dumping is a trade term ultimately meaning selling below cost. The headlines tell us again and again that Chinese manufacturers dump products on the U.S. market. In 2009 the U.S. steel industry filed a suit against China for subsidizing and dumping steel; it claimed that Chinese steel mills were selling below cost and being subsidized by the government to make up the loss.[40]

Extracting raw materials from the earth and converting it to usable steel requires immense amounts of labor; the true cost of creating steel from the ground is the cost of labor at every level, from the accounting department, to the man in the mine, to the shop foreman and truck drivers. Labor cost is ultimately the cost that determines the cost of steel as well as most other products. While labor input can be reduced through automation, if competing factories are using comparable technology, then labor cost determines the final cost difference.

In 2009, when the steel lawsuit was filed, the average wage for a Chinese factory worker was $1.74 per hour, while in the U.S. the average factory wage was $24.56 per hour. The U.S. wage was roughly 14 times that of the factory wage in China, so let's say the total amount of labor to create a ton of steel from the ground to shippable product is 25 hours—this means the cost for a U.S. steel company to produce a ton of steel would be $614. In comparison, the cost to the Chinese manufacturer would be $43. When the suit claims that China is selling below cost, which cost are they referring to? Certainly China is selling below the U.S. manufacturer's cost, but the real cost in China is infinitely lower due to the lower labor cost. In this example, the Chinese manufacturers easily sell at a lower price than their U.S. counterparts without selling below cost. They could effectively sell at $50 per ton and still be selling above cost, while the U.S. manufacturer would have to sell at over $600. If your labor cost is 14 times lower than your competition, there's no need to sell below cost. It can be frustrating to an established factory worker making almost $25 an hour to find that there are many in the world ready to work for $2, but if we chose to trade internationally, then we need to face the reality of our competition.[4142]

In 2011 four U.S. companies that manufacture towers for wind turbines filed a suit against Chinese manufacturers. They claimed that government subsidies were allowing Chinese manufacturers to sell below cost. But like the steel industry, with labor costs in China at less than 10 percent of those in the U.S., not only is the actual manufacturing cost less, but the materials and support costs are lower as lower labor costs are seen throughout the supply chain. The Chinese companies are usually not selling below cost, but they do have dramatically lower costs, and this allows them to sell products at much lower prices. The irony of the suit is that the U.S. wind industry is heavily subsidized by the U.S. government.[43]

As part of the Great Leap Forward (1958), Mao initiated a plan to have peasants make steel in backyard furnaces. While Mao was trying to produce steel in local household shops, the U.S. had state-of-the-art mills producing thousands of tons per day. The recent intense competition in steel and other industries from China is not due to some tricky trade manipulation, massive government subsidies, or selling below cost; conversely, it's simply that a previously dormant country is now catching up on industrialization and is becoming highly productive.

Finally, in 2014 the World Trade Organization ruled against the U.S. stating that there was no evidence of Chinese steel manufacturers "dumping" or selling below cost. They ruled against the U.S. for imposing tariffs on imported steel, and that the tariffs were simply an attempt to protect U.S. companies from foreign competition—there were no grounds for claiming Chinese and Indian manufacturers were selling below cost or at unfair prices. So while the headlines for several years had ranted about the unfair "dumping" of steel, in the end the WTO ruled against the U.S. claim. Unfortunately, however, after hundreds of stories about China unfairly dumping steel on the U.S. market, the headlines with the final story were few, and the opinion of the American public was fairly locked in by then. Ultimately, tariffs on Chinese imports prove to be the ultimate subsidy for U.S. steel makers, automakers, solar companies, and others, as they used lawyers, politicians and the U.S. government to slow the Chinese competition.[4445]

They Are Taking Our Jobs, But Who is 'They'?

Every American knows that the Chinese are taking our jobs—we know this because the media and politicians told us so. While there may be a small amount of truth to this claim, let's look at the bigger picture. Since 1975 U.S. manufacturing output has more than doubled, going from $1.2 trillion to $3 trillion (inflation adjusted year 2000 dollars), while the number of employees in manufacturing has gone from 17 million workers to 13 million workers. That's a lot less people making a lot more things; this means that productivity has gone up. We're told that jobs are going overseas, but the reality is that U.S. manufacturing output continues to rise.

It took ten man-hours to produce a ton of steel at a steel smelting plant in the 1980s. With improved technology and automation, it now takes just two man-hours to produce that same ton of steel. That's the same amount of steel produced with less than half the workers—40 percent to be exact. As a result of this, a U.S. steel factory that provided 1,000 jobs in 1980 can now produce the same amount of steel with only 400 workers. If the amount of steel needed remains constant, that means six out of ten workers lost their jobs due to automation. That's a 60 percent job loss. This isn't just seen in the steel industry; automation has occurred in all aspects of manufacturing, and even in office work. Watching bags of chips whisking by on a conveyor in the Perry, Georgia Frito-Lay plant is a clear reminder of how automated our manufacturing has become. The factory produces over five million cases of chips every month. From cleaning, slicing, cooking, bagging, and boxing, a bag of chips is rarely touched by human hands as they are passed from one machine to the next. The Campbell Soup factory in Napoleon, Ohio produces over 100 million cases of soup a year. A goal of plant managers is efficiency, so each year they work towards this goal. "Efficiency" is code for greater production coupled with lower cost; "lower cost" is code for fewer employees per can of soup produced.

The U.S. hasn't suffered a loss of manufacturing output; instead, we've lost manufacturing jobs. This is because with automation we produce almost three times more than in the past, and we do so with far fewer jobs. If you want to see automation in action, search the Internet for automobile factories and watch the robots at work. One of the most automated is the Tesla plant in California, where bright red robotic arms swing rapidly, grabbing five hundred pound parts and placing them into new cars with precision. The robots then switch tools and weld or bolt the component into place. An operator watches from the side as each robot does the work of 20 men. The chart below shows our continued growth in manufacturing over the last forty years.

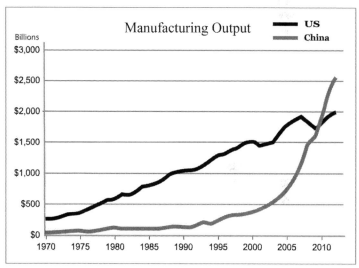

United Nations Data - 2011 dollars

While many would like to blame China for our job loss in manufacturing, the truth is that much of these losses have been due to innovation and technology, which allows each employee to be more productive.

There were 17 million Americans employed in manufacturing in 1975. Today, we manufacture about three times more than we did then. So, if there were no improvements in automation, we would have added about 34 million jobs to our manufacturing workforce. However, because of automation, each worker has become more productive and no jobs have been added. That's 34 million jobs that were not created because we became more efficient through automation. There are approximately 10 million unemployed in the U.S., so the 34 million jobs lost due to technology and automation would've easily ensured full employment. In the end, Steve Jobs and Bill Gates could bear more responsibility for our manufacturing job losses than China, as computer technology is at the core of automation. But before we are too hard on these two, consider that they have contributed heavily in creating a new industry that employs millions. So while we've had a loss of manufacturing jobs, there's been a gain in high-tech jobs.

It's true that there have been overall losses in low skill jobs as U.S. manufacturers have become more automated. Also, yes, many low skilled jobs go to low wage countries like China, India, Bangladesh, and Vietnam. However, as the U.S. has shifted to higher skilled jobs, it's more the fault of the U.S. laborer for not becoming educated and equipped to take these high skill jobs. It's estimated that over four million high-tech jobs go unfilled, as U.S. companies are unable to find qualified workers for the positions.[46]

If we're to continue operating in a world economy, and wish to continue to trade with other nations, then we must realize that the economic prosperity of our middle class lies in pursuing higher skilled labor. The days of an unskilled laborer being able to provide well for his or her family are long gone. Unless we're ready to stop participating in the world economy, we must let go of any illusions of regaining the high paying, low skilled jobs of the 1950s. From China to India to Africa, there are over two billion people in this world who are willing to work for less than two dollars an hour. To attempt to change that is futile. Our best hope is to focus on training for high skilled jobs. While it's easy to blame China and others for our job loss, remember that R2D2 has taken more jobs than Wang Chu. "They're" taking our jobs, but "they" are robots, not the country of China. With 34 million jobs lost due to automation, blaming China for our jobs losses is both foolish and misguided.

We Are Taking Their Jobs

As we complain about China taking our jobs, we neglect to see that we're also taking their jobs. With international trade, we effectively trade jobs. When Boeing sells an airplane to China, that's a job in Seattle that could have been in China. When Apple sells an iPhone to a young Chinese woman in Shenzhen, that's a design job in Silicon Valley that could have been in China. A Starbucks in Shanghai creates jobs in Seattle at the sacrifice of a teashop owner in China. A McDonald's in Beijing takes jobs from a small café owner. They're taking our jobs? It's far more accurate to say that we're trading jobs.

Trade Imbalances

The U.S. Census Bureau reports that in 2013, the U.S. exported $122 billion to China while importing $441 billion, which resulted in a trade deficit of $319 billion.[47] The media and politicians are quick to reference growing trade deficits with China as a grave threat to the U.S., but there is much more to the issue than the scary sound bites we hear. The topic of international trade and trade balances is highly complicated and controversial. Consider some issues that illustrate the complexity of measuring trade balances.

The first Ford manufacturing plant established outside the U.S. was in 1911 in Great Britain, and by the end of WWII, U.S. multinational corporations were investing heavily overseas, opening offices, starting factories and developing distribution networks. If Ford opens a factory in Europe and those cars are sold to the European market, is that considered a U.S. export? Ford has numerous manufacturing plants around the world including Thailand, Romania, Brazil, France, Mexico and Australia, just to name a few.

Toyota has factories in eighteen countries. If a car manufactured at a Toyota plant in Mexico is imported into the U.S., is that a Japanese import or a Mexican import? Or likewise what if a car is exported from the Toyota plant in Mississippi to Canada? Is that a U.S. export to Canada or a Japanese export to Canada? Let's add even more real world complexity to our trade balance equation. The parts that go into that Toyota come from the U.S., China, Mexico, Canada, and several other countries. The Ford Fiesta, which is made in the U.S., is constructed of ten percent U.S. made parts, while the other ninety percent come from numerous other countries. As large international corporations have expanded around the world, the concept of import and export has become exceedingly complicated—it's also quite tricky to measure.

Let's consider an Apple iPhone that's "made in China." When the iPhone is shipped to the U.S. it's considered an import, and about $200 is put on the books of imports from China to the U.S. However, the parts that went into making the phone are from Germany, Japan, and several other countries. When a component is shipped from Germany to China to be used in that iPhone, that goes on the books as an export from Germany to China. It's estimated that once the dust settles, the real dollar value that is contributed to China's economy is more like $10 per iPhone. However, as we've seen, the balance of trade records $200; this is because it includes all the component costs that are passed along. This ultimately results in overstating the trade deficit with China while understating the trade deficit with other countries like Germany, Japan, or Taiwan that supply components to be included in Chinese assembled products.[48]

International tourism is also a large component of cross-country exchange, but it is not measured as part of trade. In 2013 Chinese tourists spent over $100 billion around the world, and the total amount of inflows from international visitors to the U.S. exceeds $200 billion. In many ways this is international trade, but it is not counted as trade, once again skewing the real numbers.

This is all to say that international trade issues and balances are exceptionally complex. Even the most prominent economists cannot agree on the numbers, the implications, and the true advantages or disadvantages of the balance of transactions around the world. While we may complain that China doesn't buy enough from us, it's just as much an issue that others buy from China instead of the U.S. For example, in 2012 Germany imported roughly $66 billion from the U.S. and $100 billion from China—they also exported $113 billion to the U.S. and $87 billion to the Chinese. Looking at the numbers, Germany sells to the U.S. and buys from China. However, it's not just Germany, many countries are in this same situation. Although we would like to think of trade as two countries exchanging roughly equal amounts of goods and services, the German trade situation is indicative of worldwide trends.

The truth is that we, along with the rest of the world, buy a lot from China because they often have the best product at the lowest price. Labor cost is the biggest advantage. But there are other countries with labor costs as low or lower than China's. The difference is that China has been able to create the productive facilities and infrastructure to become a world-class manufacturing nation. Nonetheless, on a per capita basis the U.S. still manufactures much more than China. If we accept the general trade numbers regardless of the inherent inaccuracies as mentioned prior, in 2011 the U.S. sold $1.5 trillion worth of goods and services to the world, while China sold more at $1.9 trillion. For the U.S., that's $5,000 per person in exports, and for China it's only $1,400 per person. If we factor in population size, the U.S. is still a *much* larger exporter than China.[49]

As China and other nations catch up with the U.S. in technologies and manufacturing abilities, our portion of the world's manufacturing will continue to slowly taper down. From the post WWII high of five percent of the population producing sixty percent of the world's goods, a more realistic balance will evolve.

How China Uses its Surplus

While not as dramatic as the headlines portray, China does maintain a large trade surplus, not only with the U.S. but with most of its trading partners. When a nation ends up with a surplus balance in trade, that accumulated "cash" can be used for several things. It can be used to buy products. It can be invested in opening or expanding businesses overseas. It can be invested in overseas stocks and bonds, or even government bonds like U.S. treasury bonds. Toyota spent six billion to build an auto plant in Georgetown, Kentucky that employs seven thousand Americans. In this case, the Japanese trade surplus was used to invest in America. Most would agree this is of benefit to the U.S.

The biggest issue and potential problem is not the trade deficit, but what is done with the surplus held by others. The U.S. government has spent more than they have bought for 35 of the last 40 years, resulting in a national debt equal to a full year of gross domestic product. This 16 trillion dollar debt is financed by the U.S. government issuing bonds, which basically means taking out loans from individual investors, institutions, and other countries. If these government bonds were not issued in such large amounts to finance our growing deficit, China and others would have to explore other options such as investment in U.S. corporations or buying more products from the U.S. However, our government's spending binge causes these large reserves to be placed in non-productive assets—bonds paying interest from the American tax payer to the Chinese government. If the U.S. was not borrowing the money back, countries with a surplus like China would be buying more products from us, or they would be investing in more productive assets such as Toyota did in their U.S. factories. U.S. government deficits divert Chinese surplus dollars to U.S. government bonds that are stagnant assets.[50]

Currency Manipulation

During the 2010 presidential election, candidate Mitt Romney proclaimed that if elected he'd immediately label China a "currency manipulator." This was possibly not a great campaign position, as most voters have no idea what is meant by currency manipulation. Currency manipulation is typically when a government intentionally acts to devalue their currency against others. This makes products cheaper for foreign buyers and thus promotes exports. For example, if one dollar can buy six Chinese *yuan*, the Chinese government may try to manage its currency to change the exchange rate to seven *yuan* per dollar. By doing this, a U.S. buyer could now buy seven *yuan* worth of product with their dollar instead of just six. Countries devalue their currency by flooding the market with more of their own currency, or removing foreign currency from circulation. Think supply and demand—if there's a lot of something, it becomes less valuable, if there's a shortage of something, it becomes more valuable.

The U.S. and China are the two largest economies and exporters in the world. Because of this, the exchange rate between the Chinese *yuan* and the U.S. dollar is a critical factor in world trade. Add to that the fact that much of world's trade is done in dollars, even for non-U.S. countries, and the exchange rate between the dollar and the *yuan* becomes even more important. Because of the large amount China exports both to the U.S. and the rest of the world, many in the U.S. would like to devalue the dollar against the *yuan* to slow Chinese exports and increase U.S. exports.

The issue of currency manipulation is as complex as trade balances, and economists rarely agree on what constitutes an undervalued or overvalued currency. However, when it comes to U.S. elections, candidates can be quick to use China as a scapegoat for lost jobs and poor economic performance. The rarely understood issue of currency manipulation is an easy term to throw at the voters to convince them that China is a major economic threat. Also, candidates consistently fail to mention that we're producing three times more than we were 40 years ago, but with fewer workers. They'll also never point out that if a Chinese toy becomes too expensive due to an adjustment in exchange rates, that job won't go to the U.S., it'll most likely go to a lower wage country like Vietnam, Bangladesh, or India. A currency can't be manipulated enough to make up for a discrepancy in labor rates of $2 per hour verses over $25 per hour.

Protecting the Yuan

The media and politicians tell us that China manipulates its currency, but it's more accurate to say that China has been stabilizing its currency. While the U.S. was actively printing dollars, or in other ways adding money to the money supply for the purpose of driving down the value of the dollar against the *yuan*, China was taking action to not allow their currency to be manipulated. To avoid instability in exchange rates and thus an unstable economy, China pegged the *yuan* to the dollar at a fixed rate for ten years, which ended in 2005. When the *yuan* was allowed to float, it was only within a specified range to ensure against erratic swings. Consequently, it's more accurate to say that China was maintaining the value of the *yuan,* not devaluing it, and the U.S. government was actively trying to devalue the dollar.

Certainly China was working to keep the value of the *yuan* low, but that isn't the biggest issue causing China to be a giant exporter. Low labor rates combined with being really good at manufacturing are the reasons China has become a world leading exporter. The *yuan*, in fact, has risen in value by 36 percent over the last ten years. And that rise has had no affect on the amount of exports from China, as their exports have continued to grow. The argument that China manipulates its currency to the detriment of the U.S. is weak at best.[51]

There are several issues at play here:

First: Through China's efforts to keep large foreign reserves, they maintain the ability to buffer Western attempts to manipulate the *yuan*. China buys up dollars or sells dollars to maintain a stable exchange rate. If they didn't accumulate the reserves, they wouldn't have the power to do so, and the U.S. could easily control the exchange rate.

Second: China now holds large amounts of U.S. dollars and U.S. treasury bonds. If the *yuan* increases in value and thus the dollar decreases in value, then the large holdings in U.S. currency that they have will decrease in value. This would be a huge advantage to the U.S. as we'd effectively be borrowing six *yuan* and only paying back five. Therefore, due to China's large holding in U.S. dollars, they have a strong interest in maintaining the exchange rate. Think of it as an asset—China owns a lot of U.S. dollars and they don't want the value of that asset to go down.

Third: As mentioned earlier, the U.S. trade surplus is largely facilitated by the U.S. federal deficit, otherwise such a large trade deficit couldn't exist.

And Fourth: By any standard of measurement, the U.S. is the largest currency manipulator in the world. Due to the recent financial crisis, since 2008 the U.S. Federal Reserve has used processes like quantitative easing as well as mortgage buybacks and other methods to add an additional $4.4 trillion to the money supply in order to drive down the value of the dollar and stimulate the U.S. economy. This is the largest currency manipulation ever attempted in the history of the world.

175 years ago the West, primarily Great Britain, was destroying China by forcing them to take opium as payment for Chinese goods. In a poetic twist, today China takes U.S. dollars for Chinese goods then loans the dollars back, allowing the U.S. to deficit spend to the point that it may destroy itself. The poison comes back.

The balance of trade is tied to the exchange rate, which is tied to currency manipulation, which is tied to the national debt. If you didn't follow all of that, don't worry. The American voters didn't either, and candidate Romney lost the election.

Playing by Western Rules

Part of China's challenge in the World Trade Organization (WTO) is working within rules that were written by Western powers and based on Western political and economic structures. A subsidy, for example, is a contribution to a company by a government. It could be a government loan or loan guarantee, a grant, a tax credit, or some other type of government assistance. The WTO restricts subsidies, noting that they are unfair. But consider the difference between Western companies and Chinese companies. Western companies are founded by individuals and supported by private capital (and sometimes loans from banks). Chinese companies, in contrast, are often founded if not financed by government entities. Although China is moving away from pure communism, keep in mind that it's still a proclaimed communist country, and thus by definition, the government is heavily involved in the support and creation of businesses. Therefore, the WTO rules regarding subsidies are written from a Western point of view for Western economies. The concept of preventing or limiting government subsidies is based on the idea that a company should survive on its own merit, and should not be able to operate only through the support of subsidies; this support is seen as unfairly competitive. The unfairness here is the fact that a company can sell below cost in order to grow and build market share, and damage or eliminate the competition. But western companies do that all the time. If a company is losing money, it's selling below its cost. The only difference is who is financing or "subsidizing" the loss.

Amazon.com, which was founded in 1994, lost two billion before it finally made its first profit seven years later in 2001. And it didn't start making consistent profits until several more years had elapsed. Those early losses were subsidized by banks and investors. If Amazon wasn't making a profit for 14 years, then it was selling below cost for all those years. If government monies had been lost, it would have been called a subsidy, but because it was private money, those losses were considered an "investment." Tesla Motors, an electric car company, was founded in 2003 and has yet to make a profit. It loses money on every car it sells and the investors finance that loss.

A company's losses are a part of doing business, but telling a

country that has its origins in state-owned enterprise (SOE), that you
can't trade with us if your state is financing corporations is certainly
only to the advantage of the members who function with private
capital. What really is the difference from a competitive point if a
government gives a company $100 million or $100 million is
received from a private equity firm? If China claimed to be pure
capitalist, then one could argue they're not being honest when their
government subsidizes industry, but China does not claim this.
Rather, they claim to have elements of capitalism, socialism, and
communism; communism means that the ownership of the means of
production is held by the collective or the state. But if we're
convinced that capitalism always outperforms communism or
socialism, then why would we care if they're not pure capitalist? If
the communist structure is so bad, it should be easy to compete
against. Right?

Nonetheless, China has joined the WTO and is working to
operate in an environment that isn't consistent with their structure.
Because of this inherent difference in Chinese business vs. Western
business, China has a built-in disadvantage. Like a seven-foot man
competing on an obstacle course designed for four-foot people,
China sometimes struggles to accommodate the trade rules of the
West. But they have agreed to join, and are working to make the
square peg fit into the round hole. However, if it's a challenge for
China to accept and abide by the trade rules that the West has
established, it becomes even more so when the West shifts values
and modifies the rules for self interest.

Shifting Values

The progression of the solar panel businesses is a great example
of fickle, vacillating principles. A common value of capitalist
systems is that business should go to the most efficient provider. As
companies gain efficiencies and methods to lower their costs, they
gain market share, and the less efficient lose market share. Develop a
better, less expensive way to produce, and you win. Laws are even
created to prohibit price fixing, where a group of companies agree to
keep prices high instead of competing to be the lowest cost provider.
Laws also exist which prohibit selling below cost. Because of this, a
company with large resources can't starve the competition by selling

below cost and forcing the competition out of business. Another philosophy of the capitalist system is that it doesn't allow government subsidies to an industry—the thinking behind this is that it would provide an unfair advantage, allowing the company to sell at prices below their true cost.

In the 1980s and 1990s companies struggled to bring down the cost of solar panels, as they were just too expensive to be practical. As noted previously, governments in the U.S. and Europe subsidized these companies through a variety of grants, loans, and tax advantages, allowing them to sell at a price below their true cost. When China got involved in the solar business they had the built in advantage of low labor rates, which allowed them to sell at prices below U.S. and European manufacturers. This advantage propelled China to be a leading supplier of solar panels. When the financial crisis hit Europe and the U.S., many of the subsidies the solar companies had been receiving were withdrawn by governments, and this caused the U.S. and European solar companies to lose money. The withdrawal of subsidies made the U.S. and European suppliers even less competitive with China, so most of the business went to China.

The solar manufacturing factories in the U.S. and Europe were pushed to the brink of bankruptcy and many did go out of business. Seeing the closing businesses and lost jobs, the European Union filed suit against China in the WTO and immediately applied duties to all Chinese solar panels entering Europe. The complaint was "dumping," an amazingly vague and subjective term for a legal complaint. China in turn filed complaints against France for "dumping" wine. This was not so much a statement about dumping, but more a declaring of the fact that they will no longer accept a double standard, and that the days of unequal treaties are over. In an attempt to resolve the dispute, the EU proposed that the price for solar panels be fixed at a minimum dollar amount per kilowatt-hour (kWh). China countered with a minimum price that was lower, but was truly not interested in price fixing, preferring to compete head to head. Who's the capitalist now? A review of this sequence is a beautiful illustration of variable values masquerading as fixed values.

It's a position of the WTO that government subsidies are not good for international trade; however, as we've seen, the U.S. and the EU heavily subsidized the solar industry. When they could no longer afford the subsidies, they had a change of heart, subsidies were no longer acceptable, and they began to complain about Chinese subsidies. For many years, the U.S. and EU companies sold solar panels below their cost, but once they began to lose market share, they reverted back to the principle that selling below cost shouldn't be allowed. The value of selling at the lowest price, which is a main tenet of capitalism, was quickly abandoned when the U.S. and EU could no longer sell at the lowest price. Price fixing, another strongly held capitalistic belief, was wrong until that value was not working to their advantage, then suddenly the proposition to institute price fixing was made.

U.S. and European companies and governments found that 1: Government subsidies are OK until it's no longer giving you an advantage, then it should be stopped. 2: Competing by selling at the lowest cost is a critical value, until it's no longer an advantage to you, then it should be stopped. 3: Price fixing is wrong and illegal, until it's to your advantage, then it should no longer be illegal. When it comes to political and economic systems, what are often portrayed as fixed moral values can be more accurately described as variable opportunistic values.

While many claim to want a level playing field in trade, what they really want is an uneven playing field in their favor. It was easy to hold onto our capitalist principles when we always won, but now that there's competition, standards have quickly shifted, and many seek new values that will give the U.S. unwarranted advantages.

To Trade or Not to Trade. Are We Ready to Compete?

Free enterprise competition is about providing more for less, thus giving more value to the consumer. Henry Ford advanced the auto industry by providing more for less through efficiencies. In the years when China was pre-occupied with domestic difficulties, it was easy to "compete." But now China is becoming truly productive and therefore truly competitive.

Complaints filed against China for unfair trade practices usually involve either the complaint that they're being subsidized by government, or that they're selling below market price. But in the

Western free enterprise model, subsidies abound, and selling at a lower price is usually the goal and driver of growth. Ford built an empire because he sold cars for much less than what was currently the market price for a car. Apple Computer began by selling personal computers at such a low price that many people could suddenly afford them.

In our world of international trade, you can't have your cake and eat it too. The moment we agree to sell a Boeing airplane, an Apple iPhone, a Caterpillar tractor, or to open a McDonald's in a foreign land, that's the moment that we've agreed to compete on all levels, which includes labor rates. In that moment we effectively agree to sacrifice our low skill jobs. We can't say you should buy our Boeing 747s, iPads, and eat at a McDonald's in Beijing, but we shouldn't buy your tennis shoes or toys. We either trade with other countries or we don't. And trade means international competition, including wage competition. As long as we are trading with countries that have a large part of the population willing to work for two dollars per hour, or even two dollars per day, low skill manufacturing jobs won't be maintained in the U.S. For this reason, we can trade or not. We can't have it both ways.

For those who say buy American, remember that even when you buy American you're not *only* buying American. The Ford Focus which is "Made in America" is only 10 percent made in America, and on the other side of this, the iPhone, which we think is made in China, is actually just assembled in China with parts coming from all over the world.[52][53]

It's ironic that the most vocal advocates of "Buy American" are usually the unions claiming that jobs are being lost to overseas manufacturing. However, the largest unions such as the United Auto Workers (UAW) representing GM and Ford, propose a double standard: GM sold over three million cars to China in 2013, so ultimately the bumper sticker should say "Buy American - Sell International."

Protectionist China

During the U.S. presidential election of 2008, the candidates competed to show how tough they would be with China. They argued that China needs to stimulate domestic consumption and pursue a consumer-based economy. However, China didn't listen to this unsolicited advice because they were too busy building some of the largest shopping malls in the world. They were putting up retail stores, not only in major cities, but also in smaller cities. The advice given and still given by U.S. economists and politicians is not an informed position, as China is becoming a consumer society faster than any country has ever done.

While U.S. politicians want to think that China is opposed to buying from other countries, they need only spend a day in Shanghai, Chongqing, Beijing, Shenzhen or any other Chinese city to see that this is not the case. The Super Brand Mall in the Pudong region of Shanghai is 250 thousand square feet. It reaches thirteen stories high and as per its name does have all the major brands. On a Sunday afternoon, thousands of Shanghainese can be found shopping in the mall. With the history of China and its neighbor Japan, one would suspect that the first products they'd boycott would be from their less than friendly neighbor, but the numbers tell a different story. In 2014 Toyota was expected to sell over one million cars in China. The Chinese are true consumers, and like any good consumer, they value quality. While American politicians and union leaders tell Americans to "Buy American," the Chinese say buy the best product at the best price... even if it's from Japan.

The speakers in the Super Brand Mall in Shanghai blare loudly, extolling the features of the new Toyota Crown with six way adjustable seats. Elegantly dressed representatives are eager to assist anyone interested in the semi-luxury automobile, and then it's off to Toys R Us to pick out something for the children. While incomes vary, as they do anywhere in the world, those who can afford to—buy, and those who cannot dream and make plans.

Contrary to U.S. presidential candidates' beliefs, China couldn't be moving faster at increasing domestic consumption. On "Singles Day" 2014, China's biggest shopping day, Alibaba reported that over nine billion had been spent on their Chinese online shopping sites in a single day. Contrast this with Black Friday, the biggest shopping day in the U.S., which reported a wimpy $1.8 billion in online sales. China has become a consumer society at a rapid pace, and their consumption will continue to grow as their wealth spreads and increases.[54]

Trade Is Tricky

Trade agreements are tricky business, and like all politically charged issues, they are full of spin, special interests, and conflicts of interest. The reality is that every line item in a trade agreement hurts one party and helps another. When the U.S. imports clothing from countries with a lower labor cost, then the price of clothing goes way down, so consumers benefit, but those who would make clothes in the U.S. are hurt by the agreement. When trade agreements or U.S. law restricts certain technology such as that from Huawei and ZTE, then domestic network technology companies benefit because a major competitor is locked out, but the consumer and the users of the technology are hurt because they're unable to purchase the best products at the best price. When tariffs are placed on Chinese imported solar panels, fewer solar panels are sold in the U.S. because of the higher cost.

So, should we fear the subsidies, the selling below cost, the jobs they're taking, the trade imbalance, the currency manipulation? Should we fear trade with China? When we look past the headlines and dig deeper, again we see we haven't been told the whole story. Regarding subsidies, we subsidize more. Selling below cost? Whose cost? Trade imbalances are far more complicated than the alarmist headlines. Currency manipulation is clearly happening more in the U.S. Jobs lost to China? More accurately, jobs lost to robots.

Because Western powers like the U.S. and Britain are the leaders in world trade, we attempt to control the rules of the game with unabashed self-interest. Remember Obama's speech? He said: "We should make those rules." We talk of fair trade, but the ultimate objective of trade negotiators is to have a trade advantage. Domestic industries, with the full support of their elected officials and the media, attempt to protect themselves through any means necessary; they complain of unfair Chinese subsidies while taking their own subsidies. They work to block imports with high tariffs. They try to convince us that China is taking our jobs; meanwhile, they just let go of another 50 workers because they were replaceable—by machines. Look past the fear generating headlines and follow the money instead. Someone is trying to stop their competitor.

As China grows in economic power, trade negotiations will begin taking place on a more even playing field. The unequal treaties of the past will fade into history, and much work will be done to establish rules of mutual benefit.

Now our only question is this: to trade or not to trade. We can't have it both ways.

8

Fearing China's Product Quality and Safety

Will Chinese Drywall Make You Sick? (MSN)
Chinese Manufacturing: Poorly Made (The Economist)
Throw Away Chinese Toothpaste, FDA Warns (NBC News)
Mattel Recalls 19 Million Toys Sent From China (New York Times)
Mystery of Pet Deaths Related to Jerky Treats Made in China (Washington Post)[55]

From Toys to Toothpaste

In August of 2007, on a single day nine million Chinese-made toys were recalled due to safety hazards. Two weeks earlier 1.5 million Chinese-made toys were recalled. One Chinese-made toy caused the death of a child and required surgery for nineteen others. Another caused the death of a child and injured four more. Senator Dick Durbin demanded action: "Another week, another recall of Chinese-made toys," he proclaimed. Mattel, one of the largest toy companies in the U.S., said they had become aware of the problems at factories in China and were addressing the issue.[56]

In June 2007 the U.S. government warned consumers to throw away toothpaste made in China because it was found to contain diethylene glycol, a chemical used in automobile antifreeze and not safe for food or ingestible products. *The New York Times* reported, "Toxic Toothpaste Made in China is Found in U.S."[5758]

2009 was the year that put the spotlight on Chinese-made drywall. The building boom of 2004 to 2008 caused builders to import large quantities from China. The news reported on the smell of rotten eggs and damaging health effects of the defective Chinese-made drywall used to build as many as 100,000 houses.

Jerky dog treats made in China have caused the death of 1,000 dogs in the U.S. For several years the USDA has not been able to find the cause that is killing the pets or making them sick, but

Chinese pet treats are being removed from retail stores throughout the U.S.

The Rest of the Toy Story

It's difficult to open a newspaper or watch the news without learning of another dangerous product from China, and these headlines are disturbing. However, let's take a look beyond the headlines, dig a little deeper, and discover the rest of the story.

The largest toy recall in 2007 was for 18.5 million toys. The origin of the toys could be quickly identified by the stamp on the underside, "Made in China." The media reported the findings with headlines such as: "Unsafe from China" and "Another Safety Recall from Chinese Toy Makers." *The New York Times* reported with the headline: "As More Toys Are Recalled, Trail Ends in China."

But, too often the headlines not only miss the point, they completely distort the facts. The follow up story that didn't make the front-page headlines was that the 18.5 million toys recalled were due to design flaws, not manufacturing flaws. It wasn't the small "Made In China" stamp on the underside that really mattered; it was the big print on the side of the box and prominently shown on the toys that identified the responsible party: Mattel. Although the toys had been manufactured in China, the complete design of the toys had come directly from El Segundo, California. It was a design mistake by the U.S. toy maker that was responsible for the defects that killed and sickened children. *The New York Times* headline was wrong. The trail did not end in China, it ended in California.[59]

It wasn't until the headlines had faded and the U.S. media had moved onto the next "breaking story" that the facts surfaced. Several months after all the headlines proclaiming the danger of Chinese-made toys had subsided, Thomas Debrowski, executive V.P. of Mattel's world operations, apologized to Li Changjiang, the head of China's quality control agency. Debrowski said that Mattel was fully responsibility for the recalls and quality issues. He also apologized to Li and the people of China. But the public rarely sees or remembers the follow-up story that actually contains the facts—the breaking news headlines had already done the damage.[60]

Even today, parents in the U.S. are skeptical of the quality and safety of toys made in China. Not because of the facts, but because of the grossly misleading headlines. While skeptical of Chinese-made toys, parents still reach for the box labeled Mattel because it's a well known, established U.S. company with a reputation for quality and safety.

The headlines blaming Chinese manufacturers were a dream come true for the U.S. company responsible for one child's death and illnesses of the other children. The headlines diverted attention from the truly guilty California company to a faraway place on the other side of the world—a place that much of the U.S. public already suspected of poor quality and dangerous products.

One of the most extensive studies, which was performed by Paul W. Beamish and Hari Bapuji, researchers in Ontario Canada, found that the vast majority of toy recalls, 76.4 percent, were for design flaws, while very few recalls were made due to manufacturing defects. In addition, they found that the percent of manufacturer defects is actually lower in China than in other countries; roughly one percent of all Chinese imported toys were recalled for design flaws, while only one twentieth of one percent of the Chinese-made toy recalls were for manufacturing flaws. The overwhelming majority of toy recalls were for design defects at U.S. companies, not for defects at the Chinese manufacturer.[61]

If there is breaking news here, it's news about how the media misrepresented the facts and damaged China's reputation. It should be concerning that the Western media can so quickly destroy the reputation of a company, an industry, or even a country, with little or no liability. The public's perception on issues such as quality and safety are driven by the headlines rather than the actual facts. While sometimes deserved and other times not, there is a ready assumption of guilt when Western reporters report on Chinese product quality or safety. Additionally, far too often responsible companies in the U.S. sit quietly as the truth is distorted to their benefit.

As well as distortion of who was to blame for the toy recalls, the media also did not give the public the statistically relevant information. The U.S. media reported that 85 percent of toys recalled were for toys made in China, but they never mentioned that 85 percent of all toys purchased in the U.S. were made in China. Thus, the rate of manufacturer defects was the same for China as for most other countries, but because we purchase a greater amount of

Chinese products, it appears as though there are more defects attributable to China than any other place.

Think of it this way. There's a birthday party with twenty kids. Eighteen of the children are Chinese and two are American. When selecting between chocolate and vanilla ice cream, twelve of the Chinese children chose chocolate and two of the American kids chose chocolate. So looking at the numbers the headlines would read, "Chinese Kids Ate all the Chocolate Ice Cream." But if we look at the proportion of kids at the party, one hundred percent of the American kids selected chocolate, and only about seventy percent of the Chinese kids took chocolate.

The media's claim that 85 percent of all toy defects are Chinese is misleading because it fails to take into account how many toys are made by China compared to other countries. Or in our example, how many Chinese companies showed up at the toy manufacturing party compared to other countries at the party. China just happened to be the one making more toys.

"Chinese-Made Toys Unsafe?" More accurately: "U.S. Designed Toys Unsafe," or possibly "U.S. Media Unsafe," as they distort the facts with headlines that read: "Trail Ends in China," when in fact, the trail ends right here in the U.S.

Anti-freeze In Your Toothpaste

Who in their right mind would put auto anti-freeze in toothpaste? That's the question one probably asks when reading newspaper articles discussing the Chinese-made toothpaste recall. And, while it makes for great headlines, it is again inaccurate. Diethylene glycol, which made its way into the Chinese toothpaste, is a chemical used in a variety of products ranging from skin creams, deodorants, and glue. But for best scare impact, put in your headlines the thing someone is least likely to drink and that sounds very dangerous—go with auto anti-freeze, which actually has a very small amount of diethylene glycol.

While it was correct to recall the toothpaste, as the chemical isn't safe for consumption, the story was easy fuel for a U.S. public conditioned to believe products from China are unsafe. To keep things in perspective, the inclusion of diethylene glycol has been a mistake made by many manufacturers. One of the most interesting was the Australian "wine scandal." In 1985 Australian wine makers included diethylene glycol in wine, causing the recall of millions of bottles. In the end, not knowing what to do with all the recalled wine, the Australian electric utility developed a way to burn the 30 million liters of recalled diethylene glycol laced wine to generate electricity. Yes, 30 million liters. So, who in their right minds would put anti-freeze in a consumable product? Evidently the Chinese... and the Australians. The point here is that this is not a Chinese characteristic, but a human characteristic. Sometimes things are done incorrectly. We hope to learn and improve, and we institute methods, systems, and even government agencies to help keep us safe. But when an Australian company puts diethylene glycol into wine, the headlines call it "tainted wine." When a Chinese company puts diethylene glycol into toothpaste, the headlines read: "Chinese Toothpaste Laced with Anti-freeze."

Rotten Egg Drywall

Drywall imported from China had the same effect on U.S. headlines as Chinese-made toys and toothpaste. The media, placing more importance on being first than on being right, jumped on the stories of dangerous Chinese-made drywall with headlines like: "Will Chinese Drywall Make You Sick?" "Toxic Chinese Drywall Creates a Housing Disaster," "Sen. Nelson Calls for Temporary Ban on Chinese Drywall." Like the toy quality issues, the Chinese-made drywall headlines were fast, but the facts were slow to follow and rarely, if ever, made the front page.

CBS News, to their credit, commissioned a study by the University of Florida to test the drywall. However, they didn't just study Chinese drywall, they also looked at U.S. drywall. The study found that one quarter of the samples tested and confirmed to have a problem were actually U.S. made drywall. Similar to the toy issue, then the question becomes the total percent of defects compared to the total makeup of the products used. If Chinese imports represents 75 percent of the drywall used, and 75 percent of the defects are Chinese, then the defect rate is average.[62] But again, like the defective toy issue (or the children at the birthday party), the media conveniently neglected to provide full context for the issue. As in the Mattel case, U.S. drywall manufacturers with similar problems were silent and refused to discuss their quality issues as the media went after China. While there were serious problems with Chinese-made drywall, most reports skewed the facts, diverting attention from the broader problem to the easy target: China.

Killer Dog Food

Some jerky dog treats made in China have been determined to be unsafe, although the specific cause is unknown. While the news headlines are dramatic, like in the other examples, it's important to keep things in perspective. U.S. manufacturers of dog food have also had difficulty maintaining their product quality and safety. In 2005 one U.S. manufacturer recalled seven hundred thousand bags of dog food after the product caused the death of many dogs and was determined to have Salmonella. The company set up a phone center to help customers, with call volume exceeding two thousand calls per day. That same company had safety recalls in 2007, 2009, 2010, 2012, and 2014. Most of the recalls were for Salmonella that harmed not only dogs but also the humans who handled the U.S. made dog food. And yet, the headlines did not read: "U.S. Dog Food Manufactures Harm Your Pets." Rather, while the headlines did often contain the name of the offending company, the headlines typically read something like: "Latest Pet Food Recall." This is because a headline reading: "U.S. Manufacturers Continue to Make Unsafe Pet Foot" might actually harm U.S. pet food manufacturers.[63]

Another manufacturer of pet food that U.S. officials said may have killed up to 4,000 pets and caused the recall of over 60 million cans of dog and cat food was likewise treated differently in the headlines. The headlines read: "Pet Food Recall Widens Again on New Threat." The headlines rarely, if ever, contain the name of the offending country. If the reporting had been consistent and fair, the headlines would've read: "Canadian Pet Food Manufacturers Responsible for the Death of 4,000 Pets." The company was Canadian, but that fact was rarely mentioned in the headlines.

Agenda Reporting

Before we believe that the U.S. is exempt from such safety and quality issues, a quick Internet search on 'recalls in the U.S.' shows that we're not. Some of the highlights include over six million cars recalled by General Motors, many for serious safety issues that went intentionally ignored by GM, causing death and injury. 2014 saw the recall of 1.6 million infant car seats. In 2007, thirty-three million pounds of ground beef were recalled in the U.S. In 2010, 550 million eggs were recalled after 1,500 cases of Salmonella were reported. And as mentioned, one U.S. pet food maker has major recalls about every two years for serious safety issues.

When a U.S. or non-Chinese company has quality issues, the headlines read something like: "Tainted Pet Food Recalled," or "GM Fails Quality Test." When a Chinese company has a quality issue, the headlines read: "Chinese Drywall Can Make You Sick," in a deliberate attempt to portray China as a source of poor quality and safety concerns. The headlines and news stories from the U.S. show clearly that when reporting on Chinese product quality and safety, the media gives special treatment to China, never missing an opportunity to characterize their products as unsafe and of poor quality.[64]

In 2014 over five million automobiles were recalled, affecting almost every major car manufacturer in the world. By 2015 the recall had reached over 35 million cars. The recall was for defective airbags that shot metal debris at passengers when the airbag was deployed. General Motors issued a statement to owners of the cars affected saying passengers shouldn't be allowed to ride in the cars until the problem was fixed. The defect was serious—it caused injury and death. When the stories mentioned the company Takata as the manufacturer, the country of origin was conveniently omitted or buried deep in the article.

The treatment of this story is a typical example of how the U.S. media treats China differently when quality or safety issues arise. If it had been a Chinese manufacturer, every headline would have contained the word China, and the story would have been about unsafe products from China. The headlines would have read something like: "Another Death from Chinese Airbags" or "Chinese Airbags Shoot Metal at Your Face." But instead, the headlines read: "U.S. Expands Recall for Cars With Defective Airbags," "Are You Driving a Car With Defective Airbags?" and "Takata Faces Inevitable US Inquiry Into Airbags"

Quality Curve

The quality curve of industrializing nations is fairly consistent. Emerging markets start by producing products that require low skills and low technology. Initially, due to inexperience and lack of high tech tools, the result is low quality products. Quality quickly improves as experience is gained, equipment and skills are improved, and foreign investment is used to bring in foreign experience and technology. In this phase, customers are acquired, but not at high profit margins, because the goal is simply to attract customers. Once the business is generating volume and has a collection of customers, managers begin to look at improving those margins. The first reaction is to cut costs. This lowers the quality of the products. When the customers push back on quality, ultimately the manufacturer working with the customer is able to gradually increase price as they convey to the customer: "you get what you pay for." Over time a balance between quality and price is reached wherein the manufacturer is able to make a profit and the customer finds an acceptable quality at an acceptable price.

As countries go through each phase of economic development, they experience many of the same issues as those who have gone before them. Following WWII, with the help of the U.S., Japan began to develop its manufacturing base. Toys were an easy start, then on to household goods, then electronics, then more complicated manufacturing like automobiles. Taiwan and South Korea went through the same process. From "get it done" to "get it done right," all emerging economies go through phases of development in the quality and the safety of their products. For manufacturing, the first phase is simple, to use cheap labor and simple processes to start making something and selling it at a lower price than the competition. As progress is made, these countries start to move up the ladder to more and more sophisticated products that require higher skills and technologically advanced equipment.

Prior to WWII, Japanese products were known for their poor quality, but following the war Japan began to rapidly improve product quality with assistance from U.S. consultants like Edwards Deming. Financial assistance as well as expertise from the U.S. played a major part in the rapid economic development of Japan. Gaining from the assistance from the West, they quickly advanced up the quality curve. The strategy paid off when Honda entered the motorcycle manufacturing industry in 1955 and quickly became known for quality. By the time Japan entered the automobile industry in 1963, they were experts at manufacturing, and they experienced great success.

A key factor in the transition to industrialization is investment and influence from other successful industrialized nations, such as the support Japan received from the U.S. But in the early transition to modern industrialization, China chose isolation because their experience with Western nations hadn't been exactly positive. This isolation slowed quality improvements. China didn't have the benefit of foreign experience and capital, and their relationship with the Soviet Union wasn't of much value. Not only was China on its own, but in many ways there was opposition to their progress from the West. This isolation and opposition, along with strategic economic mistakes, caused the quality curve to be much slower than most industrializing nations.

Countries and industries go through progressive improvements in quality, and at times even go through cycles of degrading quality. Anyone who has owned an American car manufactured in the 1970s and early 1980s knows firsthand how sometimes the quality curve can dip. There were a variety of reasons for the quality drop in U.S.-manufactured cars, not the least of which was a concerted effort to drive down costs in order to compete with the emerging Japanese auto industry. The strategy backfired because it gave Japan a true edge—Japanese-made cars quickly gained a reputation for being better made than American cars. The Chevy Vega and Ford Pinto were the definition of poor quality. The Vega nearly destroyed the reputation of General Motors. So while the quality curve can be somewhat predictable, there can be surprises.

From the headlines we may be tempted to believe China is unique in their challenges in producing high-quality products, when in fact their path along the quality curve is typical. And although off to a slow start, their pace of improvements in quality and safety is now much faster than others who have gone before them.

Large U.S. retailers, like Walmart and Target, have had a huge impact on the quality of goods coming from China. This is because these retailers set high standards and require the acceptance of returns. Returns not only ensure that the manufacturer doesn't receive revenue for a defective product, but returns also allows the manufacturer to inspect the faulty products to discover what went wrong and to correct their process. According to *China Business Weekly*, more than 70 percent of the products sold at Walmart are made in China, so Walmart has contributed greatly to quality standards in Chinese manufacturing.[65]

China faces immense quality and safety challenges. In thirty years, literally tens of thousands of factories have opened in China, from the mega factories of Foxconn to the thousands of mom-and-pop operations working out of their homes. With a population four times larger than the U.S., and many more than four times the number of manufacturing facilities, quality and safety issues must be addressed on a scale never before seen in history. The pace of development along with the massive scale makes the task a true challenge.

From Western buyers setting quality and safety standards to Chinese government agencies monitoring and setting standards, the quality of products has improved rapidly in China. Add to that the true desire of Chinese factory owners and managers to continually improve their product, and we can see that the pressures pushing towards improved quality are having rapid and positive effects.

Chinese Consumers Driving Quality Higher

Even the Chinese people are aware of quality issues within their own borders. Often they prefer U.S. and European brands because these foreign brands consistently deliver higher quality goods.

Chinese parents are known for working to give their children the best. They'll spend lavishly on anything that they believe will be good for their children, from early childhood education to nutrition. Baby formula is no exception, and in 2008 it was found that some of the Chinese manufactured formula was tainted with melamine, which is a dangerous additive for formula. As news spread, mothers quickly switched to foreign baby formula, refusing to buy formula made in China. The scandal resulted in the death penalty for three Chinese executives and life sentences for others. For several years, due to fears of lack of quality, mothers boycotted Chinese-made formula, opting for U.S. and other foreign made brands instead.

However, in 2013 the New Zealand company Fonterrra, one of the biggest providers of formula to China, reported that their formula had been contaminated with a botulism-causing bacteria. This, of course, caused a re-evaluation of the choices Chinese mothers were making. While even the Chinese are sometimes quick to criticize Chinese food safety, mothers learned that problems with food safety can come from anywhere.

U.S. Exports to China – Hidden Danger

The news is filled with many stories detailing dangerous products from China, but a study of the specifics shows very little actual damage to U.S. consumers. Very few Americans have died or been injured due to quality issues in Chinese manufacturing—the headlines are bold and scary, but the issues are most often resolved quickly.

While we're made aware of quality and safety issues of products imported from China to the U.S., our headlines do not as often report the quality problems found in U.S. products sent to China. Over the last several years, fast food chains such as McDonald's, KFC, Burger King, and Starbucks have had quality issues in China. While typically these issues are traced back to Chinese suppliers, again we must dig a little deeper.

Husi Foods, a large Chinese supplier, was at the center of a 2014 food safety scare. The company sold expired meat to most of the large U.S. fast food chains in China, causing McDonald's in Beijing to stop selling hamburgers for a few days. While the U.S. companies were quick to point out that the source of the problem was the Chinese supplier Husi Foods, they were not as eager to point out that Husi Foods is a subsidy of OSI Group, a U.S. company based in Aurora, Illinois.[66] Again, the headlines are much more dramatic if they read: "Chinese Meat Supplier Sells Expired Meat to McDonald's," instead of a more accurate headline which might have read: "U.S. Company OSI Group Sells Expired Meat to Chinese Consumers."

While U.S. fast food companies work to improve quality control at the supplier level in China, there is a quality problem that goes way beyond expired meat. If we're concerned about imports from China, likewise China should be watching imports from the

West and the related safety and health effects. In 1980 the percent of the Chinese population with diabetes was about one percent. By 2012 the percentage had increased to twelve, which is slightly higher than the U.S. rate. Certainly there are many factors that contribute to this alarming trend, such as sedentary lifestyle, as more people work at desk jobs or factories instead of laboring on farms, but eating habits have just as much of an effect. And one export from the U.S. is our nutritional lifestyle and Western fast food chains. While it may be unfair to blame a few U.S. companies for the diabetes epidemic in China, certainly the growth of Western fast food is a contributor. The first McDonald's opened in mainland China in 1990, and by 2013 there were over 2,000 restaurants, with a schedule of opening 300 new McDonald's in 2014 alone. Yum Brands, which owns KFC and Pizza Hut, opened their first restaurant in China in 1987 and had over 6,000 restaurants by 2013.

The next chart shows the number of McDonald's and KFC store openings combined over the last 15 years charted with the diabetes epidemic in China. While the story of a few kids hurt by Chinese-made toys may hit the headlines, a more telling headline may be the growing diabetes epidemic in China relative to the growth of McDonald's, KFC, and Coke in Asia. The handful of U.S. children hurt by toys from China pales in comparison to the hundreds of millions of Chinese affected by Western fast food culture and companies. Salty, fat saturated, fast foods can be quite addicting; these foods produced by Coke and others also contain massive amounts of sugar. In fairness, China may have as much right to stop the importation of KFC, McDonald's, and Coke as the U.S. has to stop the import of lead tainted toys. Mexico is in fact running national ads to discourage people from drinking Coke because of the diabetic problem there. If we compare the health effects of imports from China to the U.S. with the health effects of U.S. imports to China, we will most likely see that our exports damage their health much more than theirs damage ours.

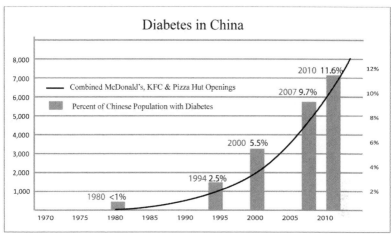

Diabetes in China

JAMA Sept 4, 2013 (diabetes data only)   http://www.eurekalert.org/pub_releases/2013-09/tjnj-sep082913.php

Good Quality and Improving

Back to our question: *should we fear the quality and safety of products made in China.* Fortunately, every consumer in the U.S. is free to choose what they purchase, and each has the full opportunity to buy or not buy products made in China or anywhere else in the world for that matter. Labeling laws require retailers to show where products are made, so the consumer can make a choice. In addition, our government agencies such as the FDA and Consumer Products Safety Commission (CPSC) have proven quite effective at protecting over 300 million people buying from hundreds of thousands of sources.

China, like any industrializing nation, has had challenges in product quality and safety; however, their overall quality and safety is comparable to most industrialized nations. And in areas where they are not, they are quickly improving. The products coming from China in the 1990s were better than the 1980s. Products in the 2000s were better than the 1990s, and products now imported from China are of dramatically higher quality than the previous decades.

Chinese government institutions are comparable to our FDA and CPSC, and they'll continue to advance in their abilities. They're learning from their own experiences and from the West. Zhen Xiaoyu was the director of China's State Food and Drug Administration. In May of 2007 he was found guilty of corruption, which jeopardized the food safety of China. In July 2007, only two months later, he was executed for his crime. Imagine being the next administrator to take that position. One would suspect that the China SFDA is at this point a very serious organization.

As discussed, the quality curve of China is typical and the trend is positive. As China moves up the value chain and produces more advanced products, the simple products will also improve. When a manager with experience running a production line of 400 workers assembling iPhones gets a new job in a toaster factory or toy factory, the quality of the toasters or toys goes up. Evaluate for yourself the products around you. For those made in China, what's the true quality? Twenty years ago you may have found that "Made in China" meant poor quality (because the country was early on the quality curve), but today most find that the quality of products made in China is very high. Walmart and Target wouldn't continue to buy 70 percent of their products from China if the quality was low. Look at the iPhone in your pocket, the lawnmower that cuts your grass, the laser printers at the office, the LED light bulb you just bought, or the toys for your child; the quality of these products is typically good and it's only going to improve.

For now we may leave the manufacturing of the products like the pacemaker that'll be placed in your body to the Germans or the U.S. But in time China will be fully at the level of Western nations in all aspects of quality, and will continue expanding their product offering. If one doesn't think the Chinese learn fast, just look at how fast they became a manufacturing giant, or at how fast they built a high-speed rail across China, or at how fast Pudong in China went from a rustic warehouse district to a first class city. Improvements in quality and safety are moving at that same rapid pace, and it is extremely likely that within 20 years "Made in China" will be synonymous with high quality.

For three decades the Western media has worked hard to "brand" China as poor quality, but the reality is starting to overwhelm the misleading headlines. When we're developing our opinions about Chinese-made product quality and safety, it's critical that we see past the headlines and discover the whole story. There are numerous companies and organizations, and yes, even U.S. government entities, that have a specific interest in making you believe that "Made In China" means poor quality or dangerous. With over \$450 billion in imported products from China each year, it's very easy to pick the one that went wrong and put it in the headlines—that is to say, if you want to find instances of poor quality and safety threats from Chinese products, you can find them. But you can also find safety hazards and poor quality from U.S. manufacturers if you chose to look. The media will pick out a few bad trees in a forest of millions of good trees, and suddenly you think the forest is dominated by bad trees; the headlines truly have the ability to not let you see the forest for the trees.

The famously successful investor Warren Buffet once said that many investment mistakes are made by mindless imitation of peers. In the media, reporters often imitate the errant headlines of their peers, causing a barrage of news stories that are misleading and damaging. Before you believe the headlines, and, more importantly, before you perpetuate the rumors, dig a little deeper. Is it really a Chinese manufacturing problem, or it is possibly a Western design flaw, as we saw in the Mattel toy recalls? Is it a mistake we've never seen before, or is it a common mistake as we saw in the toothpaste and the Australian wine? Are dangerous products only coming from China, or are they also coming from U.S. manufactures and other countries, as we find in the pet food recalls? Is the report truly indicative of the products coming from China, or is it a rare exception to otherwise high quality and safe products?

Should we fear the quality and safety of Chinese-made products?

Overwhelmingly the products coming out of China are of high quality and are safe. Just look around your home or visit your local Walmart. Oh, and those dangerous exploding airbags? You still don't know where those are from, do you? That's because the media rarely mentioned the country of origin, but you can be sure they're not from China, because the headlines would've told you so.

9

Fearing China's Pollution

China Pollution: Beijing Smog Hits Hazardous Levels (BBC)
The Biggest Polluter in China's Dirtiest City (Wall Street Journal)
Beijing Residents Gasp for Fresh Air in the City of Smog (Reuters)
Tons of Poisoned Fish Clog River in China's Hubei Province (CNN)
China's Toxic Air Pollution Resembles Nuclear Winter, Say Scientists
(The Guardian)[67]

Been There

Dead fish continued to wash up on the shores of the grossly polluted river, however, not as many as in past years. Most of the fish population had been long decimated. The surface of the river had a brown oily film, and trash frequently floated in the mucky water. For decades, industry had dumped its waste into the once fresh water, and it had been years since the water was actually drinkable. The city used the river as a method to dispose of sewage from the city inhabitants—large pipes discharged the waste directly into the river. It's not known exactly what started it on that summer day, but the oily muck on the river was so thick that the river actually caught fire. It wasn't even the first fire seen on the river—there had been many others.

On the other side of the country, children were instructed to wear masks when walking to school. Their eyes burned from the polluted air. There was no blue sky, only a foggy gray caused by the cars and factories spewing pollutants into the air. Politicians and scientists scrambled to come up with a plan, while the citizens became increasingly agitated and vocal about the devastating air and water quality.

The polluted river discussed above was called Cuyahoga, and lest you assume it's a river in China, it's not. It's in Northeast Ohio and the fire described was in June of 1969. The river was so polluted that it caught fire on multiple occasions. The polluted air described was in Los Angeles.

Pollution comes in many forms, from water pollution to waste disposal to air pollution. Within air pollution, there is carbon dioxide (CO_2), which affects the global environment. And there are small particle and large particle emissions, which affect health in local areas where the pollution is created. CO_2 emissions are caused by the burning of fossil fuels like coal and oil. These are the pollutants thought to have global impacts like ozone depletion and global warming. Unlike local pollution that affects the local environment, the CO_2 emissions of one country can affect the entire world.

Competing to be the Number One CO_2 Polluter

The two largest emitters of CO_2 pollutants are the U.S. and China. 2010 reports show the U.S. emitting 4.4 billion tons and China emitting 8.2 billion tons, so China is clearly the biggest emitter of CO_2 pollutants. But let's look closer and recognize that CO_2 emissions are primarily from energy in the form of electricity and transportation like autos, trains, ships, and planes. If CO_2 emissions are primarily for the generation of electricity and transportation, it would be reasonable to look at these emissions on a per capita basis.

Comparing CO_2 emissions per person would be more fair than comparing total country emissions. This comparison focuses on how much electricity is used per person and how much CO_2 each person emits in their choice of transportation. Looking at the numbers in this way puts the U.S. at 14.2 tons of CO_2 emissions per person and China at 6.1 tons of emissions per person. So if we in the U.S. believe that China should cut CO_2 emissions, what would we recommend? What examples and technologies would we propose? Would we propose a world standard of six tons per person? With this standard, China would be close to the goal, and the U.S. would need to cut CO_2 emissions by about 60 percent. How many hours per day would U.S. citizens be willing to turn off their electricity to accommodate this world standard? How many miles would we agree to limit ourselves in our auto or plane trips per year?

In the U.S. there are over 800 cars per 1,000 people. In China there are less than 200 cars per 1,000 people.[68] When we factor in that many children and elderly cannot drive, effectively almost everyone in the U.S. capable of driving has a car. In China it's less than one car per five. In China, when 1000 people commute the 20 miles from Yuyao to Ningbo, about 50 of them will get into their car and drive, while the other 950 will take the train. In the U.S., when 1000 people commute the 20 miles from Chino, California to Los Angeles, roughly 900 cars will be used. Over the last decade China has built the largest high-speed rail network in the world, connecting all the major cities along the East coast. And their high-speed rail is now reaching into the heart of China. While automobile sales continue to grow in China, the proliferation of the most modern rail system in the world is probably the most forward looking step that can be taken by an emerging economy to slow the increase of CO2 pollutants. Mass transit gives people transportation options that create much less CO_2 per passenger than driving individual cars.

Electricity generation is also a large emitter of CO_2 pollutants. In the U.S. the average household uses over eleven thousand kWh per year, but in China, the average household uses under two thousand kWh per year.[69] While some may complain about the CO_2 emissions from China, the reality is that the U.S. emissions of 14.2 tons per person is much worse than the Chinese 6.1 tons per person. Even though China emits less CO_2 per person than the U.S., they recently completed construction of the world's largest hydro-electric dam. The Three Gorges Dam is a very forward looking step by China in controlling CO_2 pollutants. The dam provides electricity from water power, instead of CO_2 producing coal and oil.

Outsourcing Pollution

Add another factor to this pursuit of lower CO_2 emissions. If a tennis shoe is made in Putian, China, raw materials are transported to the factory via fuel-burning ships and trucks. The lights and machinery may be kept running by coal powered electric plants. Once the shoes are complete, they're shipped across the ocean on an oil-burning freighter, then by truck or rail to the distribution center in a foreign country like the U.S. The distribution center sends the shoes by truck to the retail store. A consumer then drives to the store in their gas-burning car to buy the shoes. If we consider CO_2 emissions on a per capita basis, it would be reasonable for the end consumer to be accountable for the carbon footprint of the products they purchase. It's easy to blame China for the pollution caused by manufacturing, but it's our children that have ten pairs of shoes, each of which has its own carbon footprint.

If we add our per capita CO_2 pollutants here at home to the pollutants caused by the manufacture of the consumer products we use, then the personal carbon footprint of each American is equivalent to the combined carbon foot print of about five Chinese people. While we take pride in having reduced our air and water pollution over the last twenty years, much of that success is from moving our dirtiest manufacturing offshore, which also moves pollution off shore. It's not very accurate to claim pollution has been reduced, when in many ways, the West has simply moved the pollution elsewhere. Because of pressures by environmentalists in places like Los Angeles, some types of manufacturing became either very expensive or outright illegal, but the product remained legal. As a result of this, the pollution producer was simply moved offshore. It's quite unreasonable to complain about the pollution without complaining about the products the pollution provides.[70]

Worst Air Pollution in the World

The U.S. embassy in Beijing measures and often reports air pollution levels in the city. When it comes to pollution, a favorite media topic is air pollution in Beijing and other major Chinese cities. While these visible pollutants can contain CO_2, what's reported is small and large particle pollutants. Small particle is referred to as 2.5 because they are 2.5 micrometers in size. These are the most dangerous because they can easily be absorbed into the lungs and cause health problems. The residents of Beijing and other Chinese cities are well aware of the problems of pollution as they personally experience the burning eyes and difficult breathing that pollution causes. They worry about the damage it may be doing to their children, and they are often deprived of the beauty of a blue sky as smog flows above them. The U.S. media is saturated with reports of the unbearable smog of Beijing. By the sheer number of these reports, it's safe to assume that Beijing and other cities in China have the worst air pollution in the world. Or is it?

The World Health Organization monitors air pollution around

the world and reports that cities in Pakistan, Afghanistan, India, Iran, Bahrain, Bangladesh, Mongolia, UAE, and Qatar have higher levels of air pollution than cities in China.[71][72]

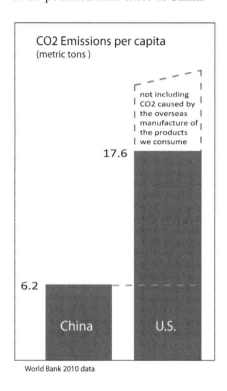

CO2 Emissions per capita
(metric tons)

not including
CO2 caused by
the overseas
manufacture of
the products
we consume

17.6

6.2

China   U.S.

World Bank 2010 data

Top 25 Most Polluted Cities		
1	Delhi	India
2	Patna	India
3	Gwalior	India
4	Raipur	India
5	Karachi	Pakistan
6	Peshwar	Pakistan
7	Rawalpindi	Pakistan
8	Khoramabad	Iran
9	Ahmedabad	India
10	Lucknow	India
11	Firozabad	India
12	Doha	Qatar
13	Kanpur	India
14	Amritsar	India
15	Ludhiana	India
16	Igdir	Turkey
17	Narayonganj	Bangladesh
18	Allahabad	India
19	Agra	India
20	Khanna	India
21	Gazipur	Bangladesh
22	Kabul - ISAF HQ	Afghanistan
23	Dhaka	Bangladesh
24	Jodhpur	India
25	Al Wakrah	Qatar

World Health Organization 2014
Based on Annual mean PM 2.5

There's no denying that China has major problems with air pollution, both in CO_2 and in visible health damaging air pollutants. However, when we look at the facts, we must recognize that China isn't, as is often implied, the worst offender. Thus, to constantly report on the pollution in Beijing without equally reporting on the even worse pollution in India, UAE, Qatar and other places, or to ignore the pollution caused by the products we import, is less than fair. It also implies an agenda other than objective reporting. The news does not report pollution measurements from our embassies in India or Afghanistan or Qatar. That special reporting is reserved for our treatment of China.

Industrialization starts with manufacturing, and manufacturing is a dirty business. As this chapter noted at the start, the U.S. at one time had the most polluted cities in the world, with rivers catching fire and unbreathable air. As other nations go through stages of development similar to ours, and as we push our dirty businesses offshore, the pollution in places like India, China, and Afghanistan will continue to pose a great challenge.

More important than the actual level of pollution is whether or not we're making progress toward a cleaner world—improvements are needed not only for our own concerns about the effects of CO_2 on the planet, but also for the health of the Chinese people and others around the globe. Our current strategy of constant nagging by politicians and the media ignores most of the facts, such as per capita CO_2 and air quality relative to other nations. Whether it's the U.S. embassy in Beijing reporting pollution measurements, or the headlines of Western papers pointing a finger at China while other worse polluters go unmentioned, our treatment is hugely biased against China.

As If They Don't Already Know

The government of China is well aware of the problem, and is seeking solutions and taking actions they find best in balancing their economy with the environment. Ultimately, the problem will be solved, partly because the citizens of Beijing will continue to put pressure on the government to improve their air quality, and also because the government truly does care about the issue. If it were easy, it would've been solved by now. And if it were easy, the industrial cities of the U.S. wouldn't have been destructively polluted for over seventy years starting at the turn of the 20^{th}century—and Los Angeles would have always had blue skies, which they can't even claim to this day.

If we care about pollution, then we have the opportunity to partner with China in seeking true technological solutions. If we truly care, we would stop the offensive reports coming from the American Embassy in Beijing. They know the measurements. They know the problem. Of what value is our nagging, other than to show how we treat China differently than other nations with the same problem? This kind of reporting is a distraction from the fact that on a per capita basis, the U.S. is still the worst polluter in the world. It's a distraction from the truth that India and others are worse polluters than China. And it's a distraction from the positive steps China has taken, such as their development of high-speed rail, which reduces the carbon footprint of the people of China as they opt for the train instead of automobiles. It distracts from the positive step China took in building the Three Gorges Dam. It distracts from the fact that the average Chinese family uses less than 20 percent of the electricity a U.S. family uses, and that almost every driving age American has a car. Finally, it distracts from the fact that much of the pollution in China is caused by the manufacturing of the products that reside in *our* homes.

Should we fear pollution in China? Our world will be better off if we stop fearing pollution in China, stop nagging and harassing China, and start working with China to find technological solutions to these difficult problems. But instead, we attempt to block China from advances in alternative energy technology, as we did when they attempted to buy A123 Battery. We attempt to stop their sale and development of solar panels, as we did with solar panel tariffs. And we complain of the people displaced by the Three Gorges Dam when they build a hydro-electric plant that will dramatically reduce the amount of oil and coal burned to create electricity. If we're to fear something, it should be that we work so hard to block China's advancements in the technologies that will be the ultimate solution to the world's pollution problems. And at the same time that we're blocking their attempts to solve the problem, we complain that they haven't solved the problem. It looks more like we should fear us.

10

Fearing China's Ethics

Caterpillar Earnings Hit by China Fraud (CNBC)
China Discloses $1.1 Billion Bank Fraud (Washington Post)
Chinese Deny Turning Blind to Investment Scams (ABC News)
500 Chinese Lawmakers Leave Office Over Election Fraud (CNN)
SEC Charges China-Based Executives With Fraud and Insider Trading (SEC)
73

Cycles of Dysfunction

Every culture has a level of ethics. A society with pure ethical behavior would be a place where there is no lying, cheating, or stealing—a utopia that does not exist anywhere in the world. Because of this, a nation's ethics become an issue of degree. When the collective ethics of a society drops low enough, the society will fail, led by economic collapse.

Dysfunction in laws and civil systems promotes corruption and unethical behavior. The more functional and practical a society's laws and systems, the more ethical a society will be. When economic society begins to fail, whether due to poor law, social structure, or disruptions like war, individuals seek options outside the laws. If getting a permit to open a new business is a 12-month, costly, 75-step process, entrepreneurs will looks for more reasonable paths, and in this situation that will mean breaking the law. As lying, cheating, and stealing become part of the individual's normal activities, the cumulative effect of corruption and degrading ethics drags down the economy. Dysfunctional laws promote unethical behavior, and unethical behavior makes the system even more dysfunctional. The two feed on each other in a rapid downward spiral.

The ethics of society follow the functionality of the system. As a legal system degrades, at first people try to follow the rules, but shortly after ethics begin to wane. This lagging effect is seen in the other direction as well. As a society improves its laws and structures, the old ethics will remain for a time due to the reality that individuals are in a habit and trend of breaking the rules. But over time, and with prodding and legal incentives and consequences, the ethics gradually improve to be commensurate with the society's laws and structure. Observe a society known for poor ethics in politics and business, and you will find a legal structure that is cumbersome and failing. As a society improves its laws and bureaucratic efficiency, an improvement in ethics will follow. Such is the current condition we find in China.

While the West was improving laws and economic systems throughout the nineteen and twentieth century, China was encumbered by Western colonial pressures, followed by civil war, only to be interrupted by WWII. If deficient laws, unstable political systems, and disruptions like war are a breeding ground for poor ethics, China was as disadvantaged as any. In China, WWII and the Civil War were followed by the social and economic experiments of the Great Leap Forward and the Cultural Revolution, both which proved to be disastrous programs. The dysfunctional laws and systems in China from 1949 to the late 1970s caused a further breakdown in political and business ethics. This was because people sought to survive in an uninhabitable environment. Part of the aim of the Cultural Revolution was to remove historic elements of Chinese culture, including religions such as Confucianism, which was a great part of China's moral underpinning. By removing Confucianism from society, much of China's moral reference was removed. With the challenges of the late Qing Dynasty, the Civil War, and WWII, and well over 100 years of system trauma, the difficulties of the Mao era solidified a culture of corruption and ethical breakdown, perpetuated by legal and system failures.

Old Habits Die Hard

In the early days of Deng Xiaoping, new laws and systems were implemented that provided rapid improvements in the economy, but the old ethics remained. Politicians and businessmen who had broken the laws to survive now continued to break the laws to realize more profits. But as any improving society learns, the lagging effects of corruption brought on by previously dysfunctional systems can be a drag on the economy and true social improvement—even worse, it can degrade the legitimacy of a government. The mud that is picked up on your shoes during the storm can slow you down once the rain subsides. To really get going again, the shoes must be cleaned, but often that can take some time.

As society improves to the point where survival does not require breaking the rules, and breaking the rules is only for additional profits, corruption will decrease. New laws also make the cost of breaking the rules much higher, which gives further incentive for people to stop the unethical activities.

China has two fundamental structures that can make fighting corruption more difficult than in some Western societies: the first is the State Owned Enterprises. The government of China has direct ownership in many companies. This gives politicians influence and control of these economic assets. They, of course, are to be used for the benefit of the people, but such large control by a bureaucrat or politician can, by nature, induce corruption. Leaders in control of these large enterprises may be tempted to act in the interest of themselves, family, or friends instead of in the interest of the people.

The second element that can be a particular challenge to fighting corruption in China is the rapid pace and scale of large government projects. Since 2007, China has installed 16,000 km of high-speed rail. The fastest way to develop this type of project is to give control of the project to one or a few people. These people will have the authority to make decisions, sign contracts, and otherwise move rapidly without the slowing influences of bureaucratic red tape or checks and balances.

Things move very quickly when the person responsible for building the rail line is the same person responsible for issuing the building permit, and also the same person responsible for acquiring land for the project. As we can see from the pace of development, it's quite efficient, but it comes with other issues in that the same authority that provides for such rapid development also can be a breeding ground for corruption.

Rapid Improvements

China has pulled out of economic despair rapidly with the help of improved law, public policy, and economic performance; due to this, ethics in China are also improving rapidly, although we do see the typical lagging effect. There are four main factors that are causing the accelerated improvement of ethics in China.

The first is that the current president of China, Xi Jinping, has made it a priority to reduce corruption at the public level. President Xi has said he will go after tigers and flies. And he started by going after some big tigers. Bo Xilai served as the Minister of Commerce from 2007 to 2012, and was thought to be a top pick to become a member of the Politburo Standing Committee. In 2012 Bo Xilai was arrested and removed from office for his corrupt practices. President Xi's campaign has not just been a campaign of words, but of actions, as indictments have been made at the highest levels. President Xi's campaign to rid the government of corrupt practices has been intentional and aggressive. Some may argue that there's an element of political motive in bringing down some of the top political leaders, and while this is possible, it's more likely that the tigers Xi has gone after were truly corrupt and destructive to the nation. Here are some of the top-level leaders in China who have been taken down for corruption:

Jiang Jiemin– Director of State-owned Assets Supervision
XuYongsheng – National Energy Administration
Zhou Yongkang – Security Chief
Bo Xilai – Minister of Commerce
Liu Zhijun – Railway Minister
Wen Qingshan – Chairman of Kunlun Energy, Co.

The second reason ethics are improving quickly in China is that it's good for business. China's new economy is driven by exports, and as any businessperson knows, the real money is made with repeat business. The way to obtain repeat business is to deliver well and honestly. As customers return and your good reputation grows, new customers are acquired, and business grows. Solid, straightforward relationships with customers and vendors are only made stronger with ethical dealings.

Early in the development of the Chinese export economy, U.S. businesses buying from China experienced the ill effects of poor ethics because factories tried to increase profits through deceptive practices. These practices included showing one material in a sample but changing to a cheaper material in the delivery, or promising delivery dates that the factory knew were impossible to meet.

In Chinese history, in particular military history, deception was seen as honorable, especially if the deception was clever and elegant. While some Western businessmen study *The Prince*, by Niccoló Machiavelli, as an inspiring business template. In China *The Art Of War*, by Sun Tzu, is sometimes used as a business reference, with quotes like: "All warfare is based on deception." While using war strategies for business may sound reasonable and clever, businesses in the West and in China are finding these strategies to be of little benefit in building long-term, successful businesses. Businesses quickly learn there's more money to be made through mutually beneficial, ethical dealings. The Chinese exporter of 2015 is a lot different than the exporter of 1985. Not only has product quality improved, but manufacturers have learned that the customer is more important than any single order. Acquire an order and make one thousand *yuan*; acquire a customer and make one million *yuan*. Thus, ethics in China are improving because it's good for business.

The third reason for rapidly improving ethics in China is their increased participation in world organizations. Joining the WTO in 2001, China agreed to be subject to the rules of the WTO. These rules not only effect top-level government relations, but trickle down to small factory exporters. As China increases its participation in world organizations and becomes more connected to the world, Chinese businesses will not only be forced to rid themselves of unproductive, unethical practices, they'll see the benefit of improved practices and will likely voluntarily pursue these changes. Participating in world organizations also encourages and requires China to reduce corruption in government. Simply working with more businesses, governments, and organizations from around the world has positively influenced business and political practices in China.

The fourth reason for rapidly improving ethics in China is Confucianism. At the end of WWII, Germany and Japan were destroyed economically and structurally. But within 35 years they were both economic world leaders. The main reason is that both countries had a culture of discipline, innovation, and a strong work ethic. These underlying cultural traits helped to propel them forward once the disruption of war was behind them. In a similar way, ethics in China have been a core value for centuries with roots in Confucianism. China was dragged into poor ethics by inefficient legal and social structures, as well as the disruptions of war, but as these deficiencies are eliminated, the core of China's beliefs will gradually resurface. Confucianism at its foundation is an ethical system, putting society above the individual. A culture will gravitate back to its roots quickly if there is obvious benefit, and there has been in China.

The implementation of the socialist market economy has been moving China from "rule of man" to "rule of law." As China learns and implements the good parts of Western law and then works to develop unique Chinese variations, the functionality of laws and society will improve—this will cause continued improvements in government and business ethics.

In 1997 when China took over Hong Kong, there was concern that Hong Kong would become more like China with its corruption, bureaucratic inefficiencies, and lack of objective and effective legal structures; a system of poor and arbitrary law. However, the opposite has occurred as the laws and systems of mainland China progress to become more like those in Hong Kong, not the other way around.

Compared to What?

While China is making fast progress in improving ethics in business and government, where is China compared to other countries? Should we fear the corruption found in the Chinese government or the ethics of Chinese businessmen and women? If poor social and legal structures promote poor ethics and corruption, there is a report by the World Bank that can give us an indicator as to where China stands relative to others.

The World Bank 'Ease of Doing Business' report which works to measure such things as the enforceability of contracts, the length of time to acquire a business license, or the ease of obtaining a building permit, gives us some indication of where China stands currently in legal and social structures. Keep in mind that when it's difficult to operate within the law (because the laws are so bad), people will go outside the laws.

We might think of it as a dysfunction index, but it's called the

'Ease of Doing Business' report. The 2014 'Ease of Doing Business' report ranked China #90 out of 189 countries with one being the best and 189 the worst. This puts China roughly in the middle, and above such countries as India at #142, and Brazil and Argentina at #120 and #124 respectively. Russia was ranked at #62. Oddly, Mexico was ranked at #39, which is difficult to comprehend when considering that more than 60,000 people were killed between 2006 and 2012 in their drug war.[74] And drug cartels in Mexico have revenues between $19 and $29 billion each year. One would think the "Ease of Doing Business" in an environment like this would be compromised. However, without arguing the methods of the World Bank study, it's important to recognize that China is ranked above or near other countries that we may not think so skeptically of, such as: Brazil, Argentina, Kuwait, Jamaica, and the Dominican Republic. The report ranked Hong Kong at #3 with only two other countries ranking higher. No, the number one spot was not held by the U.S—Singapore was #1 and New Zealand was #2. The U.S. ranked #4.[75]

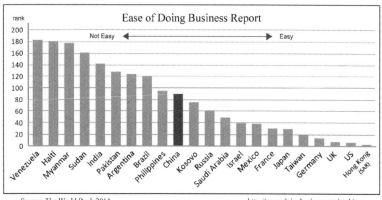

Source: The World Bank 2014   http://www.doingbusiness.org/rankings

Another report that can give us insight into ethics and corruption in China is the Transparency International's 'Corruption Perceptions Index.' While this report cannot measure actual corruption, as this would be impossible to do, it measures the perception of corruption. It effectively asks people how corrupt they believe their society is. The report gives a 1 to 100 ranking, with 100 being the least corrupt and 1 the most. China was given a score of

36, putting it above Mexico, Argentina, and Russia with scores of 35, 34, and 27 respectively. So, while China has a long way to go in reducing corruption, it is important to keep things in perspective, recognizing that while constant badgering by the media would have you think that China is one of the most corrupt countries in the world, they are not.[76]

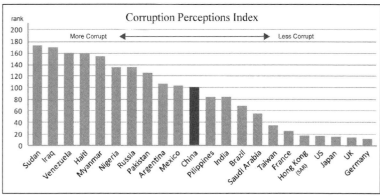

Source: Transparency International 2014   http://www.transparency.org/cpi2014

We Feel Much Better if it's Legal Corruption

The business practices of the U.S. banking industry, in combination with bad law from Washington, effectively crashed the U.S. economy in 2008. As many walked away with millions, the U.S. taxpayers were left to pay for the damage. The banking practices were highly corrupt and destructive, yet no major perpetrator went to jail for the crimes that had been committed.

Chinese students often find the U.S. system of lobbying in the democratic format to be perplexing. How can it be OK for a corporation or individual to contribute heavily to a government official's election campaign, which then gives the contributor access to the politician and the ability to influence law and allocate budget? *Isn't that corrupt?*, they might ask. Some may be quick to say no, it's not corrupt because it's legal. It's possible that U.S. citizens feel their system is less corrupt because a lobbyist has to register or a banker can create a legal argument that shows that no specific law has been broken.

Perhaps the U.S. system is so legalistic that criminals can get away with crimes against the public if they have a good lawyer. In China, the law has less patience for a complicated legalistic argument, and takes a more pragmatic approach. While their laws may be less sophisticated, in some ways they may be more efficient at stopping the bad guys. In the U.S., the "tigers," protected by massive legal teams, rarely are prosecuted. Protected by the corporate veil, criminals go unpunished while their corporations sustain small fines for "corporate misconduct." Maybe we can learn something from China when it comes to going after the tigers that are lying, cheating, and stealing.

This isn't to argue that the Chinese legal system is better than the U.S. or other Western societies; nor is it to say that there's more corruption or poorer business ethics in the U.S. than in China. Certainly China has a great deal of corruption and challenges in business and government ethics. However, while the media would have you believe they are the worst of the worst, they're not. The reports by third party organizations put them somewhere in the middle, and often better than places such as Mexico, India, Argentina, Brazil, and Russia.

With the proliferation of reports of questionable business ethics in China, should we fear doing business in China? U.S. companies are finding that China is improving in business practices every year. Major companies like Apple and HP have chosen China as their main supplier over nations like India and Brazil, and with great success. In the fall of 2014, the state of Massachusetts awarded a Chinese company a contract worth over $300 million to provide new rail cars for the Massachusetts transit system. This is a true statement on the confidence of Chinese companies to deal honestly. In the same way ethics can lag behind system improvements, reputation can lag behind reality, as seems to be the case with China.

The ethics found in Chinese business and government today aren't comparable to the practices of ten or even three years ago. That phone call to a friend in the government office that could get you a permit without going through the proper steps doesn't work as often now. And each year, more back doors are closed as the front doors become more practical.

Major changes in a society's ethics are most dramatic with new generations because it's very difficult to change the beliefs and practices of a person mid-life. China is no exception to this—we find the new generation of youth having different views about ethics than their parents and their grandparents. While prior generations had to "do what it takes" to survive, the new generation is kicking the mud off the shoes of history. Exposed to Western systems, and to the advantages of a society where the rules are good and playing by the rules is of benefit to all, a change is rapidly occurring.

Every society has its criminals. The U.S. has its Bernie Madoffs, its Jeffery Skillings, James Trafficants, and Richard Nixons. What's critical to understand is the progress China is making in addressing the problem. Improvements in law and systems have improved the economy rapidly and are giving the government the ability to fight corruption, and they are doing so in a most aggressive way. The trend is positive; as the system improves, corruption will be reduced and ethics will improve.

Companies that avoid working with China for fear of ethical concerns are losing out on opportunities that their competitors are seizing. While every business or organization must be aware of the environment they're working in and work to protect themselves from thieves, the cost of fearing China's ethics is now higher than the cost of refusing to do business with China. For those in business, of course, keep your eyes open, but fearing China's ethics and corruption may not be the wisest move.

11

Fearing China's Communism

How Communist Is China? (Slate.com)
The Death of Communism in China (CATO)
Chinese Communism and the 70-Year Itch (The Atlantic)
Hank Paulson: China Hasn't Built Better Capitalism (CNBC)
How Long Can the Communist Party Survive in China? (Financial Times)[77]

Competing Economic Ideas

Prior to the eighteenth century, kings and queens, emperors and empresses owned all the land in their kingdoms and allowed their subjects the privilege of land use in exchange for a share of their produce. For thousands of years the interest of the rulers was simply that of accumulating wealth and power for themselves with minimal regard for their subjects. This resulted in poor conditions for the masses. It was out of this condition that movements began to overthrow monarchies that had originally gained their power through wars and passed down that power to their heirs. The King and Queen of France were beheaded in 1793. The last Russian Tsar was killed in the revolution of 1917. And the last emperor of China was forced to abdicate in 1912. The wiser royalty voluntarily relinquished some power in exchange for keeping their title and certain privileges. The British royal family did this with the Magna Carta in 1215. Typically, royalty gave up power over daily laws and life, and relinquished it to a parliament or other institutions.

The 18th, 19th, and early 20th centuries saw major changes around the world as rulers were deposed by an unhappy populous. The crumbling of this old order left a void in economic, political, and social structures. It was during this era of change that great thinkers of the day began to propose ideas for the new systems that would replace the old. In politics we saw democracy begin to replace hereditary rule. In social order we saw a focus on equality, human rights, and rule of law to replace the arbitrary power of a king. And in the realm of economics was born two competing ideas: communism and capitalism. While these new ideas had not been tested on a large scale, vigorous debate was taking place as advocates on each side extolled the virtues of their proposal.

For communism, Carl Marx and Friedrich Engels proposed that all means of production be owned by a collective of the people. Effectively the government would own all the factories and land, and would use this for the best benefit of all the people. They believed that private ownership was bad for society, and that the workers should own the productive facilities through the mechanism of government. Carl Marx said, "The theory of Communism may be summed up in one sentence: Abolish all private property."

Adam Smith and others advocated for a system of private ownership called capitalism. In this system, the means of production would be owned by the individuals, not the state. They argued that if the means of production were privately owned each factory owner or farmer would be more productive. And as each sought to improve their own productivity their wealth would increase, and the wealth of society would increase. They believed that in the end this would make society most productive, wealthier, and result in the best standard of living for the masses.

Socialism, which has a more elusive definition as the word has been used in many ways, was originally a derivative of communism. However, socialism focuses more on the social structures of society, while pure communism focuses more on the ownership of the means of production. Over the last 50 years, the term socialism has come to mean somewhat of a hybrid between communism and capitalism. Usually when an American thinks of socialism, they think of the Nordic Model, as implemented by Sweden, Denmark, and the other Scandinavian countries. This model mixes private ownership with public ownership. In Scandinavia, most companies are privately owned, but heavily taxed. These taxes are used to provide such things as schooling, medical care, and social welfare benefits. This model also provides for ownership of factories by the workers, or at least strong bargaining power for employees. Proponents of this middle ground believe it'll leverage the benefits of private capital for the best interest of the people.

From the late 18th century to the early 20th century, robust debate of these ideas was at its height. The writings of the time are quite prolific, with well know titles such as "The Wealth of Nations" by Adam Smith (1776), and "The Communist Manifesto" by Carl Marx (1848). However, by the 1930s serious debate had ceased and each position had been boiled down to a simple argument: "Our way is better" and "Our way is the only way."

Redefining Terms

As has been the case too often in history, those with opposing ideas ceased to debate and reverted to the elimination of the opposition. Thinking men become frustrated with the task of changing hearts and minds, or arranging for coexistence. Such was the case in the debate between communism and capitalism.

In the pursuit of eliminating the opposition by force and propaganda, the terms communism and capitalism were redefined by the opposing parties. Communism was redefined by the West to encompass meaning well beyond its core economic idea. And in the Soviet Union and China, the word capitalism was redefined and re-characterized beyond its core meaning. From this purposeful redefining, in the U.S. the word communism has been altered to bring up broadly negative connotations that go far beyond Carl Marx's definition. At its core, communism is an economic structure wherein private capital is abolished and all means of production are owned and managed by the state. However, for the purpose of eliminating the "opposition," the West extended the definition to include violent expansionism, non-democratic rule, human rights abuses, and lack of freedom. Thus, the belief that any communist system would by nature contain these elements was born. By attaching these elements to communism, the West sought to create fear and a belief that communism was a great threat to the U.S.

Depicting communism as a violent expansionist ideology was quite easy for the West following WWII. The leading communist nation, the Soviet Union sought to expand their power and authority over neighboring countries while fighting Germany. The Soviet Union took control of their neighbors and implemented communist economies. This was partly to create a buffer between Russia and the aggressive German army, but also to expand Soviet power. By 1948 most neighboring countries were under the control of the Soviet Union.

Opponents of the communist economic model took this opportunity to link communism to violent expansionism. As the Soviet Union took control of Poland, Czechoslovakia, Romania, and other countries, the West defined this not as Soviet expansion but as communist expansion. As the Soviet Union took control of a country, opposition was eliminated through death or imprisonment. However, it was not the idea of communism that was the threat—and actually, many around the world embraced the idea as a preferred economic model. It was the expansion of a state forced onto others, and the accompanying domination, violence, and intimidation that was to be feared.

The Christian Crusades that swept across Europe in the 12th century were to be feared not due to the ideas of Christianity, but because of the mass killing and destruction in the name of Christianity. This caused people of the time to believe Christianity was violent and expansionist. Likewise, the aggressive expansionism of the Soviet Union made it easy for the West to redefine communism as violent and expansionist. In reality, it was the Soviet Union that was violent and expansionist, not the idea of communism.

In a parallel, yet opposite place, a skepticism and fear of capitalism grew as the U.S. sent 126 thousand troops to the Philippines in 1899, over 327 thousand troops to Korea in 1950, and 543 thousand troops to Vietnam in 1969. As the U.S. sent troops around the world, the task of portraying capitalism as a violent and expansionist idea was made easy. Soviet and Chinese propaganda leveraged these wars to convince their people that capitalism was a murderous ideology that in the end would establish an economic system that would only benefit a small group at the top. They portrayed this as a continuation of the imperialist activities of the British Empire and other empires of the past. On both sides, the leaders worked to make a correlation between the opposing economic models and violent expansionism. Communist leaders portrayed capitalism as a violent expansionist ideology, and in a mirror image, capitalist leaders portrayed communism as a violent expansionist ideology. And both had ample proof.

Non-democratic

As the West redefined communism as expansionist, it also attached the idea that all communist societies are non-democratic to the extent that the term 'communist dictator' is a given. However, it's important to understand that communism and capitalism are fundamentally economic structures, and both can be either democratic or non-democratic. Examples of non-democratic capitalist societies include Hong Kong, which was a capitalist country while under the rule of Great Britain, but was not a democracy. Chile, while under the rule of Augusto Pinochet, was also capitalist but not democratic. Following WWII, Singapore and South Korea developed capitalist economies without the political structure of democracy. And with full support of the U.S., Taiwan established a capitalist system while under the control of a non-democratic single ruling party. While there are many examples of non-democratic capitalist nations, there are also many democratic communist states. Examples of democratic communist countries include Venezuela, which democratically elected the communist leader Hugo Chavez. Cyprus elected communist president Demetris Christofias. Bolivia and Ecuador also freely elected communist leaders. When the Soviet Union was expanding at the end of WWII, some of those countries also democratically elected communist leaders.

So when considering China's communism, it's important to separate the issue of communism from the issue of democracy; we must recognize that neither capitalism nor communism are democratic or non-democratic by nature. While the terms may seem contradictory, there are in fact communist democracies and capitalist dictatorships. They only sound contradictory because of the efforts of each side to redefine the terms.

Also, neither communism nor capitalism are founded on human rights abuses. In the same way that the Soviet Union killed capitalists who opposed communism, the U.S. killed communists who opposed capitalism. Chiang Kai-Shek, after taking over the presidency of China, and with the support of the U.S., worked to remove all elements of the communist influence by any means possible. In Chile, Pinochet, infamous for his human rights violations, aggressively rid his society of communists through torture, imprisonment, and murder. The wars in Vietnam and Korea were for the purpose of exterminating the "communist threat," or to be more blunt, for the purpose of killing communists.

It was in the 1950s that the U.S. experienced the peak of communist paranoia. Senator Joseph McCarthy, who feared that communist elements were trying to take over, pursued the complete elimination of communism. McCarthy put on trial, and attempted to jail, any person who promoted communism or was found to be a member of the Communist Party.

At the height of the Cold War, the West pointed at Korea and Vietnam as examples of the communist's violent expansionism and human rights abuses. While at the same time, China and the Soviet Union pointed to Korea and Vietnam as examples of the capitalist's violent expansionism and human rights abuses. For over 100 years and climaxing in the 1950s and 1960s, communists have characterized capitalism as a true evil, but to no less extent, the capitalists in the U.S., Great Britain, and others in the West have labored to characterize communism as a true evil.

To Fear or Not to Fear Communism in China?

While each side has worked to redefine and package the opposing idea in a negative way, to effectively explore our question, we'll need to address separately the issues of communism, democracy, and human rights, because each is an independent issue.

In the 1950s the recent experience of WWII and Germany's pursuit of world domination put countries into a hyper-sensitive mode. As the communist Soviet Union expanded aggressively into neighboring countries, the U.S. began to characterize all communists as violent expansionists. The U.S. media and politicians labored to persuade the public that communism's aim was to take over the world, and thus communism must be stopped. The error in logic here is that the expansion was not communist; rather, the expansion was specifically a product of the Soviet Union.

At the same time, China was rebuilding from WWII and fighting economic problems of its own. It had no ambition and no resources for expansion. Even given the opportunity to expand into Korea and Vietnam, China had no interest. It considered these countries as friendly neighbors, and had no intent to expand.

However, the U.S. reached a flawed but easy correlation. If the Soviet Union was communist and wanted to expand its territorial control, then likewise China, which was communist, must have wanted to expand its territorial control as well. Regardless, China's actions and history did not back up this flawed correlation. China did not have expansionist ambitions. Because China's communists aren't expansionist and don't seek to impose their system on us, we must evaluate the idea of communism on its own. Should we fear the economic model of communism in China?

Prior to WWII the idea of communism hadn't truly been tested because wars and political disruptions interfered with its implementation. Following the war, the two ideas swung into full competition. Russia and China worked to achieve the communist ideal. Meanwhile, the U.S. and Great Britain, already well rooted in capitalism, continued to pursue the capitalist ideal. Over the next 30 years it became evident that the communist economic model didn't provide the results that the capitalist model provided. The standard of living continued to improve in capitalist economies, while it stagnated or declined in communist economies. In 1976 China had a GDP per capita of $141, while the U.S. GDP per capita was $20,747, almost 150 times larger than China's. By 1989 China's GDP per capita had only grown to $383. The Soviet Union's had stagnated at $2,693, but the U.S.GDP per capita continued to grow and had reached $28,098.[78]

Mao Zedong, the leader of China for over 40 years, had tried endlessly to make the economic model work. At first he adopted the Soviet model, then he tried implementing the Great Leap Forward, and finally he started the Cultural Revolution. But his dream of using the communist model to improve the standard of living for the Chinese people was elusive. The engine just would not turn over, and China and the Soviet Union lagged further and further behind the Western capitalist economies.

When Deng Xiaoping took control of the communist party in 1976, he recognized that results were more important than any particular ideological model. When he stated that it didn't matter if a cat is black or white as long as it catches mice, he began a path that focused on results (catching mice) not ideology (black or white). To abandon parts of a failing belief that have been held for many years is difficult, and to do it with an organization whose name (The Communist Party of China) contains within it the very idea is even more difficult. In hindsight, it's possible that a different name would've allowed them to reform their system earlier. Over the past 30 years China has dramatically modified its economic model, retaining from the communist model elements they find beneficial, and adopting from the capitalist model structures that have shown to work well in advancing economic prosperity.

Should we fear Chinese communism? Capitalists, since the days of Marx, have been claiming that communism would fail. But if capitalists are so convinced that it would fail, why then would so much effort and expense be needed to force it to fail? Wouldn't it crumble under the weight of its own inefficiency? And furthermore, why would economic difficulties in another country be cause for the U.S. to fear them?

Guns to Defeat a Philosophy

What if the U.S. position simply had been: "We're concerned that this idea will fail and that it will be bad for the people of China. Here are the reasons we believe it will fail…" Instead, the U.S. believed that guns and armies were necessary to defeat this ideology that we claimed would fall on its own. If your neighbor decides to plant orange trees and you decide to plant apple trees, each of you claiming yours is the only fruit that will grow, although you may have concerns for him, would you fear his decision? As long as he doesn't force his decision on you, why would you care? Would you beat him up until he agreed to plant apple trees? The amount of resources that have been wasted to force adoption of our political and economic beliefs is a historic catastrophe. The number of lives and the amount of resources wasted on what should have been a self-fulfilling resolution is inexcusable. When Russia went communist, most Russians believed in communism. When Mao led China down the communist road, most Chinese followed him. If we're a people of choice, why would we work so hard to force others to make the choices we've made? We've wanted to force our beliefs at the point of a gun. Constantly told to fear Chinese and Russian communism, we accepted the flawed premise that it was a threat to us, as we spent treasure and lives to defeat an idea.

Fortunately, the heat of the Cold War has subsided, but remnants of the rhetoric remain and continue to heavily influence U.S. foreign policy. Cold War mentality also continues to influence the general beliefs of the American people. Many of the current generation of politicians grew up in the Cold War era—it's difficult to change one's disposition when the ideology of the Cold War has been so integral to their past experience, education, and media exposure. Violent expansionism by any state is a threat and should be feared and protected against, but Chinese communism has never been and is not currently a threat to the U.S. or others.

From Deng's new approach, China has rapidly learned to adapt their systems based on results, not on fulfilling a target ideology. China works to identify the good and bad of each system, testing and adopting elements that work. *China Daily* reported that there are over ten million private enterprises in China and they account for over 60 percent of GDP.[79] The Chinese system has developed into a hybrid between communism and capitalism, with state owned enterprises the way Marx recommended, and private enterprises the way Adam Smith recommended. China is communist in the same way the U.S. is capitalist—not pure, but a hybrid mix. The U.S., which prides itself on being capitalist, has publicly owned and operated roads, utilities, space programs, schools, and even recently owned the car company General Motors. Agencies like Fanny May and Freddie Mac are controlled by the government, and many hospitals are government run or subsidized. Government grants and loans go to many private corporations, which is not what could be thought of as pure capitalism. Additionally, our list of welfare programs could compete with any communist country. In the past 50 years most economies have become hybrids, seeking out the best mixture of ideas to improve the standard of living for all, while abandoning the flaw of pure ideology.

Even in China a majority of the people believe that free market economies provide the best for people. A PEW research poll shows that 84 percent of Chinese believe a market economy allows most citizens to be better off.[80]

As we've seen, it's economic outcomes that must be pursued, not fixed ideological structures. When we convince ourselves that there's only one economic model that can improve the standard of living, we lock ourselves out of opportunities and provide no room for error or correction should an idea have flaws or should an alternate idea have elements of value. The Chinese communist hybrid system, which has evolved dramatically over the last 30 years beginning under the leadership of Deng Xiaoping, has shown that by selecting elements of each system, testing and fine-tuning along the way, a state can have grand economic success. In 30 years the Chinese system has brought over 300 million people out of poverty, has increased GDP per capita by a factor of 25, and has resulted in China becoming the second largest economy in the world. While capitalist societies have had great success, this hybrid system has shown to be amazingly adept at the true goal, which is rapid improvement in the standard of living of a society. Many third world or emerging capitalist economies haven't been able to compete with the success of this Chinese hybrid model.

Fearing communism is like fearing a religious belief that's different from yours. While you may be concerned about the other person's salvation, their belief is not a threat to you. The threat comes when one tries to force their beliefs on another, or seeks to eliminate those who hold different views. Over history, China has not attempted to force communism on others. While we're told to fear communism, our fear should be reserved for those who wish to force their ideas on others. If the Chinese government attempted to force us to be communist, then we should fear. And when your government says we are going to bring capitalism to the world, that is when you should fear, because when they say "bring," they actually mean force in the form of your dollars and your son's lives.

12

Fearing China's Non-Democratic Rule

When Dollars Trump Democracy in China (Washington Post)
Capitalism Is Making China Richer, But Not Democratic (NPR)
Beijing is Crushing Hong Kong's Democratic Hopes (Washington Post)
Pro-Democracy Students Are Arrested in Hong Kong (New York Times)
Macau Scholar Says He Lost His Job Over Pro-Democracy Activism
(New York Times)[81]

The Democracy

In the same way there were competing ideas in economic structures, there were competing ideas in political structures. Prior to the system of democracy, transition of political power was typically either hereditary or through violent war. Power was assumed by the son of the king or taken by the biggest army as kingdoms sought to expand or factions attempted to seize power. Transition was not for the purpose of social improvement, but for increasing the power and wealth of those who pursued power. Although forms of democracy did occur in ancient times with tribes and various societies using the vote to elect leaders and make decisions, Athens in the fifth century BC was one of the largest and best known societies to use the democratic process.

The benefit of democracy is that each citizen is given the right to have a say in selecting their leaders and making decisions that may affect their wellbeing. Democracy is thought to ensure that power is ultimately in the hands of the people, and not a ruling class. Democracy promotes equality due to the fact that each citizen has an equal vote and leaders must obey the same laws as the general citizens. Democracy also promotes peaceful transition of power.

In today's world, the primary purpose of a political system is to broadly increase prosperity, reduce suffering, and improve the standard of living of the populace. It's goal is to provide to as many as possible the opportunity to fully utilize their capabilities and pursue that which they find fulfilling. The Constitution of the U.S. puts it this way:

"We the people of the United States, in order to form a more perfect union, establish justice, insure domestic tranquility, provide for the common defense, promote the general welfare, and secure the blessings of liberty to ourselves and our posterity, do ordain and establish this constitution for the United States of America."

The goals of the writers of the U.S. constitution were: Justice, Tranquility, Defense, General Welfare, and Liberty. The U.S. Declaration of Independence called these aims "Life, Liberty, and the pursuit of Happiness."

In pursuit of the goals set out by the U.S. Constitution and Declaration of Independence, we must ask an essential question: Is democracy the only political system capable of advancing these important goals, and does democracy always advance these goals?

The Corporation

Modern day corporations like Apple, IBM, Tesla, and Boeing use a meritocratic system to hire and promote the most capable employees. Companies hire college graduates and place them in low-level positions. As these new hires gain experience and prove themselves, they're promoted to the next level. As they gain further education and experience, and show that they're capable of performing well, they can continue to advance. They're tested and their performance is constantly evaluated. The corporation, in their master goal of better company performance, promotes from within or hires from outside those who they evaluate to be a benefit for advancing the goals of the company. For a capable and well performing employee, a career is a series of advancements allowing the person to move up in position, responsibility, and pay. Although it occasionally happens, it's rare to land in a position that one isn't qualified for.

Corporations don't use a democratic system to determine who will advance. While shareholders sometimes have voting power, they rarely control a company. Corporations look to the future and strive to improve with a comprehensive plan led from the top down but with vetted players. Companies don't take a kid from the mailroom and make him the president of the company. Through systematic analysis, companies work to promote and install the most capable people using a merit based system.

The Chinese System

In the West we know two political systems. We know democracy and we know dictatorship, but there's another form of political structure that we know little about, even though it surrounds us in the non-political world and was first used over two thousand years ago. The first reported political meritocracy was in 165 BC in the Han Dynasty (206 BC–220 AD) of China and gained prominence during the Tang Dynasty (618-907 AD). Civil service exams were used to promote government officials. The Chinese philosopher Confucius argued that those who govern should attain their position from merit and not inheritance. Although the emperors of China continued to pass power to their offspring, other political positions were filled using a meritocratic system. To find competent leaders, China used an Imperial Examination, testing those who sought the offices of government leadership. Successful candidates were then given the opportunity to work their way up the meritocracy during their career, a process similar to that found in our modern day corporations.

Today in China that political meritocratic system has evolved to include every position. Even those selected for the highest positions, including the president and the premier, have worked their way up the meritocracy. The Organization Department of the Communist Party of China Central Committee is effectively the personnel department of the Chinese government; it recruits, tests, and promotes leaders through a series of steps and advancements. Eric Li, in his TED talk, gives a fascinating description of this multi-tiered system used by the Chinese government to recruit and promote political leaders. The leaders can develop through career paths in state owned enterprises, community service organizations like hospitals and schools, and through government positions like city managers or provincial positions.

The Chinese system works very much like a corporation, giving a person increasing levels of responsibility as they work their way up. Mayors in large cities have had experience running smaller cities.

Presidents of large state owned enterprises have worked their way up in the organization or have advanced through other companies. The resumes of top officials are filled with broad and extensive hands-on experience in executive management. The system is grounded in the Imperial Examination model, using merit, experience, and testing as the core method of selection and advancement.

The vast majority of Chinese leaders have competed and worked their way to the top, with competency being the standard used for promotion. For example, President Xi Jinping of China has held positions such as governor of Fujian province with a population of 37 million and a GDP of $355 billion. He was also governor of Zhejiang province with a population of 54 million and GDP of $600 billion. He was put in charge of the preparations for the 2008 Summer Olympics in Beijing—and these are just the highlights of his resume of progressive advancement.

Challenges of Democracy

In the West, we're brought up to believe that democracy is not only the best political structure, but also that it's the only acceptable political structure; we're told it's the political system that will provide the best outcome for every society. We aren't encouraged to objectively analyze the shortcomings of democracy or the benefits of alternate systems, and we're rarely taught or reminded that even the founding fathers of the United States had great concerns about democracy. If we are to compare our system with others and are anxious to judge the shortcoming of other systems, or ready to force our system on others, then we should have a better understanding of our own system and its challenges.

The ancient Greek philosophers Aristotle, Socrates, and Plato, in the midst of the Athenian democracy, did not speak highly of democracy, and some spoke against it. Socrates said that a democracy would be led by those skilled in rhetoric but not skilled or learned in the topics they are leading. Many philosophers who wrote extensively on political systems, from Plato to John Locke to John Steward Mill, had strong concerns that democracy would bring into power leaders who weren't experienced or qualified. They were concerned that the majority could vote to take away the rights of the minority. Factions fighting for their own individual interests would cause poor decisions and gridlock in the system. They also expressed concerns that an uninformed or uneducated populace wouldn't be capable of selecting the best leaders. The point here is not to challenge our belief in democracy, but to point out that democracy is not flawless and to at least give us an understanding of the non-democratic system used in China.

Influence on Elections

As Americans, we take great pride in the fact that we're able to select our leaders and particularly our president. However, it's important to recognize that every president since 1869 has been either from the Republican Party or the Democratic Party. Two parties have controlled the U.S. presidency for over 145 years—without interruption. While we express concern about the one-party rule in China, we show no concern about our own two-party rule that has lasted for over a century.

Influences on democratic elections are many. In the 2012 presidential election, seven billion was spent on campaigning. That money comes from individuals, corporations, special interests groups like unions, and numerous "non-disclosed" sources. The Koch brothers, who are large donors to political causes, have committed to spending $889 million on political campaigning during the 2016 U.S. elections; this is almost one billion dollars spent by two guys and their wealthy friends to influence the U.S. elections. President Obama joked that if he were a Republican candidate, he would be offended that someone would think it would take one billion dollars to get people to like him.

Recent studies have shown that it is half of one percent of the population that gives the majority of campaign dollars to candidates and political campaigns. So while we like to think it's "the people" that select the leaders, ultimately it's less than one half of one percent of "the people" that have the greatest impact on who will gain office. Additionally, the media controls who will advance by deciding which candidates they will report on and how they'll report on them.

Elections are determined by public opinion, and public opinion, in many ways, is determined by the media. In 2012 Facebook conducted a test to see how public sentiment could be influenced by controlling the type of news that was served to Facebook users. As expected, by controlling the news stories delivered to the users, the user's disposition was altered or one might say controlled. In 2014 when the story came out about this testing, there was outrage that Facebook would manipulate users in such a manner. It's possible those outraged should've had deeper concerns—what's upsetting is not that Facebook would do such a thing, but that the media in general has the ability to control public sentiment and opinion.[82]

Today in an election, data analysts work for candidates to determine what flyers and marketing materials will be sent to your home. If they know you're a gun-rights activist, you'll receive a flyer telling how the candidate supports your gun-rights position. If abortion rights are important to your neighbor, that same candidate will send your neighbor a flyer showing how they support their position on abortion, not mentioning the candidate's position on gun-rights because they know your neighbor wants more gun control. And if you're a military veteran, guess which flyer will arrive at your home from that very same candidate? Splitting the data and marketing to each individual, the candidate can appear to be all things to all people.

After factoring in media influence, special interests, major donors, and the two major parties' control, and as campaigning becomes increasingly scientific, calculated, and contrived, to what extent can we say the people are really in control of election results in a democracy? Influence on the elections can be a weakness of democracy.

Influence on the Elected

Once in office, what are the influences on the decisions that democratic leaders make? In a democratic system, politicians often act for the benefit of narrow special interest groups. A special interest group effectively uses their financial contributions or number of votes to influence a politician's decisions—do what they want and you'll get elected or re-elected. Don't do what they want and lose your campaign financing, votes, and finally, your position. Special interest groups can range from environmental advocacy groups to gun rights groups to farmers and can even includes corporations and investors. A report by *The Nation* says there were over 12,000 registered lobbyists in Washington. Each lobbyist can represent multiple special interests, seeking laws or government allocation of budget that would be to their client's advantage.

A representative's constituents are in fact a special interest group; they vote for and send their elected official to Washington not usually for the benefit of the country, but for what the politician can specifically do for their region. At its surface this may appear to be a good thing as it makes politicians responsive to the people who elected them, but it also opens a problematic door of competing factions and a total disregard for what may be good for the whole. A senator who has a large ship building facility in his state may fight to pass a military bill which includes the purchase of billions of dollars of ships which would be built in his home state, providing jobs and improving the economy of his region. While his arguments for passing the bill will be filled with rhetoric of how it will be for the benefit of the entire country and the vital need for such defense expenditures, in fact he's using his power for the specific benefit of his constituents. He has little true regard for the value or necessity of the project to the entire country. Too often, elected officials act in the interest of the small groups who can ensure their election or re-election, with little regard for the entire nation. Lobbyists and other influences on elected officials can be a weakness of democracy.

Gridlock

Recently the U.S. went four years without passing a federal budget because conflicting interests fought for their own piece of the pie with little ability to pursue broad objective goals. Every special interest group and every constituency kept pressure on their legislators to the point that nothing could be passed. A U.S. news commentator recently said the reason we have gridlock in Washington is that lawmakers are not doing what their constituents have asked them to do. Actually, it's the opposite. The reason we have gridlock is that the legislators are doing exactly what their constituents are asking them to do. The car is at the corner. A quarter are telling their legislators to turn hard right, a quarter are telling them to take a hard left, a quarter instructing them to go straight, and the final quarter advising them to back up. After tallying the vote, the lawmakers are doing exactly what they've been instructed to do. The cumulative decision is: don't move.

A poll that says 75 percent of Americans don't like the direction the country is headed is a useless poll. It assumes there's a particular direction the majority would like to go, but as we've seen, there isn't. With interests pulling from every direction, there's no agreement on which way to go. Thus, while the kids are arguing in the backseat over which direction to go, one can only hope there's an adult in the driver seat that can ignore the screams and make a decision, left, right or otherwise. If the leaders cannot make a decision, then gridlock has become a weakness of democracy.

Voting into Bankruptcy

Budgeting is a critical part of governance, and a primary function of political leaders, as they must set priorities that will allocate a limited budget to an unlimited list of requests. The challenge of budgeting while attempting to cater to every request of the voters, combined with a nation's ability to borrow money, can cause democracies to deficit spend often to the point of bankruptcy. This happened with Argentina in 2002, Iceland in 2008, and Greece was only held back from bankruptcy by massive bailouts from the EU as the Greek voters continue to refuse to cut benefits, which they have no ability to pay for. Voters concern themselves very little with the abstract concept of national debt while giving great concern to the check they receive from the government. Give the voters a choice between balancing the national budget by reducing their personal federal benefits, or continuing to increase the national debt and preserving or increasing their personal benefits, and most often they'll vote for what affects them most directly. They'll vote the county into bankruptcy to maintain their generous benefits, as Greece will ultimately do.

The U.S. now has a national debt equal to its annual GDP, equating to approximately $53,000 per person. If each citizen were told that they're responsible for paying back the $53,000, then they might think twice about voting for more benefits. But the voters do not find themselves personally liable for their portion of the national debt, so the spending continues. The French philosopher Lexis de Tocqueville said: "The American Republic will endure until politicians realize they can bribe the people with their own money."

In a democracy, too often voters will vote for their own special interest, even to the detriment of the whole. A weakness of democracy can be its tendency to vote itself into bankruptcy.

Tyranny of the Majority

While the theory of democracy assumes the cumulative effect of all participating in an election will result in what is best for the whole, tyranny of the majority has always been a concern of political philosophers from Plato to John Stewart Mill. In 1787 while the U.S. constitution was being written and debated, James Madison wrote in the Federalist Papers No. 10 that: "the public good is disregarded in the conflicts of rival parties, and that measures are too often decided, not according to the rules of justice and the rights of the minor party, but by the superior force of an interested and overbearing majority."

The concern of tyranny of the majority in a democracy is best illustrated in recent events in Iraq and Egypt. In Iraq, Saddam Hussein, who was a Sunni, used his power to give advantage to the Sunnis while marginalizing the Shia and Kurds. Finally, after thirty-five years of the Shia and Kurds being abused by the Sunnis, democracy had arrived. Now all could be equal, right? No. Because the Shia were the majority, it was unfortunately an opportunity for the Shia to take power and dominate the Sunnis and Kurds. This has resulted in a renewed civil war because the minority refuses to be subject to the tyranny of the majority. In Egypt a similar scenario occurred when the Muslim Brotherhood won the election and immediately pursued their own interests, not the interests of the whole. Tyranny of the majority caused the Egyptian democracy to fail, at least for now.

Tyranny is most often thought of in authoritarian rule, but it can be just as common in democracy. Tyranny of a majority over a minority can be quick to surface and just as detrimental as authoritarian tyranny. James Madison said: "Where a majority are united by a common sentiment, and have an opportunity, the rights of the minor party become insecure." Tyranny of the majority can be a weakness of democracy.

Tyranny of the Loud and Organized

A most important skill of a political leader is the ability to say no. But it's the one ability most democratic politicians don't have. Often politicians aren't capable of turning to the merits of a complaint when a mass of screaming demonstrators is on their doorstep or they're being bombarded by a well-financed lobbying campaign. Combined with the leverage of threatened withholding of their campaign contributions and possible banishment from office with their votes, the well-organized interest has great power over elected officials. While in many cases the majority may disagree with the loud minority, the majority cannot take the time to counter protest every screaming special interest group, so the organized special interest often prevails over rational objective decision making.

The National Institute of Health allocates very large budgets for scientific research to eliminate disease. Early in the AIDS epidemic the AIDS lobby organized well and to great effect. Today, the NIH spends about $330 thousand per death caused by AIDS compared to only $10 thousand per death caused by prostate cancer. The two largest recipients of research dollars per death are AIDS and breast cancer. These two causes happen to have the best organizations and largest lobbing campaigns for federal research dollars. Tyranny of the loud and organized can be another weakness of democracy.[83]

The Good Emperor Problem

Non-democratic systems are said to have difficulty in removing poor leaders; this "Bad Emperor" problem is thought to be their downfall. From experience, China is very aware of the "Bad Emperor" problem and continues to institute mechanisms such as term limits to address the issue.

While democracies may have the ability to vote out bad leaders, what ability do they have to vote in good leaders? In the same way non-democratic systems may have a "Bad Emperor" problem, democracies can have a "Good Emperor" problem; having difficulty bringing to power the best leaders. The concern that democracy can be quite deficient in its ability to bring the best and most competent leaders into high office has been a concern throughout the history of democracy.

If voters aren't skilled in the in-depth analysis that such a decision requires or can't commit the extensive amount of time that would be needed to make such a decision, then they'll often base their decisions on the marketing campaigns put forward by the candidates. They too often vote for those skilled in rhetoric but lacking other vital skills and experience, as Socrates warned. When voters evaluate a candidate, proven competence and experience are often not a big factor—the voters are quick to insert a leader with little or no record of accomplishment. Rhetorical ability and presentation are qualities that are too often rewarded in the democratic system. The philosopher John Locke called it the act of running administrations by the ignorant, others have called it government by amateurs.

For the position of U.S. President, one may expect a person with decades of experience in executive management, experience in foreign policy, experience in domestic policy, and education in fields related to the task of leadership in these areas. It would be reasonable to expect a proven track record of successful results in management on a large scale prior to being installed into the highest position. However, because the voters typically don't take a criteria based approach to the decision, often the results are not optimum, to say the least. Too often it's an unfortunate characteristic of voters to base their decisions on a surface review of a candidate's sales pitch without giving much thought to what should be the reasonable criteria of experience and proven accomplishment prior to gaining the highest political office.

President George W. Bush had only been a state governor for four years prior to running for U.S. President. Prior to obtaining the governorship he had little administrative experience in government or otherwise. His most extensive political experience was helping in his father's presidential campaign. Therefore, his real experience was in getting elected, not in governing. His successor, Barack Obama, had even less experience. Obama was a state congressman for seven years prior to becoming a U.S. senator. After being a senator for two years, he began his run for the office of president. He entered office with no executive experience, and he had minimal experience in other areas that may be reasonably expected of a President of the largest economy in the world who also controls the world's largest military.

The U.S. media makes a great deal of the presidential debates, often calculating that the performance of a candidate in the debates is one of the most important factors as voters make their decision. However, the ability to debate is only one small skill needed by a president, and in fact, one a president never uses once president. But the voters base much of their decision on this rarely used skill that has almost nothing to do with the ability to govern. This highlights the concern expressed by Socrates and others that democracy can result in bringing to power those with oratory and debate skills but little experience or skill in governing.

The examples of democracies voting in inexperienced or incompetent leaders are too many to list. India, despite years of democracy, hasn't been able to make substantial progress in improving the citizens' standard of living or in weeding out corruption. Africa has numerous examples of voters electing thieves into government. Latin America has an only slightly better record as they vote in leaders such as Hugo Chaves and Morales—both quickly destroyed the economies of their countries. Thailand has had no problem voting out their bad leader every year for the last 25 years; their challenge is electing a good leader.

Aristotle said: "Democracy arises out of the notion that those who are equal in any respect are equal in all respects; because men are equally free, they claim to be absolutely equal." His concern was that in a democracy, just because people should be found equal in many respects, there's no doubt that people are not equal in their ability to make decisions, and thus their ability to select leaders. Therefore, to allow all to have an equal vote in selecting the leaders, Aristotle argues, would not produce good results. While democracies may be quick to vote out a bad leader, their ability to vote in a good leader is often lacking. Democracy can have a "Good Emperor" problem.

Democratic Failures and Non-Democratic Successes

The West sees democracy not only as a human right, but also as a source of good governance. But what if democracy does not produce good governance? What if the arguments made by Aristotle, Plato, James Madison, De Tocqueville, and others prove true? While we point to the successes of democracy, often we ignore its failures. What if these known deficiencies of democracy prevent attaining the goals of Tranquility, Defense, General Welfare, and Liberty, the core objectives of any government and the goals put forth in our Declaration of Independence.

In China's own neighborhood, the results of democracy have been mixed. Thailand had its democratic revolution in 1932 and has had numerous elections, followed by chaos, followed by military coup. They have had over 17 different constitutions and 20 Prime Ministers in the last 24 years alone. Economic prosperity has been elusive, freedoms fluctuating, and tranquility hard to find in this democratic country. In the Philippines, Ferdinand Marcos was elected president and maintained his position for over 20 years. His rule was mired in corruption and dysfunction. Tranquility is still periodic, and the standard of living for the average Filipino has progressed little over the last one hundred years. The Philippines has been a democracy for over sixty years, yet GDP per capita remains under $3,000 per year. The correlation between democracy and economic prosperity can't be found in the Philippines.

While the flaws of democracy can cause it to fail, often economic prosperity is found in non-democratic states. Let's consider the four most successful economies in Asia, four states that became known as the Asian Tigers: Hong Kong, Singapore, South Korea, and Taiwan.

Hong Kong is an example of a highly successful non-democratic state. For over 150 years the British maintained control of Hong Kong. Being a democracy itself, it may be assumed that Great Britain sought to implement democratic principles in Hong Kong while the island was in their possession. However, this was not the case. For 150 years, the governor of Hong Kong was an appointed position—appointed by London. Great Britain was more concerned that Hong Kong be run as a capitalist economy with British laws than that the people of Hong Kong were allowed self determination. The result was that Hong Kong became one of the most successful economies in Asia, providing to its citizens the highest standard of living in the region, all accomplished without democracy.

Singapore is also one of the most successful economies in the world, with GDP per capita of $55,000. Freedom House, an organization that monitors the democracy and freedoms of countries, ranks Singapore as "Partly Free." Singapore is a controlled democracy, which means that they do have elections, but these elections are very restricted. The first elected Prime Minister of Singapore, Lee Kuan Yew, held the position for forty years. Often opponents are deemed unsuitable for office by the authorities and not allowed to run for election. Today the Prime Minister of Singapore is Lee Hsien Loong, the son of Lee Kuan Yew. This means that 50 years later the government is in the hands of the same family, making Singapore more of a democratic dynasty than a true democracy. Regardless of their method of selecting leaders, it's evident that what they're doing is working to provide a very high standard of living for the people of Singapore. A correlation between democracy and the goals of prosperity and tranquility can't be found in Singapore—Singapore thrives in its very limited democratic political system.

Taiwan, from the end of WWII until 1987, was a military dictatorship, first under the government of Chiang Kai-shek, then under the leadership of his son Chiang Ching-kuo. The father and son controlled the country from 1945 to 1987, and the first true presidential election was not held until 1996. And yet, economic prosperity as indicated by GDP per capita has been on a steady and consistent climb since the 1960s, with little if any correlation between democracy and the goals of prosperity and tranquility. The standard of living in Taiwan was well advanced prior to instituting democracy in 1996.

Shortly after the end of the Korean War, South Korea fell to a military dictator, Park Chung-hee, for 18 years. Despite South Korea's turbulent political environment, their economic prosperity began in the 1970s under the dictator's rule and really took off shortly after he was assassinated in 1979. South Korea only became a true democracy with its first direct presidential election in 1988. Of the four Asian Tigers, South Korea shows the most correlation between democracy and the goals of tranquility and prosperity. However, South Korea does lag behind the other three Asian Tigers in economic performance and GDP per capita. Today, economic progress continues under democratically elected president Park Geun-hye, who happens to be the daughter of the military dictator who held power for almost two decades.

As China observes the successes and failures of political

systems in their neighborhood, from the successes of non-democratic Hong Kong and Singapore to the economic failures in the democracies in Thailand and the Philippines, we can see why they may be reluctant to embrace the proposals of the West to rapidly implement democracy. From the examples closest to them, the non-democratic countries often outperform the democracies.

The two countries often thought to be the best examples of the benefits of democracy are the U.S. and Great Britain. However, a closer look shows us that both the U.S. and Great Britain attained their economic prosperity prior to becoming fully democratic. Early in U.S. history only white men with property could vote. Non-Whites were not ensured the right to vote until the Fifteen Amendment passed in 1870 almost 100 years after the Declaration of Independence. Even so, due to poll taxes and literacy requirements, few non-whites voted for another 70 years. Women were not guaranteed the right to vote until 1920 with the Nineteenth Amendment to the constitution. The U.S and Great Britain were the two largest economies and most industrialized nations in the world with the highest standards of living many years prior to implementing universal suffrage, the right to vote.

The Asian Tiger Model

While China maintains tranquility and drives towards prosperity, they study the successes and failures around the world. Following Deng Xiaoping's advice, they don't care if the cat is black or white, they care if it catches mice. They're looking for the best results. They observe the successful democracies of the U.S. and Britain, but also see the highly dysfunctional democracies found in Africa, the only moderately successful democracies in South America, and the trauma of the Arab world's experiments with democracy as Egypt, Libya, Iraq, Afghanistan, and Yemen pursue the Western instigated system of liberal democracy. From these numerous examples from around the world, they reasonably question if democracy is the key to success, or whether it's possible that other systems can perform better.

In Asia, and in fact around the world, the Asian Tiger model has often been proven to outperform democracy, especially in emerging market economies. This model has five elements.

1: One party or entity has full authority and accountability.

2: The authority pursues rule of law, not arbitrary rule, and fights against corruption.

3: The authority advances market economies.

4: The authority uses their power to eliminate or marginalize the disruption of political opposition.

5: The authority monitors and promotes improvements in the condition of the poor and minority groups.

These aren't benevolent dictators taking from the rich and giving to the poor. They're strategic authoritarians pursuing an economic and legal structure that leverages the power of the market economy in order to provide economic prosperity and tranquility to their nation. The Chinese system is fundamentally the five-point system used by their most successful neighbors to create the highest standards of living in the least amount of time. The Asian Tiger model bypasses the weaknesses of democracy to quickly implement proven legal and economic structures that cause rapid improvements in the standard of living for all.

With the Chinese meritocratic one party system, the problem of influence on elections is avoided because media and special interests cannot affect the selection of the leaders. Likewise, foreign powers can't use the media and hidden influences to sway an election. The problem of special interests influencing the decisions of the elected is avoided. Special interests don't have the ability to remove leaders from office; thus, they can't extort demands from them. The problem of tyranny of the majority is avoided, as the majority can't abuse a minority by way of vote. The problem of disruption by factions or gridlock due to fighting factions is avoided. As China develops and its populace becomes more educated, the people's voices are being heard. Even so, every squeaky wheel does not maintain the right to disrupt the tranquility of the masses or disrupt society.

The Chinese system also avoids the democratic weakness of government by amateurs. Zhang Weiwei, who was a translator for Den Xiaoping, tells us that almost all the leaders who have reached the central committee have held the top position in at least two provinces in China. Zhang contrasts this with the U.S. system, claiming that those entering political leadership in the U.S. are way below the Chinese standard. Zhang Weiwei said: "The Chinese model is more about leadership while the liberal democracy model seems more about showmanship. The Chinese model plans for the next generation while the democratic model plans for the next election."

China is a vast country with 1.3 billion inhabitants. While the literacy rate of 95 percent is high, by what criteria would voters select leaders who would be best for the political and economic management of the country? The prettiest picture or biggest promise may win, but the prettiest picture or biggest promise usually can't deliver. Half of the population of China is still rural, laboring on farms and working in small villages. By what criteria would they analyze political candidates? China may reasonably argue that their merit based system results in better and more qualified leaders than could be expected from a popular vote, in the end providing the people of China more rapid improvements in the standard of living for all in China, while avoiding many of the weaknesses of democracy.

Accountability

It's often argued that without democracy, a government cannot be held accountable to the people. However, consider that democratic elections cause high turnover in power and that improvements to society require long-term strategies and a single accountable entity. Many of the results of actions and new laws implemented by governments can't be seen for many years. Thus, by the time you really know how that decision worked out, the democratically elected official is long gone. The factors that caused the recent housing bubble and financial crisis in the U.S. were laws and policies that were established by government ten years before the crises that almost caused the collapse of our economy. Likewise, the Iraq and Afghanistan war decisions made by President Bush are still being dealt many years after he left office. As power is shifted back and forth between two parties, and leaders are often replaced, the high rate of turnover gives each newly elected official ample opportunity to blame current woes on prior officials. This can result in a lack of long-term accountability, because the results of their decisions will only be apparent long after they're out of office. While the Chinese system of one party rule may have other issues, "The Party" is accountable for the success or failure of the nation. They have no others to blame. They find themselves accountable and the people find them accountable.

In a democracy, if the voters are fully in control of their government, then it would be the voters that should ultimately be accountable for the success or failure of their country. However, the voters in a democracy may be the most unaccountable political body ever invented. When democracies make poor decision, is it ever the voters who are blamed? Where is the indictment and prosecution of the voters? When democracy fails, it's the elected who are always blamed, not the voters. The elected are convicted of not being able to accomplish the goals of the voters no matter how contradictory or impossible those goals. The news is filled with stories of the poor performance of democratically elected officials from Egypt to Iraq to the U.S.; however, where's the story about how the voters have failed to make a good decision? Where are the reports of how the people of Ghana, Venezuela, Egypt, or Thailand have failed to elect good governance?

Early Failures of China's System

The early leadership of the People's Republic of China had many failures that hurt the people of China. Mao, while successful as a revolutionary consolidating the country and stopping the aggressions of the West, failed at bringing economic prosperity to China. While the seeds of the meritocratic system were sewn, the leaders of China, chasing first the Soviet model then struggling to find their own way, had terrible results for the first thirty years (1949-1979). During that period the mechanism of term limits and other structures which promote good governance were not yet developed.

However, leadership since Deng Xiaoping has shown amazing ability to provide stability and economic growth. The Chinese economy has grown at an astounding ten percent per year over the last thirty years, a rate of growth rarely seen in any economy. In that time over 300 million have been lifted out of poverty. Adopting the characteristics of the non-democratic Asian Tigers with the benefits of a more structured meritocratic method of advancing leaders has proven to be an effective model. Would a democratically elected Chinese leadership be able to provide better results? Not only can we not be so sure, but a knowledge of history would suggest we bet against it as China has succeeded where many democracies have failed.

People care more about results than process or method. Surveys by Pew Research indicate that the people of China are happy with the results their government is providing. When asked: "Are you satisfied with the country's direction," the 2014 survey shows that in the U.S. 33 percent were satisfied and in Britain 40 percent were satisfied, while in China 87 percent were satisfied. When asked if the economic situation is good, in the U.S. 40 percent said yes, in Britain 43 percent said yes, and in China, 89 percent said they believe their economic condition is good.[84]

Even though the early years of the People's Republic of China showed very poor results for the people of China, today a majority of the Chinese are pleased with the results their government is achieving. Of all the countries surveyed, China had the highest rating of satisfaction by their people.

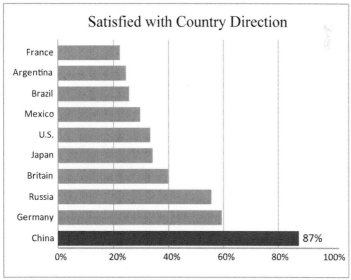

Pew Research Center, Washington, D.C. (2014)

Preoccupation with Democracy

Winston Churchill said that: "Democracy is the worst form of government, except for all the others." This quote from Churchill highlights the true issue. Churchill was committed to the results of the process, not the process itself. At the time the options were thought to be democracy, dictatorship, monarchy or war. So given the well known options of the day, in pursuit of the best results Churchill defaulted to democracy for lack of a better alternative. But his statement gives opening and even hope that one day a system may come that gives equal or better results, eliminating the known flaws of democracy. Our preoccupation with the method (democracy) distracts us from the quality of the results. We're so focused on the ideology that the leaders chosen are secondary to the process, and worse, poor results from these leaders are often excused.

What most people in third world and developing economies care about is tranquility and economic prosperity at as rapid a pace as possible because these are the things that truly affect their standard of living. They care about democracy to the extent that they've been led to believe that democracy is the key to tranquility and rapid economic development. They attempt to emulate the political structures of the U.S. and Great Britain for the hope of an end result, not realizing that democracy may not have been the driving factor in economic development and the resulting standard of living.

When we take a look at the most successful economies in the world, the U.S., Great Britain, and the Asian Tigers, we find that their growth and position weren't achieved through democracy, but most often democracy was implemented once prosperity was already achieved. History has shown us that prosperous societies do not come out of democracy, but that democracy comes out of prosperous societies. Economic prosperity is the horse that pulls the cart of democracy. Attempts to put the cart before the horse fail.

In technological innovation, the U.S. is the undisputed leader. We don't ask how an envelope can be mailed faster; rather, we ask how a message can be sent faster, and then we invent email. We don't ask how a phone line can be made longer; instead, we ask how we can build a phone without wires. As innovators, we continually ignore the tool and focus on the end results. In technology we don't look at the shovel and ask how the shovel can be made faster and more efficient, we ask how the hole can be dug faster. But when it comes to political systems, we're irrevocably attached to the tool. We study the shovel of democracy and ask how we can make it work better and if anyone dares to imply that perhaps there may be a tool better than the shovel, they are cast out as a heretic. Innovation and advancement—yes—except for our beloved political process. China, on the other hand, looks to constantly improve the end results of government; they experiment and discard the least effective, while they test and adopt the most productive.

In an interview by Lindsey Hilsum with students from Beijing, a student said: "Democracy is an absolute value in U.S., but it might not be that absolute in other countries." In the West we find this unthinkable. How could democracy not be an absolute value? How could a Chinese student, in any way, think that democracy is not a human right or of the highest value? Well, it's possible they believe this because they've studied it more than we have. Perhaps they've studied the success of the Asian Tigers. Perhaps they've studied the history of the U.S., only to find that the U.S. economy was the largest in the world prior to establishing true democracy. What if the students have studied the failures of democracy in African nations and many Latin American nations? And what if they've looked at the failure of democracy to provide a better life for the people of Thailand and the Philippines, countries in their own backyard? The Chinese students interviewed are looking at results, not methods. When they compare the results of their system to the results of others, they aren't quick to assume that replacing their systems with Western political systems would provide better results. Perhaps they've learned from Deng Xiaoping and aren't as concerned if the cat is black or white, and instead focus on whether or not the cat can catch mice.

The Value of Tranquility

America and other first world Western countries put democracy above all else. Our founding documents place the priority on tranquility and general welfare, but over time we've elevated democracy to our highest value. But what if one goal conflicts with another? What happens when one's liberty causes another to lose tranquility, or when democratic elections do not produce economic prosperity? Which do you choose?

When goals conflict, priorities must be made. Because the West has already accomplished tranquility and economic prosperity, it's easy for us to make democracy a priority. In the U.S. we highly underestimate the value of tranquility because we haven't had a war on our soil for over 150 years. When one is abundantly blessed with something, that's when one is most likely not to recognize its value; we've been abundantly blessed with tranquility and peace on our soil. With our priority being democracy, we're often anxious for revolution in faraway lands. We watch from the comfort of our tranquil lives as the "beauty" of democracy unfolds thousands of miles away, but at what price to those in the middle of violent revolution, and to what final result?

The people in these places have the same goal as we once did, tranquility, economic prosperity, and liberty. Given the choice between the economic success and peacefulness of Singapore's non-democratic system and the failures of many democratic nations, most people in the world would chose the Asian Tiger system. And now given the success of China, many would choose the Chinese system over other alternatives. With the evidence presented, many in the world are now putting economic priority above democracy. They seek tranquility over the right to vote, speak their mind, or march in the streets. They see hopeful revolutions quickly followed by chaos that correctly causes them to question the Western priority of democracy.

While we may think that dissident activities on Facebook and Twitter can be the sparks of a great democratic revolution, what if they're the sparks of 30 years of civil unrest? What if they're the beginning of years of economic stagnation as fighting democratic factions lock up the system with unending debate and dysfunction? Twitter and Facebook took great pride as they teamed up to provide dissidents in Egypt the tools to start their democratic revolution, but what do we hear from the founders of Twitter and Facebook now that democracy has at least initially failed in Egypt? Quick to take credit if things work out, but fast to disappear when they don't, the West has little personal risk when agitating the stability of other societies.

Selective Pressure

In our eagerness to spread democracy throughout the world, we put pressure on select non-democratic countries like China, leaving countries like Saudi Arabia, Singapore, and Taiwan unmentioned. But if China heeded our advice and submitted to our pressure, and a social media movement turned into a revolution, which turned into a civil war, which destroyed all tranquility and eliminated the economic progress which has been made over the last thirty years, who among us will step up to take responsibility for our actions or the actions of our government?

As much as we may want there to be a correlation between democracy and prosperity, the correlation is weak at best. There have been democratic successes and democratic failures. There have been autocratic successes and autocratic failures. Instead of fighting for democracy, we should be fighting for an improved standard of living that can only come from economic prosperity and tranquility. If other systems can compete with democracy in advancing these true goals, why do we fight so hard for a philosophical position, a method whose track record is questionable?

Non-Democratic China

It was a major breakthrough for China when Deng Xiaoping recognized that the communist economic model may not be perfect or infallible. When he gave us the Black Cat-White Cat illustration the breakthrough had been made, causing the focus to be shifted from the method (communism) to the results (economic prosperity). Deng was truly ready to look at alternatives and pursue any path that might lead to advancement. It will also be a breakthrough when the West has the same moment of clarity regarding democracy—when attention is redirected from the method (democracy) to the results in pursuit of economic prosperity, advances in true human rights and improved tranquility.

China has evolved dramatically over the last thirty years. They've learned from the success of America and Europe, as well as the Asian Tigers. They've learned from the failures of non-democratic states as well as the failures of democracies. And they've learned much from their own experiences.[85]

Non-democratic rule in China is not a threat to the U.S. because

China does not seek to impose their system upon us. China has been true to their claim of not involving themselves in the internal affairs of other countries. They don't seek to export their system. If our concern is for the welfare of the Chinese people, we'd better examine the progress that has been made in China compared to the progress in democratic places such as India, Iraq, Thailand, as well as the many struggling African democracies. We should study the successes and the failures of each system before we assume democracy will improve the lives of the average citizen of China more than their current system.

While we may not want to jettison our democratic system for the meritocracy of China, what evidence do we have that our system would provide better results for China? And by what right would we be prepared to incite and enable factions to pursue an alternate system that could result in the destruction of the stability and progress that has been the last thirty years of China? As we've seen, democracy has its advantages, but it also has its shortcomings.

If we shouldn't fear China's non-democratic system, then what should we fear? It's possible that we should fear our persistent belief that democracy is the only solution. We should fear our attempts to force democracy on every nation and the violence, destruction, and instability that too often is the result of these efforts. It might be reasonable to fear that our blind faith in a system, without thoughtful consideration and periodic review, will cause our nation to have a disastrous foreign policy as we go around the globe initiating wars and destabilizing nations, all in the name of democracy.

Our concern about democracy should be that given its known weaknesses (majority rule, special interest rule, selection not based on competency, voting into bankruptcy), what mechanisms are built-in that will guide it to evolve, improve, and reduce or eliminate these deficiencies, which were pointed out over two thousand years ago by the Greek philosophers and by many others since? Is our system gradually ridding itself of these identified pests, or is it simply becoming more evident that they exist? The Chinese system is evolving and changing in pursuit of end goals. Is democracy doing the same? Is it evolving and improving, or is it rigid and fixed?

Under any circumstances it's exceptionally difficult to establish a political system that delivers constant improvements in the goals stated by our founding fathers: Justice, Tranquility, Defense, General

Welfare and Liberty. Our hope for China and its people should be the continued improvements in achieving these goals. The methods they use to accomplish these goals, while different from ours, aren't a threat to us. To fear China's non-democratic rule is of no value. Furthermore, when those fears cause us to exert influence both in soft and hard power in the pursuit of making China a democracy like ours, it's that pursuit that should be our biggest fear because it threatens to destabilize their success as well as to damage our relationship with China.

If the Pew Research poll tells us that 87 percent of the Chinese are pleased with the way things are going in China, and that poll tells us that only 33 percent of Americans are pleased with the way things are going in the U.S., are we sure we want to force our system of democracy on them? Or is there benefit to allowing each society to make its own path?

But democracy is a human right.

Are you sure?

Let's explore the human rights issues in China, including democracy.

13

Fearing China's Human Rights Condition

U.S. Report Says Human Rights Worsen in China (USA Today)
China's Human Rights Record, 'Worst in Decades' (The Telegraph)
Biden Criticizes China on Media, Human Rights (Wall Street Journal)
Trial Begins Next Week for Human Rights Activist in China (New York Times)
China's Human Rights Abuses Demand a Tougher U.S. Approach (Wash. Post)
White House Blasts China on Human Rights Ahead of APEC Summit
(Wash. Post)[86]

Three Types of Human Rights

Following the atrocities of WWII, nations endeavored to work together towards a more peaceful world that would improve the lives of all. The United Nations Declaration of Human Rights was adopted by the General Assembly in 1948 with the specific purpose of identifying and advancing human rights. The rights identified in the declaration can be broken down into three types.

The first type is the right to be free of abusive action by others such as: slavery, genocide, war, inhumane treatment, or punishment. These are the most brutal of violations where one takes abusive action against another. The second type of human rights identified by the U.N. is the right to goods and services such as: the right to food, clothing, shelter, education, and medical care. The third type of human rights identified by the U.N. is the right to take individual action such as: reproductive rights, the right to have and express opinions either privately or publicly through media, the right to freedom of assembly and association, and the right to elect leaders through democratic elections.

#1	#2	#3
Freedom from Abuse	Right to Sustenance	Right to Take Action
Genocide	*Food*	*Reproductive*
War	*Shelter*	*Freedom of Speech*
Slavery	*Healthcare*	*Freedom of Assembly*
Torture	*Education*	*Right to Vote*

#1 Right to Be Free of Abusive Action by Others

Slavery

Abusive action by others includes modern-day slavery in the form of forced labor, child-brides, and sex trafficking. The *Walk Free Foundation* monitors and reports on modern-day slavery, and while definitions can vary and true data is difficult to acquire, their report places China at number 84, right in the middle of the 160 countries in the report. The report lists China as having an estimated 22 people per thousand in some form of modern-day slavery. This places them in the company of such countries as Chile, the United Arab Emirates, Saudi Arabia, Kuwait, and the Dominican Republic, with estimated enslavements of between 20 and 23 persons per thousand. The index places China performing much better than places like Peru at 27 per thousand, and Russia, Poland, Hungary and the Czech Republic all at an estimated 36 per thousand in some form of slavery. India, the only country with a population similar to China, had a dismal estimated 113 persons per thousand—over one in ten in some form of enslavement. While the Chinese 22 per thousand is not great, it should be kept in perspective. Critique and condemnation of China's record should be equal to critique of Chile, the UAE, Saudi Arabia, and others in the same range. Countries such as Russia, India, and others with much worse records should be condemned and pressured more on the issue of modern-day slavery. The goal of course is zero; as per the report, the U.S. had an estimated two per thousand. This either tells us something about the U.S. or something about the report.

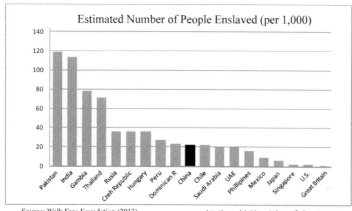

Estimated Number of People Enslaved (per 1,000)

Source: Walk Free Foundation (2013)   http://www.globalslaveryindex.org/findings/#overview

Suppression of Political Opposition

In this first human rights category of abuses of one upon another, the area of abuse of political opponents is the one that China is most often accused of. The structure of one party rule with a prohibition on political opposition which results in the strategic elimination of political opponents has been (and continues to be) a common practice throughout the world. If we're to criticize and condemn China on this issue, we must equally criticize and condemn a large list of nations, including every monarchy in the Arab world including: Saudi Arabia, Jordan, Kuwait, the UAE, and others. We must also condemn Singapore, Taiwan, and South Korea, and many others who have pursued one party or dictatorial rule by eliminating all opposition. The list of countries that aggressively eliminate or marginalize political opponents may in fact be longer than the list of those countries who don't practice this. No political philosophy has had a monopoly on the elimination of opposition. At the same time that Mao was aggressively eliminating anti-communists from China, in Taiwan Chiang Kai-shek (backed by the U.S. government) was just as aggressively eliminating, yes killing, the opposition anti-capitalists. Over time, most one party states have softened their approach; most simply imprison political opposition instead of killing, this has resulted in less condemnation from the world community. However, this softening usually occurs after full control has been achieved.

Genocide

The U.N. Declaration of Human Rights states that "Everyone has the right to life, liberty and security of person." The most egregious abuse of action by one upon another is genocide. In WWII the Nazis attempted to exterminate the Jews, and more recently in the African country of Rwanda the government attempted to eliminate the Tutsi population, killing over 800,000 men, women and children—two bloody and brutal examples of genocide.

War

If human rights includes a right to life, liberty, and security of person, then any act of war where one army or group attacks another must be thought of as a human rights violation. In the middle of war, life is threatened and taken, all are deprived of liberty, and there is no security. No matter what the justification or reasoning there is for declaring war, war itself is an attack on human rights. While the allied actions to stop the expansion of Germany and Japan are a notable exception, it's rare that the atrocities of war are lesser than the wrongs they seek to right.

It's reported that Saddam Hussein killed and tortured thousands, including 5,000 Kurds in 1988, in order to maintain his political leadership as well as the political and legal structure of Iraq. While estimates vary widely, the Iraq war started by the U.S. and its allies has resulted in the death of at least 200 thousand. When factoring in the increased lawlessness as well as the continuing conflict, estimates are as high as one million deaths caused by the U.S. initiated war in Iraq. While the U.S. keeps very close count of every Chinese dissident detained, we don't have an official estimate of the number of lives lost in the Iraq war. The military states that they don't count "enemy combatants." But if the purpose of sending hundreds of thousands of troops to Iraq is in ultimate pursuit of human rights, then the U.S. should count every life lost as a result of the war because death by violent act is the ultimate human rights abuse.

While one party rule and dictators often deprive individuals of life, liberty, and security for the purpose of maintaining their rule and their political system, many wars initiated by the U.S. and their allies have deprived individuals of these very same rights for the purpose of forcing a different leadership and a different political system. Which is more brutal, killing to maintain or killing to change? For those on the losing end of a gun, it doesn't make a difference. When President Bush went into Iraq he said, "You are either for us or you are against us." In the most clear and stark terms, this clarifies that there is no room for opposition. Those who oppose the plan of the invading army are called the enemy and are removed. If we're to condemn those who kill to maintain power and political systems, wouldn't it be reasonable to also condemn those who kill to change power and political systems?

China hasn't had war on its soil for over sixty years, nor has it instigated a foreign war in centuries. Enslavement is moderate, and genocide has not occurred. In this first category of human rights defined by genocide, war, slavery and torture, by world standards, China actually scores very high.

#2 Right to Sustenance

The second type of right identified by the U.N. Declaration is the right to sustenance, including the right to food, shelter, medical care, education, and work. These rights are, and have always been, highly supported by the Chinese government. The People's Republic of China (PRC) was founded as a communist government in 1949. As such, an improved standard of living has been and continues to be the goal and foundation of the Chinese government, although economic missteps early in the PRC under Mao made it difficult and often impossible to provide these things to the people. Past failures have not been failures of intent but failures in strategy and ability.

If we look at the results, we can observe that over the last thirty years over 300 million Chinese people have been brought out of poverty. This indicates dramatic improvements in the availability of food, shelter, medical care, and education as China makes rapid advancements in this second type of human rights.

Food

Under Mao's Great Leap Forward (1958-1961), China experienced the Great Chinese Famine, which they call The Difficult Three Year Period. Agricultural collectivization, which prohibited private ownership of farms, along with natural droughts, caused the starvation of an estimated 15 to 40 million people. Policy mistakes were the main cause of the starvation because collectivization proved inefficient. The forced use of unproven farming techniques caused yields to be dramatically reduced. Reforms since Deng Xiaoping have since corrected the policy flaws of the past, and food production has increased dramatically. In addition to improved agricultural output, reduced population growth contributed to improved conditions. The growth in exports, however, has been the largest stabilizing factor in China's ability to ensure food supply. By manufacturing and exporting, China is able to acquire buying power to import food from around the world.

Shelter

From Deli, India to San Palo, Brazil, most major cities in emerging economies are filled with slums as migration brings the rural population to the urban centers. However, in China this type of slum is hard to find. While China does have challenges in facilitating mass migration to large coastal cities, it's more common to have many people sharing a simple dwelling with running water and electricity than to have individuals building tin huts with dirt floors on the outskirts of a city.

Search the Internet for "ghost cities China" and you'll find an amazing amount of concern from the West about the oversupply of residential and commercial buildings in China. A massive building boom over the last twenty years has resulted in millions of square meters of as of yet to be filled high-rises, both residential and commercial. Speculation from the West predicts adverse consequences of such oversupply, and seeks to analyze the "error" that China has made in allowing such a building boom. However, we should consider the possibility that this hasn't been an error, but is an intentional strategy designed to leverage the unique economic growth pattern of China.

As China blasts its way into the modern world, wages for factory workers and other low wage earners are doubling every four or five years. The largest costs in construction are materials and labor. If China is able to build residential and commercial structures with emerging market labor rates, there's a huge advantage there. Even if the buildings sit vacant for ten or more years, they'll eventually be sold as increasing wages provide income to the emerging middle class. The strategy of intentional temporary oversupply is advantageous because it leverages the low labor rates of an emerging market to supply a soon to be first world nation.

This provides jobs, creates needed infrastructure, and in the end provides homes, offices, high-speed rail, and roads to the citizens of China. The alternative would be to wait until the new urban class becomes middle class then build the structures, but due to rising labor rates the construction would cost possibly ten times more, and the lack of construction activity would slow the economic growth that could propel more into the middle class. For example, consider that you're given the opportunity to build a house now for $50,000 or build it in ten years for $300,000, and that you have a reasonable guarantee that your income will rise in ten years so that it's sufficient to pay for a $300,000 house. If you are able to construct the house at the lower $50,000 price, it would save you a great amount and would be an easy decision. The critique is that the new units are too expensive to be purchased by the average Chinese, but China is constructing for future demand, not current.

While dwelling conditions aren't perfect in China, their plan is providing better than most emerging markets and they are truly building for the future. In the area of housing, China is outperforming its peers dramatically. It's most probable that in twenty years other emerging economies will still be struggling with sewage filled slums while the Chinese middle class is enjoying their first world accommodations. The west applies the common supply and demand formula while China applies a supply and future demand formula—it's only oversupply if you are measuring current demand. But if one considers future demand, the construction boom is not only correct, but highly beneficial to the future of China.

Education

In this second type of human right, the U.N. declaration includes education as a fundamental right. The literacy rate in China is 95 percent; this is a higher rate than India (74.4 percent) and Brazil (91.3 percent) which indicates success in broad education at the primary levels. In the 1980s China made many changes to their education system, abolishing government funded higher education which required students to compete for admissions and scholarships. China also began to allow private schools, which quickly increased the supply of educational options and introduced competition between those providing education. With the example set by Deng Xiaoping, educational administrators aren't concerned whether the cat is black or white, but whether it catches mice. Because they aren't tied to an ideology, they can act strategically and experimentally to find the methods that provide the best results in education. In Shanghai, high performing schools are matched with low performing schools. The high performing school works closely with the low performing school, sending teams of administrators and teachers to evaluate and improve the lower performing schools. Observing class rooms, evaluating curriculum, and teaching teachers, the high performers work to bring the low performing schools up to the highest standards. While the U.S. has "No Child Left Behind," China is working on an approach of "No School Left Behind." Competition between schools is part of the success; cooperation and mutual goals is a bigger part of the strategy.

The progress isn't only due to astute strategy by administrators, but is also advanced by supportive parents and students eager to learn. The Chinese system encourages and leverages the internal drive of students, which is often the missing factor in many first world schools.

The Program for International Student Assessment (PISA) is a test that measures the reading, mathematics, and science literacy of 15-year-olds around the world. The 2012 test results placed the students of Shanghai, China number one among all international cities. They beat every first world country including the U.S., Great Britain, and Germany. While change cannot happen overnight, the government is working actively to expand the educational successes of the coastal cities into the rural west. At the 20th High School in Dalian, China hung a banner that read: "A nation's future is determined not on the battlefield but rather in every classroom." In the human right to education, China is outperforming all of its peers and many first world nations.

Healthcare

In the area of healthcare, China has an average life expectancy of 74, which is only slightly behind that of first world countries. In China, from 1991 to 2010 the infant mortality rate dropped from 50 per thousand to 12 per thousand. As China continues to improve its medical care, infant mortality rates rapidly decline, and if they continue the trend, they'll be at first world rates within ten years.[87]

The New Rural Co-operative Medical Care System (NRCMCS), instituted in China in 2005, has the intent of bringing health care to the rural areas of China. In this system, the central government pays 40 percent of the cost, the provincial government pays 40 percent, and the patient pays 20 percent. As with many areas of Chinese advancement, China's healthcare moves in an experimental and rapid pace with a focus on results.

―――――――

China's progress in this sustenance category, the second type of human rights, has been astounding. The food supply has been increasing rapidly. Food stability is improving, and the variety on the market shelves is quickly becoming equal to the first world. The construction boom is providing housing not only for current needs, but is positioned to provide for the future as more and more Chinese move from the farms to the cities. And for the most part, China avoids the problems of typical emerging market slums as found in India and Brazil. In education, China moves with admirable intent and strategy, with Shanghai outperforming all Western cities, and rural classrooms making rapid improvements. Healthcare in China continues to improve quickly—life expectancy is on the increase and child mortality rates have improved. China's ultimate goal is universal healthcare coverage.

In this second category of human rights, the rapid advancements in providing food, shelter, education, and medical care is not often criticized by the West because China has performed better than all other emerging economies. Over the last two decades, world poverty has been dramatically reduced, and China's economic development is the reason. In our second category of human rights, China has led the way.

#3 Right to Take Action

In review of the first two types of human rights identified by the U.N., the right to be free from abuses and the right to sustenance, China measures very well, as those rights are consistent with the values of China. It is the third type of human rights for which China is most criticized. This type guarantees: the individual's right to take action in the areas of reproductive rights, freedom of speech, freedom of assembly, and the right to vote. The reason China does not excel in this third type of human rights identified by the U.N. declaration is that these rights are the most Western of values, and are not priorities of Chinese socialism.

Reproductive rights

In 1978 the Chinese government observed many countries around the world growing themselves into starvation and poverty. Both India and China were growing so rapidly in population that efforts by the government to improve the people's standard of living were challenged or cancelled out by population growth. Seeing great difficulty in feeding the growing population, China instituted the one-child policy. Singapore implemented plans to slow population growth in the late sixties with a "Stop at Two" program. The Singapore population controls were much more discriminating in that they worked to slow the population growth of poor, un-educated families. The Singapore policy was later revised to "Have Three or More if You Can Afford it." The Chinese program focused on the big cities regardless of economic status while allowing rural farm families to be exempt from the policies; if anything this policy showed discrimination in favor of the poor, not against them. The Chinese policies also exempted many minority groups, again showing favor towards disadvantaged groups.

The one-child policy is often brought up as an abuse of human rights. However, consider that the policy has contributed greatly to the prosperity of the Chinese people; it has slowed the growth of children born into poverty and has therefore placed China in a much better position to feed, shelter, educate, and provide medical services to its large population. While it may go against Western thinking, is it any more humane to allow people to have children they can't provide for, who will live in abject poverty and who face pre-mature death, or to limit the reproductive choices of individuals? In Africa and India, one of the roots of poverty is the high birth rate, in particular children born to parents who have no capacity to provide for their offspring. While the West argues for the reproductive rights of the individual with little consideration for its effect on the whole, the Chinese system places limits on the rights of the individual for the betterment of the whole. China may argue that the damage to the human rights of the whole by allowing unlimited reproductive rights is worse than the damage of putting restrictions on the individual. If unlimited population growth makes it impossible to accomplish the human rights of access to food, shelter, medical care and education, then a choice must be made—one of the human rights must be demoted or even removed from the list. While it's not consistent with the Western ideal of placing the rights of the individual above the group, the one-child policy is consistent with the Chinese ideal of placing the rights of the whole above the rights of the individual. Because population growth does affect the society as a whole, China wouldn't accept unlimited individual reproductive rights as a universal human right, and that decision has ultimately been of benefit to the people of China.

Freedom of speech and assembly

An Amnesty International article reads: "Three anti-corruption activists have been imprisoned today simply for exercising their freedom of expression and assembly." While the West insists that unlimited freedom of speech and assembly are human rights that should be guaranteed to all, China doesn't recognize these as universal human rights. As in all one party governments and authoritarian rule such as the Gulf region kingdoms and until recently the Asian Tigers, freedom of speech and assembly are restricted, especially where they threaten the government or tranquility of society. Even though the Chinese constitution adopted in 1982 Article #35 states that: "Citizens of the People's Republic of China enjoy freedom of speech, of the press, of assembly, of association, of procession and of demonstration," these rights are preempted by article one which reads, in part: "Sabotage of the socialist system by any organization or individual is prohibited." Thus, while there is a certain amount of freedom of speech and assembly, it's limited specifically to the point where it threatens the tranquility of society or the structure of the state.

While limits to freedom of speech and assembly in China may appear to be random, what one finds is that the criteria is fairly consistent. By asking four questions, we can often predict if the speech or assembly will be prohibited.

1: Is the speech or assembly disrupting the tranquility of the general public?

2: Is there intent to ultimately remove or destabilize the government?

3: Does the speech or assembly have the potential to incite the public to disrupt tranquility or attempt to destabilize the government?

4: Is an individual or group gaining a large following which ultimately could be used against the government or for political opposition?

In 2014 one thousand people gathered to protest the building of a petrochemical plant in Maoming, a city in southern China. The protest was allowed up until the protesters became violent and disruptive. When the protesters began burning cars and causing a major disturbance to the tranquility of the neighborhood, authorities brought the protest to an end. The Chinese government was listening and has in fact responded to protester's concerns about the establishment of the chemical plant. However, once the protesters turned violent, their rights to free speech and assembly were removed. The protesters broke the first rule; the tranquility of the public was definitely disrupted.

In 2012 a young man in China was sentenced to eight years in prison for attempting to form an opposition party. He broke the second rule—his ultimate goal was to remove the government.

A dissident artist became known for his confrontational writing against the government. He continually pointed out flaws in government management and his writing began to alert many to dysfunctions in the government. From his influence, people began to take notice of the issues and began to perpetuate his discontent. The third rule was broken, as he incited the public to disrupt the government.

A religious group established in Northeast China in 1992 was estimated to have as many as ten million followers within seven years of its founding. In 1999 ten thousand followers assembled in Beijing to request government recognition of the religion. The sheer number of followers and petitioners gave great concern to the government, which ultimately outlawed the religion. In line with the government's original concerns, the group has since worked to advocate the end of the Communist Party rule. The fourth rule was broken—this group with a large following had as its aim political opposition.

Religious Freedom

Religious activities have always been a concern of one party rule. In the days of monarchy, there was a strategy of aligning the rulers with religion, as the king and queen could actually use the authority and reach of the church to control their subjects—royalty claimed to be appointed by god. But where religion initiates outside the political rule or becomes unaligned with the state, one party rule can be threatened. It is not the man praying in his home that's the concern, it's massive, organized religion with a central leader at a podium with the ability to stir religious fervor or political fervor that is the issue. When an organization gains membership of millions and is led by a central figure or a common sentiment, it becomes a threat to one party rule. Whether a dissident artist with a large Twitter following or a religion with membership in the millions, any large organization with a common sentiment or central authority is seen as a threat to one party rule. Worshiping in your home—no problem. Ten thousand religious followers assembled in front of a leader—problem. China has freedom of religion; it doesn't have freedom of mass organization because mass organization can be used against the state.

The limits on freedom of speech and assembly, while not one hundred percent consistent throughout the vast nation of China, are fairly straightforward and predictable. Freedom of speech and assembly as well as freedom of religion exist, but they're not unlimited. As with most one party rule governments, if you threaten or promote the overthrow of the ruling party, you go to jail. When media incites discontent, it's quieted. When a Twitter account gains too many followers, it's shut down, and if an organization gains too many members, the threat is identified and the organization prohibited. Counter-revolution is prohibited, and counter-revolution starts with unlimited freedom of speech.

As discussed in the prior chapter on democracy, likewise the right to vote and elect leaders is not a Chinese value.

———

In this third type of human rights identified by the U.N., China scores low because China places the rights of the whole above the rights of the individual. This causes their priority of values to be different than the priorities in the West. When the West discusses China's human rights record, we point to an image of a single man standing defiantly in front of a tank. Is it possible that China sacrifices the voice of one for the lives of millions, while the U.S. sacrifices the lives of millions for the voice of one?

How We Treat China Compared to Others

U.S. leaders and media work diligently to highlight China's human rights record with constant reporting, lecturing, and badgering. The impression Americans receive is that certainly China is the worst in the world when it comes to human rights abuses. Consider the human rights records of China, India, Mexico, and Saudi Arabia. As discussed, China excels in the first two categories, but falls short in the Western values of individual rights. India fails in the first two with slavery, a cast system, and a dismal standard of living, but excels in the third with democracy and freedom of speech and assembly. Mexico, while moderate in all three categories of human rights, lost 130 thousand people in just one year of their drug war. Saudi Arabia ranks moderately in the first two categories, with very low ranking in the third category, as individual freedoms are highly restricted. With these records it's instructive to take a look at how the U.S. addresses these countries on the issue of human rights through our ambassadors.

During the senate confirmation hearings of ambassador to China, U.S. Senator Marco Rubio asked candidate Max Baucas whether or not: "U.S. ambassadors in places like China shall be freedom fighters. Do you agree that the U.S. embassy in China should be an island of freedom and that one of your primary jobs will be demonstrating to China's peaceful advocates of reform and democracy that the U.S. stands firmly with them?" The U.S. senator went on to say: "Our embassy should be viewed as an ally of those in Chinese society that are looking to express their fundamental rights to speak out and to worship freely etc." He continued: "Freedom activists are looking for an advocate and a spokesperson that will stand with them strongly. They look to America to be that."[88]

Gary Locke, former U.S. ambassador to China, in his final speech as ambassador said: "But human rights is more than economic prosperity and the economic conditions of people, but also fundamental universal rights – freedom of speech, freedom of assembly, the ability to practice one's own religion."[89] Although he also admitted there had been improvements in the quality of life and standard of living in China, we can see from his statement where his focus lies.

Hearings to confirm our ambassadors to China are used primarily as platforms to lecture China on human rights, and the ambassadorship is used as a position to support dissidents and keep a spotlight on human rights issues in China.

India's record on human rights is well documented by the organization Human Rights Watch (HRW) and others. HRW reports that India has "significant human rights problems" as they describe discrimination against tribal groups, religious minorities, women, and people with disabilities. The social structure of India is a caste system wherein a person's worth is defined by their ethnic heritage, which is a recipe for human rights abuse. The report cites restrictions on Internet freedoms and a legal system that acts to support abusive practices.[90]

The Asian Centre for Human Rights estimates that in India four people per day die while in police custody, and many of those deaths are due to the use of torture. The armed forces of India have been accused by Amnesty International and Human Rights Watch of extra-judicial executions, disappearances, and torture. Human trafficking has been reported to be a huge problem in India, with potentially tens of millions of women affected—an estimated 113 of every thousand are trapped in some form of slavery.

Given India's record of human rights abuses and the U.S. senate's outspoken position on China's human rights issues during the ambassadors hearing, we can assume the senators were equally eager to use the U.S. embassy in India as "an island of freedom," a place where U.S. values could be advanced and we could give voice to the abused in India. But while India's Human Rights record ranks below China in every category except the third, barely a word was spoken about India's human rights record during the hearing. Senator John Kerry, who was the chairman of the committee, had comments such as: "Without a doubt one of the most significant partnerships." "U.S. and Indian interests and values are converging today."

"Already India is playing a role in clean energy innovation."

When the senators spoke of issues such as human trafficking, they watered down the issue; for example, they said: "also the problem that is not just India's problem but a global problem of human trafficking." When they spoke of poverty in India the comment was: "clearly India is addressing the problem."

Senator Lugar spoke of building a strategic partnership with regards to the concerns about the growing military capability of China, so even the senate confirmation hearing for the ambassador to India was used as a platform to target China. At the senate hearing, the nominee outlined her top priorities as: 1) trade and investment and 2) defense cooperation, as U.S. defense sales to India are eight billion dollars. She concluded by saying: "We will continue U.S. engagement with India to advance human rights and freedoms that are constitutionally protected in both our countries." That's called getting a pass.

Mexico's record on human rights is moderate by world standards, with the largest problems being the murders caused by the drug wars. When senate hearings were held to confirm our ambassador to Mexico, almost nothing was said about human rights. The statement from the nominee James Jones referenced "Friendship and cooperation," and when addressing the drug war he simply said: "Illegal narcotics is a shared problem."

In Saudi Arabia women are subjected to lashings as a punishment for adultery—the accusation of adultery often means they were actually raped. Women are forbidden to drive. Practice of non-Muslim religion is prohibited and public demonstrations banned. The press is controlled by government, and anyone who speaks ill of the country or king is considered a terrorist and can be imprisoned or otherwise punished. Dissent is prohibited, freedom of speech and assembly are denied, and democracy is nowhere in sight.[91]

In a statement by Joseph Westphal, the candidate to be ambassador to Saudi Arabia, his most important point was that: "Saudi Arabia is our largest foreign military sales customer with active and open cases of $96.8 billion." His entire statement had no reference to human rights. When the senators had opportunity to address the human rights issues at the senate hearing held in February of 2014, the senators spoke only lightly of women's rights and rights of reporters. They spoke highly of the leadership of Saudi Arabia and of our "long and enduring partnership." They spoke of the Saudi commitment to political transition in Syria and their support of Egypt's democratic transition, but nothing of the repressive totalitarian dictatorship of Saudi Arabia. Nothing about freedom of speech and assembly, nothing about democracy in Saudi Arabia. This is a country where speaking ill of the king, government, or country is a crime, and the senators said nothing. No senator spoke of the embassy being an island of freedom. Nothing about the ambassador being a freedom fighter. Effectively, the ambassador was sent to Saudi Arabia to promote stability in the region, and to promote the sale of weapons to the king.

We take every opportunity to attack China's human rights record even though it's a nation that has brought hundreds of millions out of poverty and is improving daily. For those with much worse records like India, Mexico, Saudi Arabia, and others, we remain silent. Following the leadership of U.S. politicians, the U.S. media perpetuates this unequal critique. For every article about a silenced dissident in China, an article about the stabilizing effect of our gulf partner Saudi Arabia can be found. For each article about a protest in China, look for an article about the great technology coming out of India. And for each article about China censoring the Internet, look for the article about Mexico's cooperation on our "mutual" drug war "challenge."

The senate hearings for U.S. ambassadors are the most direct example of our highly biased treatment of different nations in our critique of human rights. When your favorite son gets a speeding ticket, you tell him about your first ticket and sympathize with him, telling him it happens to all of us. When your other son gets a speeding ticket, you lecture him endlessly and take away his driving privileges. Our critique of human rights around the world is grossly unjust and destructive to the pursuit of true improvements in human rights.

Western Values

China claims that U.S. attacks on their human rights record are actually attempts to promote Western values and not for the true advancement of human rights. They argue that the West has devolved from addressing human rights abuse to simply abusing the concept of human rights, making "Human Rights" a tool to promote a Western political agenda. Their claim is not without merit; we've observed that most complaints from the West address the third category of human rights—those that are ultimately Western values.

The West lectures China on freedom of speech, assembly, and democracy while ignoring the amazing record of accomplishment in the other two types of human rights. Too often the arguments from the U.S. and Western countries claiming to be advocating for improvements in human rights are actually simply advocating for the Western values of unlimited free speech and democracy, which may or may not improve the lives of the affected or cause improvements in the most critical of human rights. While the West is quick to believe that the reason the Chinese government is controlling these freedoms is to ensure their maintenance of power, it is more likely that Chinese leadership finds that unlimited individual freedoms actually slows or prevents advances in the more important first two categories of human rights. Observing the Asian Tiger one party systems, China may reasonably find that to rapidly advance in the first two categories of human rights, the third category of individual freedoms must be limited.

China may also find an additional threat from these Western values in the possibility of ceding power to the West. They may find unlimited freedom of speech and universal suffrage to be a method for western influence in China. Given the West's expertise in media, marketing, and political campaigning, is it possibly easier for a foreign power to control the "free will" of an electorate than to control a country under non-democratic rule? If you don't think this is a viable concern, consider the bags of cash the CIA gave to Hamid Karzai, the president of Afghanistan, or consider the CIA operation to establish a Twitter like service in Cuba to instigate the citizens of Cuba to revolt against their leadership.

The Chinese government and many of the Chinese people remain suspicious of the motives of the U.S. and our prioritization of democracy over other human rights. They see hundreds of thousands killed in the name of democracy and question whether true human rights are served by these Western values. The West's confidence in the superiority of democracy over the current Chinese system is rightfully suspicious to many in China. China has experienced many violent wars in its history, and has recently been enjoying a period of peace and prosperity. While the West may want and even encourage the overthrow of the government by its people using any means necessary, the Chinese government works to avoid civil unrest and drives the country toward rapid improvements in standard of living. Ignoring the West's advice to go democratic, they continue to progress towards prosperity even as they limit individual freedoms.

In the West, freedom of speech, whether for an individual, organization, media outlet, or social media platform, is the tool for change. A group advocating for change builds their case and acquires as many supporters as possible. With mass assembly, media barrages, slogans, and campaigns, the cause gains supporters and attempts to sway public opinion to their side. The ultimate goal is to force legislators to change the law in their favor. This adversarial approach is played out in media coverage, open debates, courtrooms, and legislatures. The group wanting change from the status quo presses forward, building momentum, and if they can endure, they can ultimately exhaust the opposition and prevail. While sometimes it's rational debate that resolves issues, often it's simply the loudest and most persistent group that prevails. In China, this adversarial method is avoided by limiting certain freedoms of speech and assembly. Decisions are made most often in the same manner as our modern corporations. The head of the organization listens to expert advice, reviews polls and data, analyzes the options, and makes the final decision. Merit of the argument and tested results are the preferred determining factors. In many ways the Chinese limits on free speech are a rejection of the Western adversarial method of decision making in pursuit of a more executive and corporate method. Tyranny of the loud, well organized, or well financed is denied, and the gridlock caused by opposing parties is not accepted. Where the West sees abuse of human rights when unlimited freedom of speech and assembly are prevented, China sees human rights violations when unlimited freedom of speech and assembly slow or prevent the rapid advancement of the other areas of human rights.

Freedom of speech and assembly are the foundation of Western style democracy. Western advocates for greater freedom of speech and assembly in China are ultimately advocates for democracy, and advocates for democracy are advocates for removing the Communist

Party from power. Thus, the debate regarding freedom of speech and assembly must actually be a debate with the question posed: Would democracy provide better results than China's current meritocratic political system? Would expanded freedom of speech and assembly, and ultimately universal suffrage, provide a better standard of living for the average Chinese? Would it increase the pace to prosperity? Advocating for unlimited freedom of speech and assembly is, in the end, advocating for the removal of the Chinese government with an unknown replacement. It would seek to replace the systematic, meritocratic process of selecting leaders in China with a democratic roll of the dice.

In its 2013 report on China, the organization Human Rights Watch stated that the decade long rule of Hu Jintao (2002-2012) saw little progress on human rights. However, in that decade, GDP per capita in China more than doubled, which resulted in a true increased standard of living for most Chinese. More citizens had access to food, shelter, medical care, and education as millions were lifted out of poverty. In real dollars, the purchasing power of the average Chinese citizen dramatically improved, child mortality dropped substantially, and education was greatly expanded. For HRW and others to claim that little progress has been made shows that when it comes to human rights, the West doesn't look at the full spectrum of human rights, but instead focuses solely on those rights that promote the Western values of democracy, freedom of speech, and assembly. In that decade, while the U.S. initiated the Iraq and Afghanistan wars, causing the death of hundreds of thousands, there were no wars in China, China didn't start any wars in foreign lands, and China dramatically improved the lives of millions. When focusing on the human rights that truly affect people's lives, the contrast between China's human rights record in that decade can easily compete with that of the U.S.

The Priority of Progress on Standard of Living

The ultimate goal of human rights should be the improvement of the human condition. When we become attached to tools and methods to the determinant of the end goal, we miss opportunities— worse, we cause damage by trying to force our preferred methods. On balance, what have been the results of action by the Chinese government in advancing true human rights? On balance, what have been the results of actions taken by the U.S. in places like Vietnam, Korea, Iraq, and Afghanistan in advancing true human rights?

The Road to Improvement

If there's any nation in the world that can fully understand the long road of redemption from true human rights abuses to true human rights, it's the United States. In the U.S., for over two hundred fifty years a man didn't belong to himself, but was the property of another and subject to any physical or mental abuse, any rape of body or mind. The slave had no recourse, no remuneration, no claim, no rights whatsoever. Our history is undeniable and our human rights progress has been slow. It was only 50 years ago that the U.S. put a stop to Jim Crow laws, which allowed a person to be denied service or forced to a substandard separate service due to the color of their skin.

In the last seventy-five years U.S. instigated wars have caused the death of millions. Guantanamo holds men without trial, the atrocities at Abu Ghraib are a footnote to history, and we hold over two million in our prisons. Even today those in Ferguson Missouri and Baltimore Maryland remind us that there is still much work to be done.

Whether we look back two hundred years or to just last year, our record is troublesome. What right do we have to stand at the podium lecturing and assuming leadership and authority on the issue of human rights when history distant and recent shows we hardly deserve a seat at the table:

Afghanistan War: 50,000 killed
Iraq War: 200,000 – 1,000,000 killed
Vietnam War: over 2,000,000 killed
Korean War: over 2,000,000 killed
Slavery: 1620-1865 unknown number killed. 4 million enslaved

There isn't a place in the world that has not had its abuses, wars, enslavements, and brutality. It is not a question of *if*, it is a question of *when*. We must realize that abuses won't stop overnight, and instead focus on the trend and pace of improvement. Are abuses being identified and actions taken to correct them?

China certainly has had its abuses, as has every nation, but it's critical that we see the tradeoff China has made in prioritizing human rights. Where one type of human right damages another, choices must be made. While the West's mantra may be "Give me liberty or give me death," China's may be "Give me security, peace, and prosperity, and I'll accept some limits on my individual freedoms."

Xi Jinping, the president of China, said that "protecting stability" or avoiding social disorder at all costs, is "in essence protecting human rights." The West may want to shrug off this statement as a diversion from China's human rights record, but the statement by Xi confirms that when it comes to human rights, China prioritizes stability and a continuing improvement in the standard of living over most other rights—most in China seem to agree with this priority.

The danger of our misguided focus on individual freedoms and democracy is that our constant nagging damages our relationship with China. It distracts us from a focus on true human rights abuses around the world. And most importantly, we're missing opportunities for partnerships, mutual pursuits, and benefits. Senators could be working with China to solve energy problems, advance medical technologies, and improve our educational system. The opportunities are endless, and both nations could increase the pace of advancement through mutual cooperation. The cause of human rights might be better served if we focus on true human rights abuses around the world.

If we simply want to rank China on the Western values of freedom of speech and democracy, then we can go ahead and rank them low. But considering the full spectrum of human rights and the importance of each type, China ranks very high compared to others around the word. At a minimum we need to recognize that forcing our Western values on them will have no guarantee of truly improving the full spectrum of human rights in China. And we cannot ignore that the current path they are on continues to improve the lives of millions.

14

The China Tinderbox

The Tinderbox of Slow Reform

We're told that China is a tinderbox waiting for that small spark to ignite a revolution. Analysts warn us of the tinderbox of slow reform, of inequality, of factory conditions, and of corruption. Experts tell us that each of these are coming to a flare up as the inevitable revolt of the Chinese people ignites and they reject their political system, demanding the democratic solutions of the West. But is China really at such a point? Is Chinese society on the edge of a colossal public movement?

Some tell us that the people of China are dissatisfied with the slow pace of reform, but slow compared to what? The current generation is not challenged by lack of change, they're challenged by the rapid pace of change itself, not only economic, but also political. The Communist Party of China changes very swiftly from experimentation to implementation. From the Great Leap Forward to the Cultural Revolution to the Deng Xiaoping years, fast-paced economic and political reform changed every aspect of Chinese government and economic structures. The Chinese constitution is modified not haphazardly, but deliberately, and only when they find opportunities for improvement. Term limits and mandatory retirement ages were introduced in the 1980s, preventing leaders from staying in power too long. At the same time, the leadership was split, giving two leaders different responsibilities. The splitting of roles was intentional in order to prevent one leader from becoming too powerful—it also eliminated the problem of the cult of personality. Today, political reform continues; Xi Jinping takes aggressive action against political corruption and wasteful spending, and he pursues increasing efficiencies to spread prosperity.

In every society there will always be those who are discontent, and there are always groups of radicals pursuing revolutionary change, as seen in the U.S. with the Occupy Wall Street movement, and the recent Occupy movement in Hong Kong. But while there will always be some discontent, in China an observation of the people does not show a large percentage of dissatisfaction. And in fact, the current generation has a better standard of living and more access to the benefits of modern economic society than any generation in the past 200 years. The current generation in China sees their government improving continually. When the West complains that reform hasn't been fast enough, what they are actually observing is that political reform hasn't lead to the Western structure they advocate. It's inaccurate to say that reform has been slow in China—it's only accurate to say that China isn't rapidly reforming towards the Western model. On the contrary, any analysis of the last 30 years of China indicates massive reform in both economic and political structures.

The Tinderbox of Inequality

Westerners hoping for western style political reform in China are quick to remind us that although many have prospered in China, not all have participated in the economic advancement, and that there's a growing disparity between rich and poor. However, every society has rich and poor, and often the gap between rich and poor is an unfortunate focus of attention. Deng Xiaoping recognized that economic growth would be uneven and that some would gain a higher standard of living before others. He specifically noted that economic growth would come to the large coastal cities before it reached the rural lands in the west. In 1991 he visited Pudong, a part of Shanghai, where he advocated rapid development and major construction projects. He was fully aware that development had to start in specific locations.

From the errors of the Great Leap Forward as well as the failures of Russian state planning, he knew that to attempt great change across the entire country at one time wasn't the best solution. Instead, he sought growth from economic centers such as Shanghai and Guanzhou, while ignoring the resulting disparity between rich and poor. Deng was correct; the gap is a dangerous focus, because what truly matters is the size of the middle class and the condition of the poor. The pace of progress, as more are brought out of poverty and enter the middle class, is overwhelmingly more important than monitoring the gap between rich and poor. Trying to ensure that all advance at the same pace will only ensure that there's no advancement.

The rich are always the first to obtain necessities and luxuries in society. Historically, the rural areas of the U.S. lagged behind the wealth of the city dwellers, and to some extent these areas still do. Automobiles were a luxury item only available to the very wealthy before they were accessible to the middle class. Do you remember the first cell phone you saw? Most likely it was not in the hands of a poor person. Now cell phones are accessible to most. The Gini Coefficient measures the gap between rich and poor, and it indicates that China's discrepancy between rich and poor is very close to that of the U.S. The tinderbox of the income gap is a hope of Western agitators wishing to impose Western political systems on China. Ignoring the gap between rich and poor and focusing on the progress of the poor and middle class has been a key to economic growth in China—a key that Deng Xiaoping was fortunate to find.

The Tinderbox of Factory Conditions

But what about the sweatshop conditions of the Chinese factories, and the "poor" conditions and treatment of the factory workers? That must be a tinderbox waiting for a spark. If we compare the working conditions of a factory worker in China with that of a factory worker in the U.S., yes, on par the U.S. worker has more comfortable working conditions, labor saving tools, higher safety standards, higher pay, and better benefits. However, to compare developed, first world conditions to those of an emerging economy is useless. While the utopian dream may be to snap one's fingers and have a perfect world overnight, what's realistic is continued improvement, which China is already accomplishing.

The factories of China range from the mega factories of Foxconn, which supply companies like Apple, to the small shops found scattered around the growing cities off the coast. The conditions at the large factories are typically better because they're often monitored by Western companies, which insist on higher safety standards and better working conditions. The smaller factories, which are often more rustic, typically lag behind in standards and working conditions.

Why would a young worker choose to take a position in a factory with difficult working conditions, long hours, and no air conditioning in the heat of summer? The answer is simple—it's a step up from the other opportunities available in his hometown. Many of the factory workers are young people who have come from the rural farming areas of western and central China. Their parents labor hard to cultivate small farms with a minimum of modern farming tools and technologies. If you observe a woman using a hand tool to dig trenches for planting rice, then laboring under the heat to plant each rice stock, it quickly becomes clear why the young are anxious to leave the manual farming life and head for the factories. The factories provide much higher wages, many have reasonable working conditions, and they're typically a stepping-stone for moving up the value chain. This transition has taken place in every developed country. In the U.S. it happened at the turn of the 20th century as many workers left the agricultural life for work in the big cities.

In every factory from Beijing to Guangzhou to Chongqing, there will be some happy and some less so. Although conditions aren't perfect and there may be pockets of discontent, most workers are looking towards their own future and advancement and not waiting for the conditions at their factory to change. And while they look to their own future, the factory conditions actually *are* changing. The Chinese government continues to improve factory conditions with constantly improving labor laws that stipulate minimum wage, overtime pay for hours worked over 40, and holiday pay. Safety standards continue to improve and workers rights have progressed. In 2000, the average pay for a factory worker in China was $0.50 per hour, and by 2013 it had quadrupled in real dollars to

$2.00 per hour. While these wages pale in comparison to Western pay, they represent a true and dramatic increase in pay for a factory worker over the last decade.

Are the factory conditions in China a tinderbox ripe for revolution? The answer is no. Even in the U.S., UK, and France, nations with the strongest labor rights and best benefits in the world, there's often labor discontent as workers strike or otherwise protest for improved conditions or pay. But, like the West, China's pockets of labor discontent are not widespread, and they're not a tinderbox waiting for a spark.

The Tinderbox of Corruption

We're told that corruption of the political elite is the tinderbox causing the people of China to prepare for revolt, but again, this isn't true. While the people of China are concerned about corruption, they see their president leading the way in reforms to curb corruption and bring those accountable to justice. As discussed prior in the chapter on Ethics, the transition can take time. But as the people experience real progress, the tension is reduced, and we can clearly see that the tinderbox doesn't exist.

Certainly They Talk of Revolution.

*

In a small café in Shanghai I sat sipping my coffee. I watched as the young couple across from me mapped out some type of plan on paper. The conversation started calmly, but quickly became intense. Her posture and tone of voice changed. It was clear he'd taken a position that wasn't acceptable. Was it possible that he supported rapid reform, or was she the one advocating an aggressive approach? He pulled a smart phone from his pocket, brought up some important information, and showed her the screen. She looked intently at the information that supported his position. He took a pen and drew a diagram in the margins of the paper. She studied it and questioned his proposal, pointing to each element. She took the pen from him and briskly modified his illustration. Taking caution so as not to reveal their potentially revolutionary plans I asked in a quiet tone, "Do you speak English?" "Yes, a little," the man said, looking up. "I know it's not my business, but may I ask what your topic of discussion is?" A big smile came to his face. "Our home. We're planning the decorating of our new home." I dug further into their plans. "So you're doing some remodeling?" "Yes, and my wife and I have some differences in ideas about the design." She looked at me with a smile, amused at my curiosity.

*

In Ningbo, a large city just south of Shanghai, those teenagers texting on their smart phones aren't coordinating a revolution, they're chatting about the new dress they just bought at the mall, or making plans for which movie they'll see that evening. A group of college students study together at the local restaurant working hard to prepare for next week's exam. They hop on the most modern of subway systems and race off to their preferred destinations with the swipe of a magnetic card. Professionals walk confidently to their office, pursuing careers that their parents and grandparents could have never imagined. On a Sunday afternoon in Beijing, proud parents step onto a small boat with their children—they opt for a little electric boat that'll propel them around the lake instead of the foot-propelled boats the energetic teens often choose. They dance in the parks that once were reserved for royalty and gather to play instruments and sing songs passed on from generations. The drab gray clothing of the past has exploded into bright and trendy fashion. Little girls in Shanghai dress like princesses and enjoy the parks and malls that are held to first world country standards. While every society has its discontent, by and large the people of China are working hard to improve their own lives. With a casual eye on the continued reforms in their government and their economy, they don't speak of revolution, they speak of continually improving their lives and the lives of their children.

Their Place in History

Consider a child born in China in the year 2000. Now in her teens, she observes the world around her and ponders her options, her career, her future. Her parents have found increasing stability with the leadership of Deng Xiaoping; they've lived through the greatest economic expansion in China's history. They've navigated their careers and economic choices in a rapidly changing environment, experiencing personal income growth and a continued improvement in standard of living.

Her grandparents were born around the time that the Japanese were defeated in WWII and the Chinese civil war was coming to an end. They lived through the famine and difficulties of the Great Leap Forward, where millions starved due to failed economic policies, only to be followed by the catastrophe of the Cultural Revolution.

Her great grandparents were born about the time Japan was invading China. They suffered the atrocities of the Japanese invasion and the brutal conditions in Nanking and throughout the country; they endured this suffering which was only to be followed by civil war between the Nationalists and the Communists. Towards the end of her great grandparent's life, they experienced the pain of the Great Leap Forward as they fought to feed and shelter their family.

The prior generation experienced the civil war and chaos of the post dynasty warlord era, and her ancestors prior to that were disrupted by the Boxer rebellion and the Taiping rebellion—one of the deadliest civil wars in history. The generation prior to that suffered through the Opium Wars.

To think that the current generation suffers under conditions which will ignite a tinderbox fails to take into consideration the history of China and the current unprecedented era of economic growth, prosperity, and tranquilly that began in the early 1980s. While American youth can be complacent in their advantages, the youth of China, having connection to the difficult histories of their grandparents, great grandparents, and prior generations, are for the most part aware of their place in history. They see great opportunities that the fortune of being born at the right time has brought to them. Aware that prior generations were held back by misfortune, whether from an invading foreign army or poor choices by leaders, the current generation is embracing the grand opportunity of their times. The tinderbox is a fiction of the West and a hope of those who wish to force Western systems on China, seeking to plant seeds of discontent and agitate the masses.

Western politicians often say that improvement is not just about economic conditions, but for those who have starved or been brutalized by war, tranquility and economic conditions are much more important than any particular political ideological belief. Those who think otherwise come from lands where food and tranquilly have been plentiful for generations. A 2014 survey by Pew Research asked the question: "Are you satisfied or dissatisfied with the way things are going in your country?" Of the 44 countries surveyed, China didn't just rank high on the survey, China ranked number one. A staggering 87% of the Chinese surveyed said they were satisfied with the way things were going in their country. No other country had a higher satisfaction rating.[93]

While some exuberant youth and others in China may buy into the propositions given by Western agitators, when their parents and grandparents remind them of the troubled past, the stable present, and the promising future, those with broader perspectives seek to support the current pace of reform. And they reject the proposal of a disruptive revolution. Most in China would prefer to stay on the current path, which is giving hope to a continued China Dream, while rejecting those who'd seek to light the match of a destructive radical revolution. A Chinese tinderbox should not be feared, because it does not exist.

15

Fearing China as a Super Power

Is the West Losing Out To China in Africa? (CNN)
China's Newest Sphere of Influence (Wall Street Journal)
Round Two in America's Battle for Asian Influence (Financial Times)
China Moves to Marginalize U.S. Influence in Pakistan (CBS News)
China Influence in Panama a U.S. Threat? (Christian Broadcasting News)
What the AIIB Means for the US-China Power Transition (The Diplomat)
Xi Flies to Mexico as China Battles US for Influence in Latin America'
ASSEAN Summit 2013 Sees U.S., China Compete For Influence In Asia
'(Globalpost.com) (Huffington Post)[94]

100 Years of Influence

For over 100 years the U.S. has been the most powerful and influential nation in the world. Its dominance in military, economics, politics, technology, and media has made it a true superpower. The U.S. Military budget is equal to the combined military budgets of the next seven largest nations. Not only does the U.S. have the largest GDP, but the U.S. banking system is the center of world financial transactions, and the U.S. dollar is used as the world's currency of exchange and trade.

The political influence of the U.S. is driven by its financial and military power. In WWII the U.S. military and financial resources allowed the U.S. to determine the fate of millions of people. At the end of WWII, the U.S. defined borders and promoted or established political leadership and structures in countries around the world. Even today, it's often the U.S. that decides who, what, when, where, why, and how. Whether it be denying a country economic ties to the rest of the world as it did with South Africa to force the end of apartheid; the use of military force to end a dictator's reign in Iraq or force out a government in Afghanistan; or the covert operations of the CIA supporting a military coup as happened in Chile 1973; the

U.S., whether by economic denial of access, covert operations, or brute military force, often defines borders, removes or installs governments or political leaders, and institutes legal, economic, and political systems around the world. Partly since WWI but certainly since WWII, the U.S. has had the power and influence to define the world. And while not always successful, the U.S. has not been timid in using that power and influence.

The Power of Innovation

In addition to influence by military and economic power, the U.S. has been the leader in technology for over a century. The late 19th and early 20th century saw innovators like Edison, Tesla, Ford, Rockefeller, Carnegie, Morgan, and the Wright Brothers change the world with products, processes, and business innovations. The innovation continues even today with leaders in technology like Steve Jobs of Apple, Robert Noyce, who led the invention of the micro chip, Martin Cooper, inventor of the cell phone, and countless others.

From the U.S. came inventions like AC electricity, light bulbs, the phonograph, television, GPS, microchips, computers, telephones, cell phone, mass produced automobiles, airplanes, refrigerators, air conditioning, digital cameras, motion pictures, the credit card, birth control pills, software like spreadsheets and word processors, the Internet, modems, the computer mouse, and thousands of other world changing inventions. Changes in business models have also had a large influence on the world, from consumer product companies like Proctor & Gamble and Hershey to franchise chains like McDonald's and Starbucks to the big box stores like Walmart and Home Depot.

As U.S. inventions spread throughout the world, the world is influenced and changed. Tesla's AC electricity and Edison's light bulb changed the world dramatically in a short period of time. Airplanes cut travel time between faraway lands from days to hours. The cell phone has allowed those who never had access to a telephone to suddenly be connected to anyone anywhere in the world, a U.S. invention that's changed the lives of millions. For many years, the U.S. has been the world's frontrunner in technology and innovation.

The inventions of television and motion pictures gave rise to another U.S. influence—the media. By the 1950s much of the world was directly connected to the U.S. through movies exported around the world. And as TV became common, viewers were exposed to U.S. TV shows and news programs. The saturation of U.S. media greatly influenced the world—it spread Western ideals, culture, and the U.S version of reality. Even in the last twenty years the cultural influence of the U.S. has rapidly grown with the invention of the Internet, which brought us new platforms such as Facebook, Twitter, email, and Web sites providing instant access to information.

While some of the power and influence simply evolves without specific intent, such as the influence of the light bulb, the TV, or the cell phone, other power is wielded with a specific political agenda. Often U.S. presidents and political leaders make decisions about how military, financial, and other powers will be used to affect the course of history. Whether it be the hard powers of military and economics or the soft powers of innovation and media, the U.S. has shaped the world for over 200 years and has truly been the world's superpower.

The Costs and Benefits of being the World's Superpower

As China grows in economic, military, and political power, they threaten our position as the world's only superpower. But what are the true benefits of being the world's superpower, and what are the real costs?

While it's difficult to estimate what our condition would be if we weren't the world's "superpower," we can observe that there are many other nations that have a standard of living comparable to ours without the cost of being the leader. Western European countries like Germany, France, the United Kingdom, and Scandinavian countries as well as Australia and the Asian Tigers have a standard of living comparable to the U.S. As many seek to ensure that the U.S. maintains a leadership role in the world and retains its superpower status, it's rare that we truly analyze the benefit of this status against the cost. To what benefit do we seek to maintain our position as the world's sole superpower?

Often in international conflicts it's said that the U.S. is the only nation with the ability to take action. But this ability is defined by our military expenditures and our willingness to accept responsibility. The U.S. spends four to five percent of GDP on military, while other first world nations typically spend less than two percent.

While the Iraq war was called a coalition, by 2012, 4,486 U.S. military lives had been lost, accounting for 93 percent of the "coalition" casualties. Considering that Europe has roughly the same population as the U.S., calling the Iraq action a coalition isn't accurate. The dollars spent on the war were of the same proportion. U.S. expenditures, while not yet fully counted, easily exceeded $1.5 trillion when factoring in the long term care of the military disabled returning from war. In the Afghanistan war, 67 percent of the casualties were U.S. troops, and the U.S. has paid the vast majority of the cost. The United Nations is composed of 193 member nations with the U.S. representing half of one percent of the total membership, yet the United States pays 22 percent of the general UN budget and 26 percent of the peacekeeping budget, resulting in billions of dollars spent by U.S. tax payers.

The Cost of NATO

Another world organization, NATO, was established after WWII as an agreement between member states. The agreement was that if one member was to be attacked, all NATO members would come to their defense. While NATO has 28 members, the U.S. pays one fifth of the direct NATO budget. However, that isn't the most expensive part of the deal. NATO members are expected to maintain defense expenses of at least two percent of GDP; however, most do not. And when one is attacked, other members are bound by the treaty to volunteer their military to come to their aid. The reality has been more an agreement that if any member state gets into trouble, the U.S. and U.S. tax payers will come to their aid. The U.S. has never been invaded and is virtually unassailable, so for the U.S. to be a part of NATO is effectively to the benefit of European nations that can have access to U.S. military might, but of questionable value to the U.S. When the U.S. was attacked on 9/11, NATO did invoke article five of the NATO treaty, declaring that the attack on the U.S. was an attack on all NATO members. However, after some initial troop participation by member states, in particular the UK, which had over 500 casualties in Afghanistan, the U.S. was left as the only remaining participant in the operation.

The United States spends $2,250 per year per person on national defense while European and other nations that are at a much greater risk of invasion and attack spend much less. The UK and France spend less than $1,000 per person; Germany and Italy spend roughly $600 per person; and Spain about $250 per person. Because about forty percent of U.S. households pay no income tax, the burden falls on the remaining citizens. Thus, there are large numbers of U.S. earners that pay $5,000, $10,000 or more per year towards the U.S. military. This isn't to say that other nations should spend more, but perhaps when the U.S. spends so much, others are incentivized to cut back and rely on the U.S. military and U.S. taxpayers for protection.

In 2014 the Islamic group ISIS took over a Syrian town near the border of Turkey. The president of Turkey, a country that spends about two percent of its GDP on the military, complained that the U.S. was not doing enough to stop the aggression. The comments were made while the Turkish military stood silent, taking no action. No mention was made of the other 27 members of NATO, or of other Middle East Nations such as Saudi Arabia, Iran, Jordan, or Israel. While the U.S. is farther away from the conflict than any other NATO country and Middle Eastern nation, the expectation was that this was a U.S. responsibility. The cost of being the world's superpower is incredibly high.

Borrowing for National Defense

It's interesting to observe that the U.S. annual federal deficit is roughly equivalent to what we spend on national defense. This isn't to say that our defense expenses are responsible for all of our deficit. However, if the U.S. spent a little less than two percent of GDP on military, as do most of our "allies," then our annual deficit would be cut in half—in that respect military expenses are responsible for a good part of our deficit spending. Thus, one of the costs of being the world's superpower is a continually mounting national debt. Too often, being the world's "superpower" means doing most of the work and paying most of the bills. The more we do, the more we are expected to do, as others turn to us to solve every problem. This makes us the superpower, or quite possibly the superfool. Superpower status often causes the U.S. to act alone, making decisions and taking action without the full participation of other countries, which further exposes us to risks that others don't share.

As we go further into debt, covering a disproportionate share of the world's security bill, not only in dollars but in lives, we're told we're the only ones who can afford it. But a national debt equal to our annual GDP is not "affording it." It's passing financial problems onto future generations. So in fact, we can't afford it. As we spend over $2,000 per person every year on our military, others have the luxury of spending $1,000, $500, or even $200 per person. Whether one is for or against a national healthcare system, if we cut our military expenditures equal to our allies, that would leave an extra $1,000 per person, which could go a long way towards having the same national healthcare coverage that our allies have. Or that $1,000 per person could go towards reducing our national debt. There are other costs to being the world's superpower, but military expenditures are the most prominent and obvious. Therefore, it's reasonable to question the costs and benefits of maintaining this position.

As other nations, who are at much greater risk, are able to accomplish security for a fraction of what we spend, we can conclude that we could also maintain our security with a much smaller budget. The question isn't what would happen to the U.S. if we lose our superpower status, but rather, what would happen to the world? In retrospect, we could ask ourselves what would have happened if we hadn't invaded Vietnam. What would've happened if we hadn't invaded Korea? And what would have happened if we hadn't invaded Iraq and Afghanistan? Opinions will vary, but there is reasonable argument to be made that in too many of these cases our actions had little, if any, benefit. When looking at the cost of lives and dollars, the return on our sacrifices is questionable. We watch as our allies spend their money on healthcare, education, high-speed rail, and other social benefits, and we spend ours on costly wars with questionable benefits. The cost of being the world's superpower is very evident, but the benefits are often hard to discern.

A Shift in Power

The real question is not what would happen to the U.S. if we were not the world's superpower. All indications suggest that we'd be fine. Rather, the question is: what would happen to the world if the U.S. was not the only superpower? And more to our concern, what would happen to the world if China became a superpower with military, economic, and political power comparable to, or even greater than, the U.S.?

As any nation gains influence and power there's always concern that it won't be used responsibly, that it may be used in the same manner as Germany or Japan in the 1940s, or as Great Britain in the 18th and 19th centuries when they sought to expand their empire. At its most basic level, a good power would seek to promote peace throughout the world. It would help struggling neighbors to resolve differences, while stopping one sovereign nation from invading another. A good power would work to improve health throughout the world, working to eliminate diseases, lower infant mortality, and reduce poverty. A good power would advance technologies that benefit humankind. A good power would work to promote the most important of human rights. A good power wouldn't abuse its power for selfish gain, but would instead work for justice in international relations. A good power would show restraint in seeking to spread values that might not be universal. Finally, a good power wouldn't seek to write the rules, but would seek to work with others in writing mutually beneficial rules.

To consider whether we should fear China as it rises in military, economic, and political power and influence, we must estimate how China may use its growing power. What aims will it pursue and what methods will it use to advance those goals. What would China do as a superpower?

China's Growing Economic Power and Influence

While it may be fifty or more years before China has economic power and influence comparable to the U.S., certainly China's growing economic power will reduce the relative power the U.S. currently has in international finance and economics. This increasing economic power will give China more voice in world financial institutions, banking regulations, currency exchange, and trade agreements. This can already be seen with China's establishment of the Asian Infrastructure Investment Bank (AIIB), a bank comparable to the World Bank. Even though the U.S. encouraged other countries not to join, 57 founding members quickly signed up for this new world financial institution created by China. The founding members included many close allies of the U.S. such as the United Kingdom, France, and Germany.

The most reasonable prediction about China's use of economic power is that China will maintain the course and character it has held for decades. It's logical to predict that the growing power will be used to continue their goal of improving the lives of the people of China as well as improving the lives of others around the world. Their power will be used to promote their self-interest, yes, but more importantly, it'll be used to push back against U.S. domination in trade and financial rule making. China will push back against the U.S. when it says, "We should write those rules." Over time China will use its economic power to level the economic playing field, insisting that negotiations be set up between equals and not skewed by one dominant player against another.

Military Power and Influence

As we've observed in the prior chapter on military, China's growing military power will be used to defend the people of China. They'll very likely maintain their position of non-aggression, but they'll no longer be bullied by foreign militaries. The growing military power of China will be used in the same manner as their economic power to ensure negotiations are between equals. And they'll continue their history of restraint as they adhere to their policy of not interfering with the internal affairs of other sovereign nations.

Political Power and Influence

International political power is the ability to sway the actions of other political leaders around the world. It's the power to build coalitions between nations, and even coalitions against nations. Whether it's humanitarian, trade-focused, financial, or military, political power can greatly affect a nation's position in the world.

For decades the U.S. has wielded more political power than any other country. It has defined world financial systems, as it did with its creation of the Bretton Woods agreement. It has ensured the viability of nations, as it has accomplished through its financial and political support of Israel. And it has changed political structures around the world, as it did with South Africa, Iraq, and Afghanistan.

The U.S. may have more hard power through economic and military strength, but people around the world are starting to find value in China's style of leadership. The world sees the U.S. sending bombs and guns, starting wars and destabilizing regions, and they see China improving their own economy, bringing trade to other countries, and leading by quiet example. China is now a larger trading partner with Latin America than is the U.S., so while those south of our border know that the U.S. has more hard power, they might seek Chinese leadership in world political issues because they see increasing direct benefit from their relationship with China. European nations and African nations may be coming to the same conclusion.

It is very likely that China's use of political power will be in the same manner as their growing economic and military power. It'll be used to level the playing field, push back against Western domination, and demand a true seat at the table when negotiations are taking place. It's likely that the political power of China will ultimately be used to temper the quick aggressive actions of the West as China seek the same goals outside their borders as they do within—tranquility and prosperity.

Power Shift

The shift that's occurring is described as a decline in U.S. influence and power, but more accurately it's a catching up of others. We're not becoming weaker; they're becoming stronger. In this way, our power relative to others is in fact reduced. Although claiming allies, many times over the last 60 years we have acted on our own. As U.S. military, economic, and political power diminishes and our unilateral power fades, much more true negotiation and alliances will be required.

As some in the U.S. leadership fight desperately to hold onto our position and our unilateral, disproportionate powers, we must question whether or not we really want to continue to be the one and only superpower. Are the costs to maintain or slow the diminishment of our power worth the benefits? Will these expenditures make America a better place, and will they make the world a better place? What opportunities will we be missing by diverting resources to what may very well be unproductive pursuits of power?

In a ten-year period, we'll spend another six trillion on our military, and the pivot to Asia is intended to place 60 percent of our military resources toward Asia. But let's be more specific. The pivot is reallocating resources to counter China's growing power. Thus, in ten years $3.6 trillion U.S. tax payer dollars will be spent specifically to counter China's growing power, and that's the just military. Is this the best use of our resources? Is it even necessary? What are we countering? What's the real benefit here? What's our return on investment? If we seek a pivot, perhaps we should pivot inward. Could $3.6 trillion cure cancer? Could $3.6 trillion build high-speed rail throughout the U.S.? Could $3.6 trillion be better spent on educating our youth? Could our national debt be reduced? As we pivot from one questionable allocation of resources to another, we miss historic opportunities. Our chase for power makes us less powerful. Our fight for influence makes us less influential. The benefits to maintaining our disproportionate military, economic, and political power must be reevaluated against the true cost, not only in hard dollars, but in missed opportunities.

Fearing the China Superpower

In 2014 the president of China, Xi Jinping, and Li Kequiang, China's Premier, visited numerous countries as they worked to build strong relations directly with the political leadership of other nations. In a speech by President Xi given to Mongolian lawmakers, Xi said: "China has always regarded its neighbors as cooperative partners and sincere friends for common development, peace, and stability." He went on to quote an old Chinese proverb: "A good neighbor is not to be traded for gold." Xi continued to speak of mutual benefits: "We will never do things that could result in 'one wins and the other loses' or 'one wins more and the other gets less.'" "China will unswervingly follow the path of peaceful development and in the meantime, it will push for peaceful development among all countries,"[95]

President Xi's words aren't empty. They're backed up by China's current actions and its history. When we observe China's recent military activity, we can see that they are consistent with Xi's statements. When we look at China's recent economic and political use of power, we find it consistent with Xi's claims. And the long history of China also confirms that this is the character of China. To fear China's world influence and power is unfounded. China's military doesn't seek to destroy and dominate, but to protect and provide stability. China doesn't seek to destroy with economic power, but to improve the lives of the people of China as well as the lives of others around the world. China doesn't use its political power to manipulate or "write the rules," but to seek true, mutual benefits among equals. To continue to accept the position that China's rising power must be countered would be a wrong and costly choice.

If we embrace China as a rising superpower, together taking on the challenges that are common between us and sharing in the burdens of being a world leader, then the opportunities are endless. What if China partners with us as a military superpower in keeping the world safe and secure? What if China partners with us as a super power in reducing poverty?

Two superpowers in technological development.

Two superpowers promoting true human rights.

Two superpowers against terrorism.

Two superpowers against disease.

As President Xi said, "A good neighbor is not to be traded for gold." China is offering to be a good neighbor to us. The question is: what will we do with this opportunity? If we persist in thinking that we're on opposite teams, then the rise of China will be seen as a threat. But if we can recognize that we're on the same team, then the strength and power of this partnership will become a huge advantage as we work to make the world a better place.

We have a choice; we can fear China as a superpower and spend our resources fighting their rise. We can continue our allocation of $3.6 trillion in ten years to counter their growing military power. We can continue to accept the disproportionate burden of being the world's peacekeepers in Europe, Asia, and the Middle East. We can fight to prevent China from growing to an economic superpower status that'll ultimately bringing hundreds of millions out of poverty. We can continue the fear that drives our misguided, wasteful spending.

Or we can stop fearing China as a superpower and accept them as a partner in the real challenges of our world.

When we consider the cost of being the world's only superpower, we can see that they're quite high. When we look at the benefits of being the world's only superpower, we can see they're minimal. Looking at what China will do with its growing power, we may find that to fear China becoming a superpower would be the worst possible decision we could make.

16

From Fear to Opportunity

Each year the research group Gallup polls Americans and asks a simple open-ended question: "What one country anywhere in the world do you consider to be the United States' greatest enemy today?" In February of 2014 more respondents selected China than any other country.

From our review of the U.S. headlines and U.S. political treatment of China, it's no wonder that many Americans consider China our greatest enemy. Our view of China is defined by the media, which conveys the Cold War thinking of many of our politicians as well as the negative and fear instilling story lines that interested organizations and corporations seek to perpetuate.

The motives for this misguidance can often be difficult to obtain, but in this journey we find hints when we see U.S. corporations writing the reports that congressional committees submit to Congress, or when we observe the contributions from corporations to political candidates, or when we see presidents seeking advice from generals who have studied war, but haven't studied peace. We find clues when we see domestic corporations seeking tariffs against China and remaining silent when the media incorrectly reports stories about their Chinese suppliers or competition. While neither the media nor its motives are likely to change, the question becomes: will we the people change our view once we look beyond the headlines to a more objective and fact based analysis?

The Power of Fear

To understand the power of fear, we can use a simple metaphor of a lion and lion tamer. In order to coax a lion into a cage, the lion tamer cracks the whip. The loud sound of the whip (the headlines) instills fear in the lion, as the lion believes the whip can cause pain. Fear causes the lion to seek options, placing it further from the threat of pain, and the lion, keeping a close eye on the whip, will back into the cage.

To use fear as a motivator, a solution (the cage), must accompany the fear. As a person experiences fear, the mind seeks a way out, a solution to the stress, a resolution to the fear. Once a person is fearful, then the solution can be presented as the way out. Fear causes us to take action or causes us to allow others to take action. It forces us to focus on the threat in the same way the lion keeps a close eye on the whip. While the desire to seek improvements can be a motivator, like offering food to the lion, fear is often a more direct and effective tool for those wishing to motivate or control others.

A U.S. consumer products manufacturer may want you to fear foreign made products so that you'll buy American. A weapons company may want you to fear attack so that you'll agree to spend more on the military. A cyber security company may want you to fear hackers so more will be spent on cyber defense. A group of anti-government activists in a far away land may want you to fear their government so that you'll accept U.S. forces being used against that government. The U.S. sources in Iraq who reported that Saddam Hussein had weapons of mass destruction wanted U.S. forces to invade Iraq. After the U.S. invaded, it was shown that the information obtained from the informants had been completely made up. But those sources knew fear was a great motivator, and they used it successfully, which caused the U.S. to invade Iraq. Today, ISIS releases videos of brutality with the specific intent to create fear in the American people in order to provoke the U.S. into entering another war. While fear may not always be the first tool of choice, those wishing to motivate find a ready and willing accomplice in the media, making fear not only an effective motivator, but an inexpensive one.

A company may spend millions proclaiming the benefits of a product, but one exaggerated leak to the media can result in tens of millions in free advertising against their competition, be they Chinese or otherwise. A country that may benefit from having the full force of the U.S. military at their disposal, saving them billions in their own military budget, will benefit if fear causes the U.S. military to pivot resources to their region. And those with political ideological pursuits can use fear to sway political action and thus public resources. The tool of fear is used by any wishing to protect their markets, advance their markets, force change, or sway allocation of resources. Fear is cheap and effective.

The media is a willing accomplice in the headlines of fear because it not only causes action, it captures attention, and attention means ratings, which is the measurable goal of media. The combination of the media using fear to capture our attention with others using fear to sell their products or ideas is a marriage of convenience and mutual benefit.

U.S. – China Relations, Defined by Fear

For the last seventy years U.S.–China relations have been defined by fear as politicians, businesses, and organizations perpetuate that fear using the media as their willing accomplice. It's a tool used to get Americans to follow an expensive, often wasteful, and non-productive path.

The headlines tell us to fear China's growing military, but when we look at history and look past the headlines we find that China, which has been brutally attacked by its neighbors and the West, not only has a right to defend itself, but has a responsibility to the people of China to have one of the largest militaries in the world, ensuring that the atrocities of the past are not repeated.

The headlines tell us to fear China in cyberspace, but when we look past the headlines we find that the American government is the largest cyber spy in the world, while little evidence is shown that China is a true cyber threat. We find that it's our insecure systems that are the real threat, not China.

The headlines tell us to fear China's intellectual property theft, but when we look past the headlines we find that while China does have room for improving their IP laws, too often it's our defective laws that seek to give corporations a monopoly on the most obvious of ideas. It causes the Selden effect, which slows innovation, when the purpose of IP rights is to promote innovation.

The headlines tell us to fear China's technological products, but when we look past the headlines we find U.S. corporations seeking to block competition like Huawei from selling in the U.S. We find the U.S. refusing to sell a simple battery company to China due to security concerns, yet we provide Japan the plans to our most sophisticated fighter planes.

The headlines tell us to fear Chinese-made toys, but when we look past the headlines we find that the real problem was the design of the toys that came from U.S. manufacturers. The media made a big issue of Chinese-made toothpaste that contained a harmful chemical, but reported very lightly on the thirty million bottles of wine from Australia with the same chemical. We find when dangerous products are reported on, if they're from China, then "China" will be in the headlines, and if they're from any place else, often the country of origin is buried in the details or never even mentioned.

The headlines tell us to fear the pollution of China, with our embassy constantly reporting air pollution levels in Beijing, but when we look past the headlines we find that our embassies in places like India and Pakistan make no mention of air pollution in their cities, which have worse air quality than Beijing or any other Chinese city. The headlines proclaim China to be the biggest greenhouse gas polluter, neglecting to mention that the U.S. has a higher per capita CO^2 pollution rate, and neglecting to report how the U.S. has effectively outsourced pollution.

The headlines tell us to fear China's growing economy, but when we look past the headlines we find that we're ignoring the fact that a Chinese GDP equal to the U.S. would mean that the GDP per capita in China would still be one quarter of that in the U.S. We ignore the fact that China could only have our standard of living once their economy is four times the size of ours.

The headlines tell us to fear poor ethics and corruption in China, but when we look past the headlines we find China taking dramatic action to improve the ethics and stop corruption—we see China making great progress. We watch while U.S. bankers and other financial industry executives, whose corruption nearly destroyed the U.S. economy, not only are absent from the news, but they are not even legally prosecuted. When we look past the headlines we find that corruption in China ranks very average and is better than places like Brazil and Argentina, but that detail is rarely reported.

The headlines tell us to fear China's growing world influence, but when we look past the headlines we find we're ignoring what that influence may bring, and neglecting to evaluate the cost and benefits of our own world influence.

The headlines tell us to fear communism in China with no room to evaluate its successes, its failures, or to discover how it's been modified over the past thirty years.

The headlines tell us to fear China's non-democratic rule, while refusing to explore China's unique meritocratic system, and ignoring the challenges and defects of democracy with its mixture of successes and failures around the world.

The headlines tell us to fear the human rights abuses in China, while ignoring that China has brought over 300 million people out of poverty. And at the same time, we ignore the reality that some of our allies around the world have much worse human rights records. We find the headlines defining human rights in the Western terms of democracy and capitalism; the more important issues of standard of living and the elimination of poverty are ignored.

But facts be damned, the political proclamations and headlines of fear define what Americans think about China, which causes many to select China as our greatest enemy.

Negative about all things China

As we convey every optimism about the Arab Spring countries, wishing for their success as they attempt to implement the Western values of democracy and capitalism, we're disheartened by their stumbles and difficulties, hoping it's only a temporary setback. Equally in our attempt to validate our Western beliefs, the West shows unwarranted skepticism towards any accomplishments made in China, hoping the Chinese system will fail, and along with it China, because if they succeed, it challenges our deeply held Western beliefs.

In the Shanghai Pudong district, run down warehouses and farmland have been turned into a first world Boston-like city within the short span of fifteen years. Upon seeing the impressive buildings, one of the most outspoken proponents of capitalism, Milton Friedman, discounted the accomplishment, calling it "a statist monument for a dead pharaoh on the level of the pyramids."

When they build buildings we critique that they're empty. When they build world-class factories and become the most productive manufacturer in the world, we critique that their labor isn't paid equally to our first world countries, and that manufacturing creates pollution. When they bring 300 million people out of poverty, we want to talk about the lack of democracy. When they build the largest hydroelectric dam in the world, we complain about those who've been displaced by the construction. Too often we criticize their accomplishments and lack praise for their advancements.

From fears of war, cyber attacks, unfair trade, currency manipulation, loss of technological leadership, unsafe toys, the stealing of intellectual property rights, pollution, human rights abuses, the fear of China's world influence, and the raw threat of this thing called communism, Americans have been convinced that China is our enemy, a great threat, and should be feared.

When asked: "What one country anywhere in the world do you consider to be the United States' greatest enemy today?" We respond: "China."

A Different China

In our journey together we've discovered a China different from what we've been told. We find a people that wish us no harm, a people that hope the best for us, themselves, and the rest of the world. We've found a nation that has experienced a difficult past, a nation striving to prosper, and a nation now coming into its stride. While we've been told they're not like us, we find a people and a society that is very much like us. They seek to protect themselves, they seek peace, and they seek prosperity.

In military they seek to protect themselves from foreign invaders. In intellectual property they seek to improve the world and improve their own economic condition. In trade they hope to improve their standard of living. When a toy harms a child, the people of China feel pain for that child. The people of Beijing suffer when air pollution harms their health in the same way children in Los Angeles suffer from polluted air. China pursues economic growth as we do, to improve the lives of all. With the same ambitions for their society and for future generations, they are very much like us. Their student protest in Beijing was our 1970 student protest at Kent State, and we see in both how every government seeks to keep peace. China's Bo Xilai, a politician who accepted millions in bribes, is our James Traficant. The propaganda of China promoting communism during the Mao era is only equaled by the propaganda of the U.S. as we sought to advance capitalism.

The moral authority of Mao was the moral authority of Reagan. For many readers, this statement will be the most difficult to accept. It goes against our core ideological beliefs, as we've elevated capitalism and democracy to the status of human rights. But it's that error that has caused us the pain of war and unneeded conflict for almost 100 years. The moral authority of Mao was the moral authority of Regan because they both sought prosperity for all but with different tools and with different beliefs about how that could be accomplished. Some tools work better than others, and each society selects the tools they believe are best, sometimes making the right decision, other times not.

Some Wish Us Harm

In 2001 Arab radicals hijacked U.S. airplanes, flying them into buildings and causing the death of almost three thousand Americans. In November of 2013 a rally was held at a foreign U.S. embassy with the crowds chanting "death to America" and other anti-American slogans. The embassy protest was in Pakistan, a country which has received an average of $10 billion in U.S. aid every year since 1951, while most of the Arab radicals which perpetrated the 9/11 attacks were from Saudi Arabia, a country claimed as one of America's closest allies. We work so hard to be friends with countries who clearly want to destroy us, while we work equally hard to not be friends with China who wishes us no harm.

The history of China shows us that the people and the leaders of China are truly a peaceful people, seeking prosperity for all. Where we're aggressive, they seek isolation. Where we're bullies, they seek to defend themselves, and when we propose unequal treaties, they refuse. When we claim human rights abuse, they ignore us, knowing our history and questioning our definition of human rights. But they do not seek to destroy us. They do not wish us harm. They, like us, seek peace and prosperity for all nations and all people.

Beyond the Headlines – Beyond Fear

Modern history has given several countries the chance to propel the world forward in technological, social, and political advancement. For several centuries Great Britain played a major role in developing corporate, banking, and governmental systems that advanced modern society. Great Britain was also the instigator in helping world trade advance to a new level. But the history of Great Britain isn't pure and free of blemish. Like any country, they've committed their sins from empire building to the forcing of opium on China to supporting the U.S. slave trade. Great Britain has contributed much, but not without errors.

In 1776 a new nation was established with the United States' Declaration of Independence. The United States' influence and contribution to the world has been staggering. The first exceptional contribution was the U.S. Constitution, which has been a resilient document that has in large part been the foundation for what would become the most powerful country in the world.

While our innovation and accomplishments have been the envy of the world, like Great Britain and other world leaders, our path hasn't been without error. Despite a founding document extolling the virtues of a man's freedom, the U.S. somehow found slavery to be acceptable for over 100 years. Our early industrial revolution, like Great Britain's, saw brutal conditions for child labor and other laborers. Like Great Britain, our contributions to the world have been great. It would be an understatement to say the U.S. has had an influence on the world. The U.S. has truly changed the world, but not without mistakes.

However, great opportunities come even to the flawed and imperfect, as we can fully attest. In China the fundamental errors in economic and political structures are being corrected, a better course is being taken, and a nation that's had its internal and external difficulties is now seizing great opportunities to improve themselves and the world. But while they adopt some of the ideas of the West, they also make their own path, discovering what works and what doesn't work. What if they don't take the path we've taken? What if they make choices different from ours?

Leading up to the U.S. invasion of Iraq, President George W. Bush stated: "You're either for us or you are against us." As politicians advance their careers they learn that there are only three relationships, your friends, your enemies, and the irrelevant. For the 25 million Iraqi citizens, this was a brutal choice. When Hitler's Germany invaded France, they told the French people: you're either for us or against us. When Japan invaded Korea certainly they told the people: you're either for us or against us.

This is a great error of our time. We have accepted that there's only one system, focusing on the color of the cat while ignoring whether or not it actually catches mice. We accept the proposition that others are either for us or against us. If they accept our way, they're a friend, if they do not accept our way, they're an enemy.

By accepting this flawed idea, we place ourselves in a position to be misled by the creators of fear, appealing to our less than perfect core beliefs. Sometimes fear can keep us safe, but more often than not fear causes us to miss opportunities.

Skeptical of the headlines and focused on the facts, with a review of our successes and our failures, our view of China must change. Our view has been distorted by the headlines and agenda of those who would benefit from our fear. Once we look beyond those headlines, we can reject the fear, reject the attempt to define China as our enemy, and accept them as a friend. *We can and must stop fearing China*. We can because we are learning to discover the rest of the story, and we must because if we don't, we'll miss historic opportunities. Imagine the possibilities available if we refuse the narrative of fear, seek the facts, accept that other paths may succeed, and stop fearing China.

Welcome the Great Opportunity

In this time of prosperity after centuries of external disruptions and recent internal missteps, great opportunities have come to China—China is seizing those opportunities. Xi Jinping, the president of China, has spoken of the "Chinese Dream" saying: "Dare to dream, work assiduously to fulfill the dreams and contribute to the revitalization of the nation."

On the surface, this theme may simply sound like guidance for the future path of China, but more than a guide for the future, it's a recognition of the historic place China stands now. President Xi encourages citizens today and generations to come to recognize the good fortune of living in tranquil and prosperous times. He encourages them to seize their advantage in history and pursue personal dreams to their own benefit and to the benefit of China.

While China embraces this historic opportunity, there's an even greater opportunity presented to us, and that's for the United States to accept China as a true friend and join with them in meeting the challenges of our world. While the Cold War model presumes that the two strongest nations, having the two largest militaries, should be in opposition to each other, the U.S. has the chance to change that wasteful dynamic and gain from the opportunities of cooperation and friendship with China.

In Shanghai fifth graders rank the highest in the world in academic performance, while higher education in the U.S. is thought to be the best in the world. Imagine the opportunities if China helped us improve our primary education, and we worked with them to improve their higher education.

In the U.S., the dream of high-speed rail connecting our cities has been elusive for 40 years. By the end of 2015, China will have over 11,000 miles of high-speed rail connecting major cities, reducing the growth of CO^2 pollutants, and all while providing one of the best rail transportation systems in the world. What opportunities await if we partner with China and learn from their great success in high-speed rail development?

While the job isn't done, the U.S. has made great progress in reducing pollution in our air and water. As a friend of China and with our past experience, how can we truly help China with this challenge? What technologies can we jointly work on to improve the lives of children in Beijing and Los Angeles at the same time? Imagine the opportunities if we change from our badgering and critical tone to a true spirit of cooperation to take on this mutual problem of pollution.

China now has the world's fastest super computer. What can we learn from them? They have the longest bridges. How can we gain from their expertise and experience? Both China and the U.S. have challenges in delivering healthcare. How can we work together to experiment and explore healthcare systems that will improve not only both societies, but the world?

The U.S. has been working to eliminate poverty in Africa for decades with moderate success, while China has brought over 300 million out of poverty in China in thirty years. Imagine the U.S. working with China to eliminate poverty in Africa, or working together to help other struggling nations come into the benefits of the modern world.

The U.S. has been the most innovative nation for over a century, and we continue to lead the way in science and business. Our ability to develop new technologies is unmatched. Imagine the opportunities if we help China to harness the power of invention and innovation.

If the American Dream converges with the Chinese Dream, and we seize this historic opportunity for friendship and cooperation, the next one hundred years will be the world's greatest century as these two superpowers join together to take on the world's greatest challenges.

The Cure

In a small town in the middle of the U.S., there's a lady by the name of Eva who suffers from cancer. The disease has been attacking her for five years and has caused her great pain. She spends many hours in the hospital undergoing treatment, and the cost is high to her, her family, and to society. She has access to the latest drugs and technologies available, which have slowed the cancer and have eased her pain. But cancer will eventually win.

In 2015 it is estimated that almost 600 thousand people will die of cancer in the U.S. On the other side of the world in the city of Shanghai, women have a much higher rate of breast cancer than is found in other nations. The people of China, like us, would like to find a cure for cancer.

The U.S. is the leading spender on cancer research, with more people working to solve the problem than any other country. Currently there are approximately 80 thousand people in the U.S. working on cancer research. Those people are working to discover drugs and technologies that can slow the progress and pain of cancer as well as find a true cure for cancer. Their work has made Eva's life better, but there is much work to be done.

If China had the same number per capita of people working on cancer research, that would be another 320 thousand people working to eliminate cancer. Would Eva and others with cancer be better off if another 320 thousand people joined our 80 thousand to push towards a final cure for cancer? Would our children and grandchildren benefit if China and the U.S. took on this great challenge together? Imagine the opportunities if we partnered with

China to take on these grand challenges like diseases, pollution, education, poverty, and war.

Our view of China determines the allocation of our resources. If we choose to fear China and treat them as an enemy, trillions will be spent to counter their inevitable growth. But, if we treat them as a friend and celebrate their successes while helping them through challenges, not only can we stop the wasteful spending of another Cold War, we can partner with them in solving great problems and making the world a better place. This is the choice given to our generation. Will we seize the opportunities presented to us in this historic time of China's rise, joining with them as a friend in building a better world, or will we choose to continue fearing China?

Paul Harvey, a U.S. radio commentator, used to sign off all his radio addresses with: "And now you know the rest of the story." Unfortunately Paul Harvey is no longer with us, and very few are telling the rest of the story. The headlines hit and they affect our opinions and beliefs, but the more important "rest of the story" rarely comes, so we base our opinions on skewed, agenda driven headlines.

But now that you know the rest of the story, which will you choose: fear or opportunity?

234

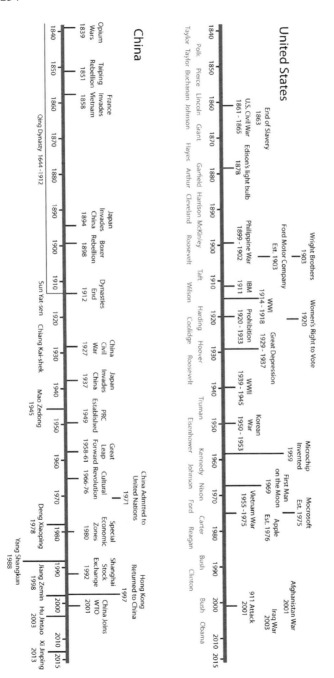

United States

1840	1850	1860	1870	1880	1890	1900	1910	1920

End of Slavery 1863
U.S. Civil War 1861 - 1865
Edison's light bulb 1878
Philippine War 1899 - 1902
Ford Motor Company Est. 1903
Wright Brothers 1903
IBM 1911
WWI 1914 - 1918
Women's Right to Vote 1920
Prohibition 1920 - 1933
Great Depression 1929 - 1937
WWII 1939 - 1945
Korean War 1950 - 1953
Microchip Invented 1959
First Man on the Moon 1969
Vietnam War 1955 - 1975
Microsoft Est. 1975
Apple Est. 1976
911 Attack 2001
Afghanistan War 2001
Iraq War 2003

Taylor Taylor Buchanan Johnson Hayes Garfield Harrison McKinley Roosevelt Taft Wilson Harding Coolidge Hoover Roosevelt Truman Eisenhower Kennedy Nixon Ford Carter Reagan Bush Clinton Bush Obama

Polk Pierce Lincoln Grant Garfield Arthur Cleveland

China

1840	1850	1860	1870	1880	1890	1900	

Opium Wars 1839
Taiping Rebellion 1851
France Invades Vietnam 1858
Japan Invades China 1894
Boxer Rebellion 1898
Dynasties End 1912
China Civil War 1927
Japan Invades China 1937
PRC Established 1949
Great Leap Forward 1958-61
Cultural Revolution 1966-76
China Admitted to United Nations 1971
Special Economic Zones 1980
Hong Kong Returned to China 1997
Shanghai Stock Exchange 1992
China Joins WTO 2001

Qing Dynasty 1644 -1912

Sun Yat-sen
Chiang Kai-shek
Mao Zedong 1945
Deng Xiaoping 1978
Yang Shangkun 1988
Jiang Zemin 1998
Hu Jintao 2003
Xi Jinping 2013

INDEX

238

REFERENCES
Direct URL links to references may be found at:
www.FearingChina.org/references

1 Adam Lashinsky, "Is China an Economic Threat?" Fox News (2005, November 17)
  Aurelia End, "China seeks to upend economic power of US," The Standard (2015, April 20)
  Minxin Pei, "How the U.S. should counter China's economic power play," Fortune (2015, April 3)
  John Elliott, "U.S. Eclipsed as Allies Line Up to Join China's Asia Bank," Newsweek (2015, Mar. 31)
  Linda Stern, "China Gaining on U.S., Now World's Second Largest Economy," CBS (2010, Aug. 16)
  Jonathan Weisman, "At Global Economic Gathering, U.S. Primacy Is Seen as Ebbing," New York Times (2015, April 17)
2 "Data:China," The World Bank
3 International Monetary Fund (History) imf.org
4 "Facts and figures on EU-China trade," Official website of the European Union (2014, March)
5 "GDP Per Capita," International Monetary Fund (2014)
6 Chen Weihua, "Stiglitz has harsh words for US policy makers on China," China Daily USA (2014, December 25)
7 "Millennium Development Goals," USAID (2014)
8 "Data:China," The World Bank
9 Barack Obama, "Remarks by the President in State of the Union Address," U.S. Government (2015, January 20)
10 Yang Yi, "Welcome aboard China's train of development: President Xi," Xinhuanet (2014, August 22)
11 Gary Wolf, "Steve Jobs: The Next Insanely Great Thing," Wired (2002, March)
12 Franz-Stefan Gady, "How Threatening Are China's Missiles?," The Diplomat (2015, April 7)
   Julian E. Barnes, "U.S. Plans Naval Shift Towards Asia," Wall Street Journal (2012, June 1)
   Bret Stephens, "How Many Nukes Does China Have?," Wall Street Journal (2011, October 25)
   Calum MacLeod and Oren Dorell, "China navy makes waves in South China Sea," USA Today (2013, March 27)
   "For Xi, a 'China Dream' of Military Power," Wall Street Journal (2013, March 13)
   James A. Lyon, "How to neutralize China's military threat," The Washington Times (2013, March 29)
   Gregory Korte and Tom Vanden Brook, "China, U.S. head toward faceoff in South China Sea," USA Today (2015, May 14)
   Elisabeth Bumiller, "U.S. Official Warns About China's Military Buildup," New York Times (2011, August 24)
13 "List of countries and dependencies by area," Wikipedia
14 "SIPRI Military Expenditure Database," Stockholm International Peace Research Institute
15 John Vause, "Chinese hackers: No site is safe," CNN (2008, March 11)
   E.H., "How does China censor the Internet," The Economist (2013, April 21)
   Calum MacLeod, "China military involved in U.S. hacking," USA Today (2013, February 19)
   Charles Arthur, "Is your Gmail being hacked from China?," The Guardian (2010, March 25)
   Danny Yarron et. All, "China Hacking Is Deep and Diverse, Experts Say," Wall Street Journal (2014, May 29)
   Julian Barnes, "U.S. Says China's Government, Military Used Cyber espionage," Wall Street Journal (2013, May 7)
16 Jordy Yager and Carlo Munoz, "Intelligence chiefs warn that cyberattacks are nation's top security threat," The Hill (2013, March 12)
17 William Wan and Ellen Nakashima, "Intelligence chiefs warn that cyberattacks are nation's top security threat," The Washington Post (2013, February 19)
18 Mark Milian, "One-Third of Cyber Attack Traffic Originates in China, Akamai Says," Bloomberg (2013, January 23)
19 Mark Milian, "Indonesia Passes China to Become Top Source of Cyber-Attack Traffic," Bloomberg (2013, October 16)
20 Siobhan Gorman et. All, "China Hackers Hit U.S. Media," Wall Street Journal (2013, January 31)
21 Ian Trynor, "Airbus could sue following allegations Germany spied on them for the US," The Guardian (2015, April 30)

22 "NSA 'asked' Germany's BND to spy on Siemens over alleged links with Russian intel," Russian Television (2015, May 10)
23 Scott Shane, "No Morsel Too Minuscule for All-Consuming N.S.A.," New York Times (2013, Nov. 2)
24 David E. Sanger, "Obama Order Sped Up Wave of Cyberattacks Against Iran," New York Times (2012, June 1)
25 "2012 Report To Congress;U.S.-China Economic and Security Review," U.S. Government (2012, November)
26 "US report warns on China IP theft," BBC (2013, May 23)
   Richard A. Clarke, "How China Steals Our Secrets," New York Times (2012, April 2)
   Leo Kelion, "Cheap 'Apple Watch' copies on sale via Alibaba site," BBC (2015, March 11)
   Larry Dignan, "Microsoft's Ballmer: Piracy killing our China revenue," ZDNet (2011, May 26)
   Jim Michaels, "China's theft of business secrets is beyond espionage," USA Today (2014, May 19)
   Terril Yue Jones et.all, "Chinese hackers steal U.S. weapons systems designs, report says," NBC (2013, May 28)
27 Jay Yarow, "Apple Wins A Patent For Rounded Corners," Business Insider (2012, November 9)
28 Michael Riley and Ashlee Vance, "Inside the Chinese Boom in Corporate Espionage," Bloomberg Business (2012, March 15)
29 Ian O'neill, "NASA Banned From Working With China," Discovery (2011, May 10)
   Matthew Pennington, "US panel: China tech giants pose security threat," Yahoo News (2012, Oct. 8)
   Shannon Tiezzzi, "US Admiral: China Counter-Space Threat Is 'Real'," The Diplomat (2015, Mar. 26)
   Mark Clayton, "A123 sale to China: threat to US security?," Christian Science Monitor (2012, December 11)
   "China's Huawei and ZTE pose national security threat, says US," The Guardian (2012, October 8)
   "Lawmakers Press Huawei, ZTE Amid Probe About Possible Threats to U.S. Security," Wall Street Journal (2012, June 13)
30 Wall Street Journal (2013, March 28)
31 Alina Selyukh and Doug Palmer, "U.S. law to restrict government purchases of Chinese IT equipment," Reuters (2013, March 27)
32 "US approves A123 sale to Chinese firm despite security concerns," Fox news (2013, January 29)
33 "Don't Sell Bankrupt Battery Maker A123 to China's Wanxiang: Rep. Blackburn," The Daily Ticker (2013, Januay 29)
34 John Culberson, "Letter to the President," Political News.ME (2010, October 13)
35 "2015 Research and Innovation Tour: Where Europe and China connect," European Union (2015, April 15)
36 Ashley Killough, "Biden: 'Name one innovative product' from China," CNN (2014, May 28)
37 Zoe Chace, "Are Chinese Exporters Cheating?," NPR (2012, September 20)
   "US Questions China Aviation Subsidies," Leeham News
   Johathan Katz, "Chinese Steel Subsidies Out Of Control," Industry Week (2007, July 30)
   Scott Horsley, "Obama Gets Tough On China's Auto Subsidies," NPR (2012, September 18)
   Peter Whoriskey and Anne Kornblut, "U.S. to Impose Tariff on Tires From China," Washington Post (2009, September 12)
   Niraj Chokshi, "Trade with China has cost 3.2 million American jobs," Washington Post (2014, December 15)
   Karla Murthy, "Chinese 'currency manipulation' and what it means for U.S. trade," PBS (2010, Apr. 15)
   Keith Bradsher, "U.S. Solar Panel Makers Say China Violated Trade Rules," New York Times (2011, October 19)
38 Martin Feldstein, "The American Economy in Transition," University of Chicago Press (1980)
39 Yuki Noguchi, "Solyndra Highlights Long History Of Energy Subsidies," NPR (2011, November 16)
40 Robert Guy Matthews, "Steelmakers Accuse China of Dumping in the U.S.," The Wall Street Journal (2009, April 9)
41 Tim Catts, Peter Robison and Ilan Kolet, "No Renaissance for U.S. Factory Workers as Pay Stagnates," Bloomberg Business (2013, November 21)
42 Judith Banister, "China's manufacturing employment and hourly labor compensation, 2002-2009," Bureau of Labor Statistics (2013, June 7)
43 Mathew L. Wald and Keith Bradsher, "4 U.S. Makers of Towers for Wind Turbines File Complaint Over China's Steel Subsidies," New York Times (2011, December 29)
44 Robert Evans, "WTO faults U.S. over duties on Chinese, Indian steel goods," Reuters (2014, July 14)
45 "WTO supports China, India in steel subsidies case," Inchin Closer (2014, July 8)

46 "The Employment Situation-March 2015," Bureau of Labor Statistics (2015, April 3)

47 "Trade in Goods with European Union," United States Census Bureau (2015)

48 Zachary Karabell, "The "Made in China" Fallacy," Slate (2014, March 11)

49 "Exports of goods and services," The World Bank (2014)

50 Joseph P. Quinlan And Marc Chandler, "The U.S. Trade Deficit: A Dangerous Obsession," Foreign Affairs-Council on Foreign Relations (2001, May/June)

51 "The cheapest thing going is gone," The Economist (2013, June 15)

52 Galina Hale and Bart Hobijn, "The U.S. Content of "Made in China"," Federal Reserv Bank of San Francisco (2011, August 8)

53 "What Percentage of Your Car Was Made in America?," ABC News

54 Heng Shao, "$9.3 Billion Sales Recorded In Alibaba's 24-Hour Online Sale, Beating Target By 15%," Forbes (2014, November 11)

55 Will Chinese Drywall Make You Sick," MSN
"Chinese Manufacturing: Poorly Made," The Economist (2009, May 14)
"Throw away Chinese toothpaste, FDA warns," NBCNews.com (2007, June 1)
Louise Story and David Barboza, "Mattel Recalls 19 Million Toys Sent From China," The New York Times (2007, August 15)
"Mystery of pet deaths related to jerky treats made in China continues to stump FDA," The Washington Post (2014, March 28)

56 "Mattel issues new massive China toy recall," NBCNews.com (2007, August 14)

57 "Throw away Chinese toothpaste, FDA warns," NBCNews.com (2007, June 1)

58 Walt Bogdanich, "Toxic Toothpaste Made in China Is Found in U.S.," New York Times (2007, June 2)

59 Eric S. Lipton and David Barboza, "As More Toys Are Recalled, Trail Ends in China," The New York Times (2007, June 19)

60 Christopher Palmeri, "Mattel Takes the Blame for Toy Recalls," Bloomberg Business (2007, Sept. 21)

61 Jamie Ferman, "Industry Report Dolls, Toys, Games, and Children's Vehicles," U.S. Department of Commerce (2013, April 22)

62 "Homeowners Charge U.S. Made Toxic Drywall," CBS News (2009, November 23)

63 Carla Gillespie, "Before Salmonella Outbreak, Diamond Pet Foods Had History Of Trouble," Food Poisoning Bulletin (2012, June 4)
Steven Reinberg, "Pet Food Recall Widens Agaoin on New Threat," abc News (2012, May 3)
"Toxic Pet food may have killed dozens of dogs," NBCNews.com (2006, May 10)

64 Gil Aegerter, "U.S. Expands Recall Warning for Cars With Defective Air Bags," NBCNews.com (2014, October 22)

65 "Wal-Mart Company Statistics," Statistic Brain (2015, April 12)

66 Abram Brown, "Wealthy Illinois Tycoon Appears At The Center of Chinese Meat Scandal," Forbes (2014, July 22)

67 "China pollution: Beijing smog hits hazardous levels," BBC (2015, January 15)
"The Biggest Polluter in China's Dirtiest City," Wall Street Journal (2014, September 17)
Natalie Thomas and Kim Kyung-Hoon, "Beijing residents gasp for fresh air in the city of smog," Reuters (2015, March 4)
Jethro Mullen, "Tons of poisoned fish clog river in China's Hubei province," CNN (2013, September 5)
Jonathan Kaiman, "China's toxic air pollution resembles nuclear winter, say scientists," The Guardian (2014, February 25)

68 "Motor Vehicles per capita," The World Bank

69 Lindsay Wilson, "Average household electricity use around the world," Shrink That Footprint

70 "Key Events in the History of Air Quality in California," California Environmental Protection Agency (2015, January 6)

71 Richie King and Lily Kuo, "Key Events in the History of Air Quality in California," Quartz (2013 October 18)

72 Madison Park, "Top 20 most polluted cities in the world," CNN (2014, May 8)

73 "Caterpillar Earnings Hit by China Fraud," CNBC (2013, January 28)
Peter S. Goodman, "China Discloses $1.1 Billion Bank Fraud," Washington Post (2006, June 28)
Matthew Mosk and Brian Ross, "Chinese Deny Turning Blind to Investment Scams," ABC News (2013 January 10)
Joseph Netto and Ralph Ellis, "500 Chinese lawmakers leave office over election fraud," CNN (2013 December 28)
"SEC Charges China-Based Executives With Fraud and Insider Trading," SEC (2013, Sept. 26)

74 "Mexico Drug War Fast Facts," CNN (2015, March 10)

75 "Doing Business," World Bank Group (2014, June)
76 "Corruption Perceptions Index 2014," Transparency International (2014)
77 Christopher Beam, "How Communist Is China?," Slate.com (2010, July 26)
   James A. Dorn, "The Death of Communism in China," CATO (1999, March 5)
   Larry Diamond, "Chinese Communism and the 70-Year Itch," The Atlantic (2013, October 29)
   Mathew J. Belvedere, "Hank Paulson: China hasn't built better capitalism," CNBC (2015, April 15)
   Jamil Anderlini, "How long can the Communist party survive in China?," Financial Times (2013, September 20)
78 World Bank Data, "compiled by," GapMinder (2014)
79 Xinhua, "China has 10m private enterprises," China Daily (2013, February 2)
80 "Country's Economic Situation," Pew Research Center (2014)
81 Harold Meyerson, "When Dollars Trump Democracy in China," Washington Post (2014, July 2)
   Frank Langfitt, "Capitalism Is Making China Richer, But Not Democratic," NPR (2014, November 7)
   Editorial Board, "Beijing is crushing Hong Kong's democratic hopes," Washington Post (2014, September 2)
   Chris Buckley and Alan Wong, "Pro-Democracy Students Are Arrested in Hong Kong," New York Times (2014, September 26)
   Austin Ramzy, "Macau Scholar Says He Lost His Job Over Pro-Democracy Activism," New York Times Blog (2014, August 18)
82 Robert Booth, "Facebook reveals news feed experiment to control emotions," The Guardian (2014, June 29)
83 "Fair Allocations In Research Foundation," The Fair
84 "Global Attitudes & Trends," Pew Research Center (2014)
85 Simon Denyer, "In China, Communist Party takes unprecedented step: It is listening," The Washington Post (2013, August 2)
86 Calum MacLeod, "U.S. report says human rights worsen in China," USA Today (2015, January 13)
   Malcolm Moore, "China's human rights record, 'worst in decades'," The Telegraph (2014, March 2)
   Carlos Tejada and Lauri Burkitt Carlos Tejada and Laurie Burkitt, "Biden Criticizes China on Media, Human Rights," Wall Street Journal (2013, December 5)
   Editorial Board, "China's human rights abuses demand a tougher U.S. approach," Washington Post (2014, September 14)
   Chris Buckley, "Trial Begins Next Week for Human Rights Activist in China," New York Times (2014, January 17)
   Carol Morello, "White House blasts China on human rights ahead of APEC summit," Washington Post (2014, November 7)
87 "Children in China: Infant mortality rate, 1991-2013," Unicef (2015, January 10)
88 "Max Baucus U.S. Ambassador to China Confirmation Hearing," C-SPAN (2014, January 28)
89 "Outgoing US envoy Gary Locke in China rights call," BBC News (2014, February 27)
90 Human Rights Watch
91 "Westphal Hearing," U.S. Dept. Of State (2014, February 13)
92 David Shambaugh, "The Coming Chinese Crackup," Wall Street Journal (2015, March 6)
   Ho-Fung Hung et.all, "When Will China's Government Collapse?," Foreign Policy (2015, March 13)
   Gordon G. Chang, "McCain to Beijing: Revolution is Coming," World Affairs (2012, February 7)
   Katie Holliday, "Is rising unrest in China a threat to the economy?," CNBC (2014, August 18)
   Stephen R. Platt, "Is China Ripe for a Revolution?," New York Times (2012, February 9)
   "China's ethnic tinderbox," BBC (2009, July 9)
93 "Global Public Downbeat About Economy," Pew Research Center (2014, September)
94 Teo Kermeliotis, "Is the West Losing Out To China in Africa?," CNN (2011, September 9)
   Ilan Berman, "China's Newest Sphere of Influence," The Wall Street Journal (2015, January 22)
   David Pilling, "Round two in America's battle for Asian influence," Financial Times (2015, April 1)
   Farhan Bokhari, "China moves to marginalize U.S. influence in Pakistan," CBS News (2015, April 20)
   Laura Robertson, "China Influence in Panama a U.S. Threat?," CBN (2009, March 1)
   Jin Kai, "What the AIIB Means for the US-China Power Transition," The Diplomat (2015, March 27)
   Kaitlin Funaro, "Xi flies to Mexico as China battles US for influence in Latin America," Global Post (2013, June 4)
   Jim Gomez and Matthew Lee, "ASSEAN Summit 2013 Sees U.S., China Compete For Influence In Asia," Huffington Post (2013, October 9)
95 Xinhua, "President Xi welcomes Mongolia to 'board China's train of development'," China Daily (2014, August 22)

Printed in Great Britain
by Amazon

64700125R00147